REASONING, ARGUMENTATION, AND DELIBERATIVE DEMOCRACY

In light of the latest research from cognitive and developmental psychology, this key text explores reasoning, rationality, and democracy, considering the unique nature of each and their relationship to each other.

Broadening our understanding from the development of reasoning and rationality in individuals to encompass social considerations of argumentation and democracy, the book connects psychological literature to philosophy, law, political science, and educational policy. Based on psychological research, Moshman sets out a system of deliberative democracy that promotes collaborative reasoning, rational institutions such as science and law, education aimed at the promotion of rationality, and intellectual freedom for all. Also including the biological bases of logic, metacognition, and collaborative reasoning, Moshman argues that, despite systematic flaws in human reasoning, there are reasons for a cautiously optimistic assessment of the potential for human rationality and the prospects for democracy.

Reasoning, Argumentation, and Deliberative Democracy will be essential reading for all researchers of thinking and reasoning from psychology, philosophy, and education.

David Moshman is Professor Emeritus of Educational Psychology, University of Nebraska–Lincoln, USA.

REASONING, ARGUMENTATION, AND DELIBERATIVE DEMOCRACY

David Moshman

Routledge
Taylor & Francis Group
NEW YORK AND LONDON

First published 2021
by Routledge
52 Vanderbilt Avenue, New York, NY 10017

and by Routledge
2 Park Square, Milton Park, Abingdon, Oxon OX14 4RN

Routledge is an imprint of the Taylor & Francis Group, an informa business

Library of Congress Cataloging-in-Publication Data
A catalog record for this title has been requested

ISBN: 978-0-367-31276-3 (hbk)
ISBN: 978-0-367-31277-0 (pbk)
ISBN: 978-0-429-31602-9 (ebk)

Typeset in Bembo
by Newgen Publishing UK

CONTENTS

PREFACE

Somewhere around 1980 I had the idea of writing what would have been my first book: a small text on the development of reasoning, called simply "The development of reasoning." I had been doing research on the development of logical and scientific reasoning in adolescence since graduate school in the early 1970s, and was also very interested in the development of moral reasoning. The book would have traced the developmental course of several types of reasoning (covering literatures here addressed in Chapter 2 and part of Chapter 3) and would also have addressed some of the associated matters of metacognition, development, and education discussed in Chapters 4, 7, and 8, respectively.

Over the past four decades I have continued to study and write about reasoning. Portions of what I had in mind for my reasoning book showed up in other publications, including my books *Adolescent Rationality and Development* (Moshman, 2011a) and *Epistemic Cognition and Development* (Moshman, 2015). I continued to think about a book that would look directly and comprehensively at the development of reasoning and associated progress in rationality, but my conception of this book gradually shifted in three major ways.

First, I increasingly found that there was much to say about adult reasoning and rationality, without which the developmental picture is incomplete. But it was not just developmentalists who needed to see an account of human reasoning and rationality that integrates the cognitive and developmental literatures. I wanted to write a book for cognitive, developmental, educational, and other psychologists interested in a broad perspective on reasoning. Thus the term "development" does not appear in the title of this book and the book is not primarily about children, though the perspective throughout is substantially developmental.

Second, I have appreciated the efforts of psychologists and philosophers working to extend the study of reasoning from individual to group reasoning and to develop new conceptions of reasoning as a social process of argumentation. I have also appreciated the work of theorists of democracy to develop models of deliberative democracy in which argumentation plays a central role. I wanted to provide a comprehensive account that construes reasoning and rationality as no less social than individual, encompassing inter-individual processes of argumentation, which can be seen as collaborative reasoning, and rational social institutions, including deliberative forms of democracy. I ultimately decided I could best communicate the focus of the book with a title that proceeds from reasoning to argumentation to deliberative democracy.

Finally, as I thought about the extended picture of reasoning, and about the state of the world, I realized I also had an argument to make about the role of reasoning in democracy and the promotion of rationality at both individual and social levels. I have tried to present the psychology of reasoning in a way that not only extends to the social but also illuminates the potential for enhancing democracy.

Reasoning, Argumentation, and Deliberative Democracy provides an integrated treatment of the reasoning and rationality of individuals, as studied in the largely distinct literatures of cognitive and developmental psychology. Going beyond these psychological literatures, it also considers social aspects of reasoning and rationality, drawing not only on social psychology but also making connections to philosophy, law, political science, and educational policy. The book has nine chapters, beginning with an introduction that summarizes the argument and introduces the main concepts. The second chapter reviews research on the development of logical reasoning. Chapter 3 expands the conception of reasoning beyond logic to other forms of reasoning. Chapter 4 develops the conception of rationality beyond various forms of reasoning to include metacognitive knowledge about and control of reasoning. Chapter 5 expands the conception of reasoning beyond individual cognition, the focus of most of the cognitive and developmental literature, to include collaborative reasoning. Chapter 6 extends this social conception of rationality beyond interindividual argumentation to societal aspects of rationality. Chapter 7 goes beyond earlier descriptions of developmental progress to look more directly at the process of developmental change. Chapter 8 goes beyond the explanatory focus of the previous chapters to consider the deliberate promotion of reasoning, rationality, and democracy. Finally, Chapter 9 turns to science fiction to understand our world of persons and reasons.

This book is aimed in part at researchers, theorists, and students in cognitive, developmental, and educational psychology concerned with reasoning, rationality, metacognition, and/or advanced levels of development. I hope cognitive psychologists will see the importance of a developmental perspective in understanding human rationality and that developmental psychologists will see the importance of a serious look at adult cognition in understanding the reasoning of children and the nature of developmental change. I also hope all psychologists will see the importance of conceptualizing reasoning socially while maintaining a focus on individuals.

The book is also intended for audiences beyond the field of psychology. In particular, the focus on deliberative democracy connects the psychological study of reasoning to questions of law, philosophy, and political science. For anyone aiming to develop a psychologically plausible account of deliberative democracy, or simply concerned about the state of democracy in the 21st century, recent psychological claims of human irrationality may be disheartening. I show in this book that there is much evidence supporting rationalist assumptions and much we can do to promote the sort of reasoning that makes democracy possible and productive.

The book may serve as a supplementary text for students in upper-level and graduate courses, especially in psychology and education, including courses in cognitive psychology, thinking and reasoning, cognitive development, or lifespan development. Because it is substantially interdisciplinary, it does not assume readers will be expert in any particular discipline. In the introductory chapter I provide an overview of the book's main argument and an introduction to 15 central concepts from several relevant disciplines. I have also carefully defined all terms as I proceed and included a glossary for reference. I hope this book will help readers see the big picture of reasoning and rationality in a way that connects theories, concepts, and evidence from a variety of fields.

For early guidance in the study of reasoning, I am grateful to Edith Neimark, my graduate adviser at Rutgers University, whose work spanned cognitive development (Neimark, 1970) and adult thinking (Neimark, 1987; Neimark & Santa, 1975), including Piaget's conception of formal operations (Neimark, 1975) and related work on logical reasoning (Neimark & Slotnick, 1970). She was hard to please but I always hoped for the best when I gave her the latest draft of whatever I was writing, and I was always delighted if she thought it was not too bad.

I am grateful to Deanna Kuhn for detailed and helpful feedback on the manuscript. I also thank Rick Bady, Austin Dacey, Wim De Neys, Jeff Fraum, John Gibbs, Charlie Hauss, Peter Levitov, Rick Lombardo, Henry Markovits, Hugo Mercier, Adam Morfeld, Bill Overton, Harvey Siegel, Les Smith, Rich Stamler, Keith Stanovich, Joe Starita, Truong Thi Nhu Ngoc (Ruby), and Sam Walker for comments on various chapters.

As always, I am grateful to my wife Sara for everything and more, even if that's a logical impossibility.

1

INTRODUCTION

Research on reasoning has undermined traditional assumptions of human rationality. The concept of democracy, however, assumes that people are rational agents, competent to govern themselves individually and collectively. If humans are not rational agents, we must reconsider the political ideal of democracy.

I argue in this book that, despite systematic flaws in human reasoning, there are three reasons for a cautiously optimistic assessment of human rationality and the prospects for democracy. First, research and theory in cognitive and developmental psychology provide the basis for a more positive assessment of individual rationality. Second, groups of people, under the right circumstances, reason better than individuals. Third, developmental progress toward greater rationality can be promoted through education. Psychological research provides a basis for conceptualizing a system of deliberative democracy that relies on and promotes collaborative reasoning, rational institutions such as science and law, education aimed at the promotion of rationality, and intellectual freedom for all.

I begin this chapter with a nontechnical overview of the book, supporting and fleshing out the argument summarized in the two paragraphs above. This is followed by three sections providing a more technical introduction to 15 central concepts: reasoning, rationality, reasons, persons, bounded rationality, heuristics and biases, dual processing, metacognition, epistemic cognition, developmental progress, developmental process, argumentation, deliberative democracy, education, and intellectual freedom.

Overview

The remaining eight chapters of the book begin with the biological bases of logic and proceed from there to reasoning of several sorts, metacognitive

aspects of rationality, rational argumentation, the ideal functioning of democratic societies, the nature of development at individual and social levels, the role of educational institutions in the promotion of rationality, and defending against the Borg.

Chapter 2 (Development of Logical Reasoning) considers the development of logical reasoning, beginning with Piaget's conception of logic as intrinsic to biological self-regulation. Psychological research reveals a sensorimotor logic of action already developing in infancy and shows that even preschool children routinely make logically correct inferences. The development of logic is in large part the development of (metalogical) understanding about the nature of logic and associated regulation of one's inferences. Research shows systematic and universal progress in logical reasoning over the first 12 years of life, leading to the ability (beginning about age 11 or 12 years) to determine the logical implications of ideas one deems hypothetical or even false. Development beyond that is much less universal and related more to experience and education than to age. There is extensive evidence that even adults fall far short of logical perfection, with substantial individual differences. Mathematical reasoning, which also involves matters of logical necessity, shows a similar developmental pattern of universal childhood progress over the first 12 years, with substantial individual differences in further development and systematic errors at all ages.

One might think the development of logical reasoning is the basic story of reasoning and rationality. Perhaps all we need to complete the picture is more detail about logical functioning at various ages across the lifespan.

Chapter 3 (Reasoning Beyond Logic) argues to the contrary that, even if we interpret logic broadly to go beyond deduction, reasoning is more than logic. Causal reasoning is discussed as a form of reasoning central to science that cannot be reduced to logic because it involves matters of empirical fact and theoretical interpretation that go beyond logical necessity. Reasoning beyond logic also includes principled reasoning, which is central to morality, and reasoning on the basis of precedent, which is central to social tradition. Logical, causal, principled, and precedent-based reasoning are all concerned with matters of truth and justification, though they conceive of such matters differently. Reasoning is defined as epistemologically self-regulated thinking, meaning it involves a focus on the justification and truth of one's conclusions. This involves the generation and use of reasons, including but not limited to logical reasons. As with logical reasoning, research on causal, principled, and precedent-based reasoning shows systematic and universal progress in the first 12 years of life. Here too, however, adults show substantial individual differences in the extent of development beyond that, and all fall far short of rational perfection.

One might think this expanded conception of reasoning, in which logical reasoning is one of several forms, provides a comprehensive framework. Perhaps all that remains is to flesh out the picture with detailed research on the development and functioning of various sorts of reasoning.

Chapter 4 (Metacognition and Epistemic Cognition) argues to the contrary. Taking into account the psychological reality of logical inferences in very young children, it makes the case that the development of reasoning is in large part the development of metacognition, expanding on the discussion in Chapter 2 about the development and role of metalogical understanding. Of particular importance to reasoning is the aspect of metacognition concerned with the justification and truth of beliefs—epistemic cognition. The chapter traces the development of epistemic cognition in childhood and beyond. Drawing on a variety of theorists, it suggests there is a theoretical consensus that epistemic development is largely a process of recognizing subjectivity and then re-establishing a basis for objectivity (at least as a meaningful ideal) in multiple domains and at multiple levels of abstraction. Looking across Chapters 2–4, cognitive development is presented as progress toward rationality, thus distinguishing it from other cognitive changes. A distinction can be made between basic development, referring to the universal progress in rationality across the first 12 years of life, and advanced development, referring to further progress that is highly variable across individuals.

Again one might think we now have the basic framework of reasoning and rationality with only specifics left to be filled in about our understanding and regulation of our various inferential processes across development. What more could there be?

Chapter 5 (Argumentation as Collaborative Reasoning) notes that the picture so far presented, consistent with the literatures of cognitive and developmental psychology, construes reasoning as a process that takes place in an individual mind. An emerging literature, however, suggests that argumentation among people can be construed as a process of collaborative reasoning. The chapter reviews evidence that when small groups engage in reasoning they are sometimes more rational than any of their individual members. Of course it is also true that groups can be less rational than their members. Examination of the conditions that foster group rationality suggests the importance of respect for reasons and persons. It appears that rationality can be enhanced through argumentation, but the possibility and quality of argumentation depend on the size, circumstances, and functioning of the group, including the respect of group members for each other's intellectual freedom.

Having supplemented the standard individualistic picture of reasoning and rationality with a social picture, it might appear that the account is now comprehensive. Again, what more could there be?

Chapter 6 (Democracy as Collaborative Rationality) adds another whole dimension to the discussion by distinguishing two meanings of social (following Piaget and many other theorists): (1) interindividual and (2) societal. Argumentation among individuals in small groups (the topic of Chapter 5) addresses the social aspect of reasoning only in the first sense. What remains is the nature and role of society. Many theorists in philosophy, law, and political science (especially neo-Kantians such as John Rawls) have construed democracy as a project of collaborative rationality based on respect for reasons and respect for persons, and some in this tradition have specifically advocated "deliberative democracy" as the ideal form of democracy. This chapter connects democratic theory to research on reasoning and rationality. Along the way, it examines identity as a theory of oneself that coordinates the personal and the social, notes the dangers of identity for rationality and democracy, and proposes a concept of rationalist identity consistent with deliberative democracy. Argumentation is crucial to social institutions, such as legislatures, law, and science, that play important roles in the rationality of democratic social systems. Intellectual freedom, seen in Chapter 5 as crucial to argumentation, is correspondingly crucial to democracy, especially deliberative democracy.

We now have an account of reasoning and rationality extending from the biological bases of logic early in Chapter 2 to the ideal functioning of democratic societies and rational institutions in Chapter 6. Now, one might think, we must surely be done, unless we want to talk about rationality across the galaxy or in nonbiological forms. But the picture remains incomplete even if we remain on Earth and stick to human rationality.

Chapter 7 (The Rational Construction of Rational Agency) turns our attention to processes and patterns of development. Previous chapters described the course of developmental progress in logical reasoning (Chapter 2); in scientific, moral, and social conventional reasoning (Chapter 3); and in the metacognitive basis for reasoning (Chapter 4). Chapter 7, however, looks more directly at fundamental processes of developmental change and general patterns of progress in rational agency. Drawing on Chapters 5 and 6, moreover, it considers the role of argumentation and democratic institutions in the development of individuals and the possibility that groups and societies might themselves show developmental change. I argue that rationality is neither inherent in the human genome nor learned from human environments, though genes and environments are obviously important. Rather, rationality is constructed over time by increasingly rational agents through rational and social processes of reflection and coordination. Subjectivity is inevitable but reflection on subjectivity enables progress to metasubjective forms of objectivity and increasingly rational self-governance at individual, social, and societal levels.

And what remains beyond this seemingly comprehensive account of the development of reasoning and rationality? What more is there to be said?

Chapters 2–7, even as each went beyond the previous one, remained focused on *describing* and *explaining* reasoning, rationality, and development. What remains for Chapter 8 (Education for Rationality) is the question of how we can *promote* the development of reasoning and rationality. The chapter begins with the concept of critical thinking, which has long been popular in education and, although variously defined, is closely connected to rationality in its concern for reasons. Peer argumentation is proposed as an educational approach that promotes the development of rationality. The chapter also notes the prevalence of indoctrination in curriculum and instruction, especially in elementary and secondary education. Extending previous discussions about the role of intellectual freedom in collaborative reasoning (Chapter 5), deliberative democracy (Chapter 6), and the development of rational agency (Chapter 7), Chapter 8 addresses the central role of intellectual freedom in any educational program aimed at the promotion of rationality. The chapter concludes with a brief sketch of the ideal rational agent.

And finally, I do turn to questions of rationality across the galaxy and in nonbiological forms. But my focus remains on human rationality on the planet Earth, which I now reconsider from the perspective of science fiction.

Chapter 9 (Reasons and Persons) begins with the Borg, a collective entity introduced in the television series *Star Trek: The Next Generation.* The Borg is composed of biomechanical life forms with limited individual agency. Within the *Star Trek* universe, the Borg is a fearsome threat because it assimilates all societies and civilizations it encounters. In the real world, I suggest, the more immediate threat is not that the Borg will arrive from elsewhere and assimilate us, but rather that we ourselves will turn into the Borg. Resisting that tendency requires active reflection on rationality. It also requires efforts to support reasons and persons, neither of which can exist without the other. I illustrate the importance of personhood with two legal cases in which a court faced specific questions as to whether a particular individual was legally a person. In 1879, the Ponca chief Standing Bear was found in a federal court in Omaha, Nebraska to be a person within the meaning of the law and thus entitled to determine where he would live. Nearly five centuries later, the android Data is likewise found, in an episode of *Star Trek: The Next Generation*, to be a person with the right to make his own choices. Turning finally to an episode from the original *Star Trek*, I illustrate the centrality of truth and justification. The alternative to the Borg is a world of persons and reasons.

Reasoning and Rationality

In the remaining three sections I introduce the major concepts of the book. First, I consider the nature of reasoning, especially in relation to rationality. I then turn to cognitive and developmental psychology, which have generally focused on the reasoning, rationality, and development of individuals. This individualist account is then supplemented by social considerations of argumentation and democracy that extend and enrich standard cognitive and developmental accounts of reasoning and rationality.

I begin with reasoning, a central concern of philosophy at least since Aristotle and a major topic of psychological research since the 1930s. The study of reasoning raises questions of rationality, leading to further discussion concerning the nature and role of reasons, agency, and personhood.

Reasoning as Epistemologically Self-Regulated Thinking

I use the term "reasoning" in much the way it is used both in ordinary discourse and in the scholarly literatures of philosophy and psychology. Although reasoning has been defined in a variety of ways, I attempt here to capture what I believe to be something close to a consensus. Reasoning is generally seen to be (1) inferential; (2) under the control of an agent; and (3) aimed at reaching conclusions that are true or at least justified. With respect to the first, reasoning is generally seen as a process by which we infer something that goes beyond what we have perceived. With respect to the second, automatic inferences play a crucial role in cognition but are usually distinguished from reasoning, which is deliberate. And with respect to the third, reasoning provides *reasons* for belief or action, which is why it makes good sense to call it *reason*ing.

With that in mind, I define *reasoning* as epistemologically self-regulated thinking. I define *thinking* as the deliberate application and coordination of one's inferences to serve one's purposes. I define *inference* as going beyond the data. And I use the term "epistemological" to refer to matters of truth and justification, based on a definition of *epistemology* as the study of knowledge, especially with regard to normative matters of justification and truth (Moshman, 2011a, 2015).

These definitions recognize that inferences can be entirely automatic. People routinely make inferences that they did not mean to make without any awareness that they have made them. You are making a variety of grammatical and semantic inferences right now as you extract meaning from the sequence of words in this sentence (Graesser, Singer, & Trabasso, 1994). Even young children routinely make a variety of inferences, including logical inferences (more on this in Chapter 2).

We do not generally regard our ongoing inferential processes as thinking, however. Rather, we reserve the term "thinking" for cognitive acts aimed at serving some purpose, involving some degree of awareness and control of our inferences. If you stop reading to study a particular sentence that confused you, focusing on specific words and grammatical relations, we might say you are thinking about that sentence. But it would seem odd to say that you have thought about every sentence you have read. Reading always involves the processing of information and is always inferential, but it seems useful to distinguish (a) a deliberate effort to make sense of something confusing from (b) the ongoing and largely automatic processing of text. More generally, it is important to distinguish acts of deliberation from automatic processes. Thus, following common (but not universal) practice, I reserve the term *thinking* for deliberate actions that serve the purposes of an agent.

Reasoning, in turn, is a type or aspect of thinking, but not all thinking is reasoning. Thinking may be aimed at practical goals, such as solving some problem or making some decision, and may be satisfied with pragmatic solutions. But sometimes we think in order to determine the truth of some matter, or at least to reach the most justified conclusion. Thus, again following common (but not universal) practice, I have defined reasoning as a subset of thinking in which we regulate our inferential processes for epistemic purposes—that is, to reach conclusions that are true, or at least justified.

Given this definition, multiple forms of reasoning can be distinguished. I consider logical reasoning in Chapter 2. I then proceed in Chapter 3 with causal, principled, and precedent-based reasoning, which are central, respectively, to the domains of science, morality, and social convention (Moshman, 2015). Later, in Chapter 5, I turn to argumentation, which I construe as a collaborative form of reasoning.

Good Reasoning, Bad Reasoning, and Not Reasoning

Reasoning of all sorts serves epistemic purposes. Thus we can evaluate it with respect to how well it serves those purposes. This suggests a distinction between good reasoning, which reaches justifiable conclusions, and bad reasoning, which reaches conclusions that cannot be justified. Such a distinction is indeed meaningful and important, but conceptual and empirical considerations complicate the picture. Sometimes what looks like good reasoning or bad reasoning is actually not reasoning at all. Thus we need an additional distinction: We must distinguish reasoning from not reasoning. Only if someone is actually reasoning is there a legitimate question of whether the reasoning is good or bad.

Consider a mathematical example: What is 4×3? An answer of 12 is correct, but if this answer comes to you immediately you are not reasoning. Right answers do not necessarily show good reasoning. This is not only because the reasoner may have been reasoning poorly and got lucky but also because the person in question may not be reasoning at all. Suppose, however, the question were asked of a child of about 8 years who had not memorized basic multiplication facts but understood the logic of multiplication. If the child determined that 4×3 means $4 + 4 + 4$, added $4 + 4$ to get 8, and then added another 4 to get 12, this would indeed be good reasoning. And if the child made a mistake along the way and ended with an answer different from 12, that would be less than good reasoning, maybe bad reasoning, but still reasoning.

Just as right answers do not necessarily show good reasoning, wrong answers do not necessarily show bad reasoning. One outcome of research in cognitive psychology is evidence that much of what might seem at first to be bad reasoning is actually not reasoning at all. Much of our cognition consists of automatic processes, including a variety of heuristics and biases, that are often helpful but may also lead us astray (Kahneman, 2011).

These considerations about reasoning raise questions of rationality, which can be seen in two ways. In the next subsection I present an objectivist conception of rationality as a matter of good reasoning rather than bad reasoning. The subsection after that supplements this with a subjectivist conception of rationality as a matter of rational agency, which is what makes reasoning (good or bad) possible at all.

As discussed above, we must distinguish good reasoning from bad reasoning, and must also distinguish reasoning (whether good or bad) from automatic cognitive processes. The objectivist aspect of rationality enables us to do the first. The subjectivist aspect enables us to do the second.

Rationality as Good Reasoning

Perhaps the most common conception of rationality, at least among psychologists, is that it is a matter of good reasoning. This conception of rationality is objectivist in that it assumes reasoning can be evaluated objectively against logical, statistical, or other norms. There is sometimes dispute about what norms apply in particular cases, but the concern with norms connects empirical psychology to the normative considerations of philosophy. To what extent, asks the objectivist conception of rationality, do people reason the way logicians and other philosophers say they should?

The answer is we often do and often don't. Sometimes when we don't conform to logical or other norms it is unclear whether we should have done so. But in many cases there is a consensus among experts that the failure to conform to normative standards cannot be justified. Both good reasoning and bad reasoning are common. The objectivist conception of rationality highlights the rationality of good reasoning.

Rationality as Rational Agency

The objectivist conception of rationality, as just seen, evaluates reasoning by applying standards proposed by logicians and other philosophers. But why should we listen to logicians and philosophers? The short answer is that they are operating at a higher level of understanding with regard to logical and epistemological matters (more on this in Chapters 2, 4, and 7). But they are people, nonetheless. Without people there could be no reasoning or rationality at all. Rationality does involve objective norms but it is not a set of pre-existing rules. Rationality, in its subjectivist sense, is a characteristic of people, who, even when they reason badly, are rational agents.

To be a person, then, is to be a rational agent. To be a rational agent is to act on the basis of reasons. To act on the basis of reasons is to form, maintain, revise, and act on one's own beliefs rather than to have one's beliefs and actions caused by physical, biological, social, or other forces beyond one's control. Working through what we mean by reasoning and rationality takes us, it seems, beyond the causal universe to a world of reasons and persons.

Reasons and Persons

The human body is a physical object subject to causal forces. But we rarely explain the movements of human bodies in causal terms. Instead, we generally think and act on the presumption that we and others are *persons* who engage in *actions* on the basis of *reasons*.

If a tornado were to blow me across a field, for example, no one would ask *why* I crossed the field. The motion of my body was caused by strong winds. But in most cases where I cross a field, there would indeed be an expectation that I have and could provide an explanation. Maybe I was playing a game. Maybe I was going someplace. Maybe I was looking for something. Maybe I was avoiding someone. Maybe I was taking a walk. In each case I had a *reason* for crossing the field. Crossing the field was an *action*, not just a movement of my body, and is explained by my reasons, not by a physical or other force causing something to happen. This is what it means to be a rational agent.

This picture of persons as rational agents is not entirely true, but it is not simply a fiction. The presumption of rational agency is perhaps best described as an idealization. We are part of the causal universe, even when we think we are determining our own beliefs and behavior, but we are also, to some extent, rational agents. To the extent that we recognize and value our rational agency, we respect both reasons and persons. Respect for reasons and persons enhances our rational agency and, in the ideal, creates a world of reasons and persons in which reasoning and rationality flourish.

The opposite of this is the world of the Borg. In Chapter 9, using examples from *Star Trek*, I conclude the book with an idealized vision of a world of persons and reasons.

Cognition and Development

Reasoning has long been a major topic of study in both cognitive and developmental psychology, with substantial attention given to issues of rationality in both fields. In this section I discuss theoretical conceptions from cognitive and developmental psychology that play important roles in the present analysis of reasoning and rationality. Drawing first on cognitive psychology, I consider the bounded nature of human rationality, the role of heuristics and biases, and the plural nature of cognitive processes. Drawing on developmental and educational psychology, I consider metacognitive, and especially epistemic, aspects of reasoning and rationality. Finally, I consider what it means to make developmental progress, and what processes account for such progress.

Bounded Rationality

Our concern in this book is with *human* rationality, not all possible forms of rationality. Human reasoning is limited by the human information processing system. In evaluating human reasoning against rational ideals, we must recognize that not all ideals are humanly achievable. There may be some value in evaluating human reasoning against standards of rational perfection, but it is also important to evaluate human reasoning against what a human mind could reasonably be expected to achieve in a reasonable period of time. In fact, it is rational to do the best one can with the mental resources at hand and to reach a conclusion while there is still time to act on it. Sometimes people properly settle for a satisfactory solution rather than continuing to search for an ideal one.

One well-established constraint on human cognition, for example, is working memory (Barrouillet & Gaillard, 2011). Is it rational to consider only a small number of items at once rather than taking everything into account simultaneously? For a human being, there is often no choice but to simplify or approximate. Even if we should consider everything at once, we can't.

Limitations, however, can often be overcome. If you ask me to multiply 8,756 by 3,472 in my head, the best I can do is provide an approximate result, not because I don't understand multiplication but because the information processing demands of the task overload my working memory. But I can provide an exact result using pencil and paper, or more easily with a calculator. Rationality is not just doing the best possible under the circumstances but creating better circumstances. Thus, the limitations of the human information processing system are not the last word, but they are a factor to be considered.

Heuristics and Biases

One might hope that, even if our information processing systems must function within strict constraints, such as working memory limits, our inferential processes are all rational at least in the sense of conforming to logical or other norms. Alas, as we will see in Chapter 2, research and theory since the 1930s have suggested that our inferential processes often lead us astray. Serious doubt about human rationality became increasingly prevalent and influential beginning with research by Peter Wason in the 1960s (Wason & Johnson-Laird, 1972).

Beginning in the early 1970s, Kahneman and Tversky (Kahneman, 2011) were particularly important in providing evidence that inference often involves heuristic processes that are subject to a variety of biases. To refer to these processes as "heuristic" suggests that they are pragmatically useful in providing satisfactory answers to questions we are likely to face. To refer to "bias" suggests that our inferences generate conclusions that deviate systematically from what rational norms require. Much research in the latter third of the 20th century suggested that human beings, far from being rational agents, are largely driven by nonlogical processes beyond our control.

Dual Processing

Dual process theories construe cognitive functioning as an interaction between distinct systems or levels of inferential processing. Such theories arose in cognitive and social psychology in the 1970s and have increasingly dominated the psychological study of reasoning since the 1990s (Barrouillet & Gauffroy, 2013; Evans, 2007; Evans & Stanovich, 2013; Kahneman, 2011; Klaczynski, 2000; Markovits, Brunet, Thompson, & Brisson, 2013; Ricco, 2015; Ricco & Overton, 2011; Stanovich, 2004, 2011). Current philosophical accounts of reasoning are also generally consistent with dual process conceptions and sometimes refer to them explicitly (Richard, 2019; Siegel, 2019; Staffel, 2019).

Dual process theories generally distinguish two systems or levels of processing. Despite differences in the precise characterization of these systems or levels, there appears to be a widely accepted distinction between a system of automatic and intuitive processes (often just called System 1) and a system of deliberate and reflective processes (often just called System 2). System 1 involves heuristics and biases that are often highly adapted to the cognitive issues we face but may also lead us astray. System 2, relying on deliberation and reflection, may overcome the limitations of System 1 but is itself subject to systematic biases due to strong commitments to protect and maintain our theoretical beliefs and personal identities.

With regard to rationality, then, System 1 is often rational in the objectivist sense but is not rational in the subjectivist sense. There is no agent responsible for its operations. System 2 is rational in the subjectivist sense of agency and respect for reasons but can be systematically biased by self-serving motivations, such as the human tendency to apply critical thinking selectively to disfavored ideas (Klaczynski, 2000). Human rationality relies on the interplay of both systems (Stanovich, 2004).

But human rationality, as already noted, is bounded by human constraints. Even if System 2 functioned perfectly, it could not replace System 1. Given the stringent limits of working memory and the effort required for self-regulation, ongoing application of System 2 to everything is not psychologically realistic for human beings. To function adaptively we rely largely on System 1, which involves automatic and intuitive processes not subject to the metacognitive demands of self-regulation and the strict constraints of working memory. The deliberate and reflective processes of System 2 are profoundly important but are just the tip of the cognitive iceberg, most of which operates below the surface of consciousness.

Further examination of System 1 shows it to be a collection of systems rather than a single system. There are many systems of automatic inference and associated intuitions. Inferring basic emotions from people's facial expressions, for example, is a complex cognitive task that nearly all of us perform automatically and effortlessly. It appears that evolution and early development provide us with a special system of inferential processes highly adapted to the specific task of inferring emotions from facial expressions. Similarly, speaking a human language requires complex linguistic transformations that are routine among 4-year-old children, though even adults are mostly unable to explain or justify their grammatical intuitions.

The diverse subsystems of System 1 operate autonomously, independent of each other and beyond the reach of System 2 (Stanovich, 2004).

There is reason to believe that System 2 is also internally complex (Ricco, 2015; Ricco & Overton, 2011; Stanovich, 2011). System 2 is generally seen as both deliberate and reflective. Thinking, as defined earlier in this chapter, is deliberate, and thus associated with System 2. Reasoning, defined as a form of thinking, is also deliberate and thus associated with System 2. But reasoning, as defined earlier, involves epistemological reflection on one's inferences, whereas thinking need not be reflective. Most versions of dual processing conflate two distinctions: (1) the distinction between automaticity and deliberation and (2) the distinction between intuition and reflection. This leads to a conception of just two systems, one automatic and intuitive and the other both deliberate and reflective. A distinction of reasoning from thinking, however, reminds us that thinking can be deliberate without being reflective. Thus, we need to distinguish (1) multiple systems of automatic inference and associated intuitions, (2) deliberate but pragmatic processes of thinking, and (3) reflective processes of reasoning.

Research on dual processing has important implications for understanding the development of reasoning and rationality. In demonstrating the major role of automatic, intuitive processes in human cognition at all ages, dual process conceptions remind us that deliberation supplements automatic inferences rather than replacing them, and that reflection supplements intuition rather than supplanting it.

Metacognition and Epistemic Cognition

Metacognition is cognition about cognition, including (1) conceptual knowledge about knowledge and inference and (2) procedural knowledge implicit in cognitive self-regulation (Moshman, 2011a, 2015; Schraw & Moshman, 1995). Thus defined, it is a very broad concept, including much that is discussed using related terms, such as self-monitoring, self-knowledge, introspection, reflection, cognizance, consciousness, metarepresentation, attribution, perspective taking, theory of mind, executive function, and executive control. Under varying terminology, metacognition has been a central topic of developmental and educational psychology since the 1970s. The human mind's understanding of itself and its ability to regulate itself show dramatic and universal age-related progress over the first 12 years of life. Metacognitive development often continues well beyond that, but there are substantial individual differences in the nature and extent of further progress (Demetriou & Spanoudis, 2018; Moshman, 2011a, 2015).

Thinking is metacognitive in that it involves the deliberate control of inferences to serve the purposes of the thinker. In the case of reasoning, this self-regulation is epistemological, meaning that it is particularly concerned with truth and justification. This requires knowledge about matters of epistemology—that is, *epistemic cognition* (Greene, Sandoval, & Bråten, 2016; Moshman, 2015). Thus epistemic cognition is the subcategory of metacognition most directly relevant to reasoning. Of course, few people other than philosophers read the literature of epistemology. But beginning in early childhood, we all think about matters of justification and truth and we all make dramatic progress in our understanding of these matters.

Early development of epistemic cognition can be seen in children's increasing recognition of their own subjectivity in a variety of situations, their progress in recognizing the legitimacy of multiple perspectives, and their later progress in understanding that, even if there isn't always one true answer, some ideas may be better than others. Adolescents and adults go beyond this in recognizing more abstractly that knowledge is frequently subjective, perhaps inherently subjective, raising general questions about the status of objectivity. Some come to understand the challenge of subjectivity more fully than others and some, to varying extents, respond to that challenge by constructing rationalist epistemologies that motivate and support better reasoning (Chandler, Hallett, & Sokol, 2002; Moshman, 2015).

Thus, there is great potential for development in epistemic cognition beyond childhood and associated progress in reasoning, but great variability in the extent to which that potential is realized (Greene et al., 2016; King & Kitchener, 1994; Kuhn, 2005; Moshman, 2015). Metacognition and epistemic cognition are the topic of Chapter 4, with further discussion about the development and promotion of epistemic cognition in Chapters 7 and 8.

Developmental Progress

Development is change, but not all change is development. The prototypical example of developmental change is the case of an immature organism over some portion of the lifespan making anatomical and physiological progress toward maturity, as in the attainment of sexual maturity over the course of puberty. Four aspects of such change are particularly notable, providing the basis for a definition of development that distinguishes developmental changes from other sorts of change. First, the change takes place over an extended period of time. Second, the change is regulated by internal organismic processes rather than imposed directly by the environment. Third, the change involves a succession of qualitatively distinct structures or modes of functioning rather than simply a process of growth in the quantitative sense of getting larger or faster. And finally, the change is progressive, rather than arbitrary, neutral, regressive, pathological, or specific to particular environments or cultures. *Development*, then, is a type or pattern of change that is extended over time, self-regulated, qualitative, and progressive (Moshman, 2011a).

Developmental change extends far beyond anatomy and physiology to psychological realms of behavior and cognition (Piaget, 1967/1971). As we will see in Chapters 2–4, children show systematic age-related changes in logical, scientific, principled, and precedent-based reasoning and in associated conceptions of knowledge. By the age of 12 or 13 years, nearly all individuals have achieved a level of rational agency virtually unseen in children under the age of 10 years, with strong potential in most cases for substantial further development in adolescence and adulthood. Development beyond age 12, however, is far from universal and is less related to age than to experience and education.

Developmental Process

The accounts of developmental change provided in Chapters 2–4 are largely descriptive, consisting mostly of a succession of stages or levels through which the individual passes in the course of development. But what explains such development? To explain development requires an account of the process itself, not just descriptions of a series of outcomes.

Research looking closely at developmental transitions suggests that progress in reasoning and rationality comes about through rational processes of coordination and reflection that transform earlier structures into better ones and make implicit knowledge explicit. The full discussion of developmental process is deferred until Chapter 7, however, because it needs to incorporate considerations mostly absent from Chapters 2–4 because they are mostly (though not entirely) absent from the literatures of cognitive and developmental psychology. The missing considerations are social considerations, including both interpersonal rational exchanges (discussed in Chapter 5) and the rational institutions of society (Chapter 6).

Argumentation and Democracy

Argumentation is both cognitive and social. It is closely associated with reasoning but not always seen as a form of reasoning. I suggest that it be seen as collaborative reasoning, and that such reasoning can be seen as the foundation of democracy or, specifically, of an ideal form of democracy known as deliberative democracy.

Argumentation as Collaborative Reasoning

Argumentation is often seen as a matter of dispute. To argue is to disagree, which is to be disagreeable. But disagreement is a fact of life, and verbal dispute is far from the worst response to it.

Argumentation may thus be seen, somewhat more positively, as a matter of debate. Given two positions held by two different people, we argue to determine which, and thus who, is right. Even if neither person changes position, the debate may help others choose the better alternative. Thus, argumentation potentially serves a rational purpose.

But sometimes both positions have some merit, and neither debater is entirely correct. This may render the argumentation inconclusive and perhaps seemingly pointless. But if the process of argumentation is seen as collaborative reasoning, the arguing parties may find a way to coordinate their perspectives to create a new position better than either of the original positions, and thus may both profit from the exchange. As discussed in Chapter 5, research shows that, under the right circumstances, groups may use argumentation to operate more rationally than any of the individuals composing them.

Deliberative Democracy

Democracy is commonly seen as majority rule. But majorities may vote to ban minority religious and political views or to act against minority groups of all sorts. If rule of the majority is all there is to democracy, then democracy is a danger to minorities.

Liberal democracy may be defined as a social system based on equal respect for all persons. Equal respect for all persons entails a right of each to participate in democratic decision-making, including a right to have your vote count equally to others, which is the basis for the democratic principle of majority rule. But equal respect for all persons also entails respect for the fundamental rights of each individual, which constrains what democratic majorities may legitimately do (Rawls, 1971, 2001). These fundamental rights are typically specified in democratic constitutions protecting freedoms of belief and expression, legal equality, and rights to privacy and due process.

Many theorists of democracy have argued for some version of what has been called *deliberative democracy* (Bächtiger, Dryzek, Mansbridge, & Warren, 2018b; Nino, 1996). A *deliberative democracy* is a form of liberal democracy that takes as its ideal the achievement of consensus through rational processes of argumentation. If we think of democracy as rooted in respect for persons, deliberative democracy is equally rooted in respect for reasons. Respect for reasons, and associated processes of argumentation, serve to generate better decisions and are thus in the best interest of the social system. By recognizing persons as rational agents, moreover, respect for reasons furthers respect for persons. To respect a person is not just to allow that person a vote but to seriously consider his or her beliefs and reasons.

Ideally, deliberation leads to consensus. When it fails to do so, majority rule remains the basis for making decisions that must be made. Even when a decision must be made, it ideally remains clear that the majority could be wrong. Ideally a consensus remains that the process of argumentation followed, if necessary, by a vote, is the rational ideal, and that we are all best off in the long run if we respect that process even when we disagree with particular outcomes.

Deliberative democracy rests on a conception of persons as rational agents. The conception of persons as rational agents, like the corresponding conception of societies as deliberative democracies, is an idealization. People and societies routinely fall far short of rational norms. Nonetheless, I argue in Chapter 6 that people are sufficiently rational for deliberative democracy to be the ideal form of collective governance. Acknowledging systematic and pervasive human irrationality, I suggest three reasons for cautious optimism. First, as seen in Chapters 2–4, people are not as utterly irrational as some have claimed. On the contrary, adults at their best are rational in ways beyond the competence of children, and even children show increasing rationality over the course of childhood. Second, as seen in Chapter 5, argumentation under the right circumstances enhances reasoning. Deliberative democracies draw in multiple ways on the rational powers of argumentation to operate more rationally than the individuals who compose them. Finally, as discussed in Chapter 8, democratic societies can promote rationality, and thus democracy, through education.

Education for Rationality and Democracy

Education potentially serves many purposes. Two widely accepted purposes for education in democratic societies are the promotion of rationality and democracy. We can foster both through education aimed at the promotion of (1) the rational agency of individual students; (2) the social competencies that enable collaborative reasoning; and (3) the civic understandings and values that enable deliberative democracy.

Education may also undermine rationality and democracy, and often does, through indoctrination and censorship. In Chapter 8 I discuss both the problems of actual schools at all levels of education and the ideal of an educational system aimed at the promotion of rationality and democracy.

Intellectual Freedom

A recurring theme of the book is that rationality requires intellectual freedom. This includes freedoms of belief, expression, discussion, inquiry, and access to information and ideas. Intellectual freedom is crucial to rational argumentation (Chapter 5), deliberative democracy and rational institutions (Chapter 6), developmental progress (Chapter 7), and academic work at all levels of education (Chapter 8).

Intellectual freedom can be justified on at least three grounds. First, intellectual freedom is a fundamental right of individual persons as it respects their rational agency, which is what defines them as persons. Second, intellectual freedom serves the pursuit of truth by enabling collaborative reasoning. Third, intellectual freedom is necessary for democracy, especially deliberative democracy. But intellectual freedom is not just the absence of government censorship. Intellectual freedom, broadly defined as freedom to engage the intellect, is presented throughout much of the book as the basis for reasoning, rationality, argumentation, democracy, development, and education.

Conclusion

The remaining eight chapters are meant to be read in order but don't have to be. This first chapter provided an overview of the argument and an introduction to the central concepts of the book. That should suffice so readers with particular interests may sample from the remaining chapters as they please. Readers interested in individual cognition and development may wish to read Chapters 2, 3, and 4 most closely, and then proceed as their interests direct. Readers most interested in social cognition, democracy, or education may want to skim or skip Chapters 2–4 to focus on later chapters. *Star Trek* fans are free to go right to Chapter 9.

2

DEVELOPMENT OF LOGICAL REASONING

There is a long history of psychological controversy regarding the origins, nature, and development of logic, and its relation to thinking and reasoning (Braine & O'Brien, 1998; Evans, 2007, 2017; Henle, 1962; Inhelder & Piaget, 1955/1958, 1959/1964; Johnson-Laird, 2006; Johnson-Laird & Byrne, 1991; Langer, 1980, 1986; Mercier & Sperber, 2017, 2019; Markovits, 2014, 2020; Moshman, 1990, 2004b; 2015; 2018; Noveck, 2019; Overton, 1990; Piaget, 1928/1972, 1967/1971; Ricco, 2015; Ricco & Overton, 2011; Rips, 1994; Smith, 1993; Wason & Johnson-Laird, 1972). In this chapter I present theories and research concerning the early emergence of logic, developmental progress in logical reasoning, and associated developmental progress in knowledge about the nature of logic. I then turn to the extensive literature on logical reasoning in adults, showing that it is best understood in a developmental context. Finally, I raise questions about the scope of logic in relation to reasoning, leading to Chapter 3, which considers reasoning that goes beyond logic.

Early Logic

Logic, one might think, is the culmination of the development of reasoning. But one would be wrong about that. Logic, it appears, is where it all begins.

Consider this deduction: If an object is *here* or *there*, and it is not *here*, it is *there*. A logician might call that a disjunctive inference, but you don't need to be a logician to act on a sensorimotor understanding that if something is here or there, and not here, look there. In fact, you don't even need language. Disjunctive logic can be observed in the behavior of infants still in the first year of life (Cesana-Arlotti et al., 2018; Piaget, 1937/1954).

The Origins of Logic

The most systematic and convincing answer to the question of the origin of logic, in my view, comes from Jean Piaget's (1967/1971) classic *Biology and Knowledge*, which addressed the fundamental question of how a living organism could have knowledge, especially what he called logico-mathematical knowledge, which concerns matters of logical necessity. Living things, Piaget argued, are, most fundamentally, self-regulating systems, and logic is intrinsic to self-regulation at physiological, behavioral, and cognitive levels. Among their many logical aspects, self-regulating systems include structures of inclusion (classification) and structures of ordering (seriation).

With regard to inclusion, after detailed analysis of multiple examples, Piaget (1967/1971) concluded:

> Thus, the classificatory function seems to be found in every organization structure, and this fact constitutes a remarkable structural isomorphism between biological and cognitive organizations. Of course, we are not talking of the same kinds of classification; sometimes the inclusions of the subclasses or substructures within classes or structures are, as it were, incorporated in a material organization . . ., sometimes they are an immanent part of a functioning . . ., [and] sometimes they arise out of it.
>
> *(pp. 163–164)*

Similarly, concluding a section on structures of ordering, Piaget (1967/1971) wrote:

> To sum up, order structures do seem at the outset (from the DNA stage) to be inherent in every biological organization and in its functioning. At the other end, order structures are produced by thought, but a thought which also is ordered in its functioning. Between these two extremes are found all the intermediary stages, and the parallelism between these and inclusion structures could be described in greater detail. Here again we are confronted with a fundamental isomorphism between biological and cognitive structures.
>
> *(p. 166)*

Transformation of biological (including behavioral and cognitive) systems tends to maintain or enhance their equilibrium. Logic is implicit in biological systems, including their psychological functioning, and becomes increasingly explicit at more advanced levels of equilibrium. In Piaget's words, "thought starts in structures that are immanent to the living organization, but by reconstructing them at its own level it extends and enriches them in endless ways" (p. 164).

McCulloch and Pitts (1943) published a classic analysis of the logic inherent in neural networks that was favorably cited by Piaget (1967/1971) as an example, at the level of nervous functioning, of his thesis that logic can be found in biological structures at all levels. McCulloch and Pitts (1943) wrote:

> Because of the "all-or-none" character of nervous activity, neural events and the relations among them can be treated by means of propositional logic. It is found that the behavior of every net can be described in these terms, with the addition of more complicated logical means for nets containing circles; and that for any logical expression satisfying certain conditions, one can find a net behaving in the fashion it describes.
>
> *(p. 115)*

But Piaget (1967/1971) cautioned:

> The first question to ask is whether this is indeed a case of "logic" or of a cognitive mechanism. One can certainly speak of some kind of logic, but only on condition that a careful distinction be made . . . between the structures inherent in a function, which thus intervene as factors in its internal mechanism, and the structures produced by the function, which inaugurate functioning of a higher order, that is, "behavior."
>
> *(p. 222)*

In other words, even if there is a logic intrinsic to the functioning of the nervous system, this does not mean an organism is making logical inferences, much less engaging in logical reasoning. To understand the transition from the logic implicit in all biological functioning to the increasingly explicit logic of human childhood, we must consider the sensorimotor logic of infancy.

Sensorimotor Logic

Piaget (1936/1963) conducted longitudinal observations of each of his three children over the course of infancy, resulting in a detailed account of the development of what he called "sensorimotor" intelligence, beginning with the elementary reflexes of newborn infants and culminating in the emergence of what he called "representational" intelligence in the latter part of the second year of life. Much of the analysis focused on how infants devise means to serve their ends. "Deduction," Piaget wrote, "appears at its beginnings as the direct extension of earlier mechanisms of assimilation and accommodation, but on a plane which begins to become differentiated from direct perception and action" (p. 349). Thus "sensorimotor deduction" (p. 347), involving observable trial and error, is transformed in the second year of life into "mental deduction" (p. 348), which requires representational intelligence. In related work, Piaget (1937/1954) looked at how infants, through the coordination of their increasingly intelligent sensorimotor action-schemes, construct increasingly objective sensorimotor conceptions of space, time, objects, and causality. Such conceptions include matters of implicit logic, such as the reversibility of displacements in space.

The most thorough and systematic investigation of infant logic can be found in a series of two volumes by Langer (1980, 1986). The study involved 12 infants at each of the ages 6, 8, 10, and 12 months (reported in the first volume) and 12 older infants/toddlers at each of 15, 18, 21, and 24 months (reported in the second volume). The sample was mostly cross-sectional but included a longitudinal aspect in that some of the 10-month-olds had previously been assessed at 8 months. Over multiple trials, each participant was presented with a series of carefully devised combinations of a diverse set of objects, varying in arrangement and subject to a variety of manipulations, with interventions by the experimenter on some trials. Children's videotaped actions were analyzed with respect to logical considerations, such as classification, ordering, mapping, equivalence, replacement, substitution, commutativity, combinativity, correlation, negation, reversibility, and exchange. The results showed ongoing progress in logic throughout the period of 6–24 months.

Langer's interpretation of his results is generally consistent with Piaget's account of sensorimotor development but more directly focused on specific matters of logic. On the fundamental issue of the origin of logic in relation to language, the substantial logic already seen in children of 12–15 months strongly supports Piaget's (1967/1971) claim that "logico-mathematical structures are extracted from the general coordination of actions long before they make any use of language, either natural or artificial" (p. 181).

Critics of Piaget's account of infant development have argued that he underestimated the extent of innate knowledge and/or the rate of early development. Such claims generally refer to new evidence that competencies observed by Piaget appear to be present even earlier than he acknowledged (Gopnik, 2009). But virtually no one has argued that Piaget overestimated infant competence. The consensus among developmentalists is that infants of any age are at least as logical as Piaget thought.

Preschool Inference

Though logic can be seen prior to language, there is no doubt that the representational intelligence and emerging language of 2-year-olds have major implications for the nature and scope of logic, and for our ability to study it. Scholnick and Wing (1991) analyzed uses of the word "if" in conversations involving 4-year-olds and adults (mostly their parents and teachers). They found that the 39 4-year-olds (as well as the adults) used "if" commonly, in most cases in sentences that "resembled the first premise of a conditional syllogism" (1991, p. 249). The children made inferences that were classified as *modus ponens* (of the form *If p then q; p; therefore q*) and *modus tollens* (of the form *If p then q; not-q; therefore not-p*), both of which are consistent with the logic of conditional relations. They also made *biconditional* inferences, which involve interpreting *If p then q* symmetrically to entail *If q then p*. There is room for considering how much logic should be read into such isolated inferences, but it seems clear that preschool children make logical inferences at least in the sense that they often make inferences consistent with rules of logic.

In closely related research, longitudinal analyses following three preschool children from ages 2 to 5 years (Scholnick & Wing, 1992) showed early progress from (1) comprehending adult use of *if* to (2) making inferences from adult *if* sentences to (3) child production of *if*. "Within 6 months of speaking their first *if*," Scholnick and Wing (1992) concluded, "children produced *ifs* at the same rate and in the same forms as adults" (p. 1). Further longitudinal analyses including two additional children (for a total of five) showed, "By the time the children produced their own *ifs*, their inferences resembled adults." (Scholnick & Wing, 1995, p. 319).

Another line of research on preschool logical inference concerns transitivity. Transitive inference involves the logic of ordering (seriation). If A is larger than B, and B is larger than C, we can conclude that A is larger than C. But even without making a transitive inference, a child who is told that A is larger than B and B is larger than C might conclude A is larger than C simply because she has heard about A being large (in the first premise) and C not-large (in the second premise). Bryant and Trabasso (1971), in a study of 4-year-olds, provided a way to address this problem. In what has become a standard methodology, children learn (for example) that A is larger than B, B is larger than C, C is larger than D, and D is larger than E. They are then asked the relative size of B and D, which have not been compared directly. In this expanded format, the child has learned about B being both not-large (first premise) and large (second premise) and about D being both not-large (third premise) and large (fourth premise), so a conclusion that B is larger than D cannot be based on a categorical distinction between things that are or are not large. The children's success on this task was attributed to genuine transitive inference.

Going beyond human cognition, researchers using nonverbal variations on Bryant and Trabasso's (1971) methodology have found what many deem evidence for transitive inference in a variety of mammals and birds, and even in fish and insects (Tibbetts, Agudelo, Pandit, & Riojas, 2019), though skeptics have proposed and provided evidence for alternative interpretations (Zentall, Peng, & Miles, 2019). Regardless of what inferences we attribute to various species, however, it seems clear that preschool children make logical inferences, including transitive inferences, by the age of 4 years.

Braine & O'Brien (1998; see also Rips, 1994) developed a theory of "mental logic" that helps explain both preschool logical competence and subsequent development. The theory has three components. The first is a set of elementary "inference schemas" such as *If p then q; p; therefore q* (*modus ponens*) and *p or q; not-p; therefore q* (disjunction) that are assumed to be available to everyone beginning in early childhood. The second component is a "reasoning program" that applies the schemas in lines of reasoning. This includes a relatively effortless "direct-reasoning routine" that is also assumed to be universal beginning in early childhood. The reasoning program also includes some more effortful "indirect-reasoning strategies" that develop later, if at all. Finally, the third component of mental-logic theory involves pragmatic considerations of meaning, comprehension, and conversational expectations.

Thus in Braine and O'Brien's (1998) mental-logic theory, which is supported by substantial research, the inference schemas and direct-reasoning routine together comprise a basic mental logic. Inferences that can be made on the basis of this logic are routinely made beginning in the preschool years, whereas other inferences, which require more effort and control, are seen less routinely and only later in development, if at all.

Progress in Logical Reasoning

As we have seen, human development is rooted in the implicit logic of self-regulatory systems and proceeds through the sensorimotor logic of infancy to the verbal inferences of preschool children. What, one may ask, remains to develop?

Knowledge of Inference

Perhaps the most important initial development marking progress beyond the preschool years is emerging knowledge of inference. Although preschool children routinely make inferences, it appears they do not know they are making inferences, do not attribute inferences to others, and fail to recognize inference as a source of knowledge for themselves and others. Beginning at age 6 years, however, children are aware that they and others make inferences and show increasing knowledge about the nature and role of inference (Miller, 2012; Moshman, 2015; Pillow, 2012; Sodian & Wimmer, 1987).

Knowledge about inference includes knowledge about the logical properties of inferences, a matter of *metalogical understanding*. Metalogical understanding concerns the necessary truth of logical knowledge and the special kind of justification provided by logical proofs. We will consider metalogical understanding in Chapter 4 as part of *epistemic cognition*, people's knowledge about the justification and truth of beliefs and claims. Metacognition, including epistemic cognition, is no less important than logic for rational agency and thus democracy.

Classification and Seriation

In a series of studies with multiple collaborators, Inhelder and Piaget (1959/1964) interviewed over 2,000 children ranging in age from 3 to 9 years as they examined and manipulated assorted objects that could be classified and ordered in a variety of ways. The objects, presentation, and questions were designed to elicit behavior and explanations from the children relevant to class inclusion, hierarchical classification, complementary classes, multiplicative classification (matrices), seriation, and multiple seriation.

The studies showed a regular progression from preschool "graphic collections" and isolated inferences to behavior and explanations that show children understand and apply the logic of classification and seriation beginning at age 7 or 8 years. Understanding the logic of hierarchical classification, for example, includes understanding that a class may be divided into subclasses and logically must have at least as many members as any subclass within it. Inhelder and Piaget interpreted their results as part of Piaget's general theory of the emergence of what he called "concrete operations," emphasizing the role of logical structures in providing for a level of logical reversibility and equilibrium that is typical by age 7 or 8 years but not seen in preschool children.

Critics of Piaget's account have questioned his structural analysis of logical reasoning and devised tasks to show that logical competencies associated by Piaget with concrete operations are already available in the preschool years. In a classic early example already noted, Bryant and Trabasso (1971) interpreted their evidence for transitive inference in 4-year-olds as a challenge to Piaget's theory that the logic of seriation is not understood until age 7 or 8 years. Of course there is more to the logic of seriation than making a transitive inference, which raises complex theoretical issues. For present purposes, however, what is notable is that in childhood, as in infancy, critiques of Piaget have overwhelmingly focused on showing logical competence earlier than he acknowledged. Thus there is a longstanding consensus that 8-year-old children are at least as competent as Piaget's evidence indicated.

Hypothetico-Deductive Reasoning

The evidence seems clear that children are capable of logical reasoning by the age of 7 or 8 years (Inhelder & Piaget, 1959/1964)—if not even earlier, as proposed by many critics of Piaget's stage theory. What, then, if anything, remains to develop? Obviously, we may learn various new facts and skills useful in particular environments, and we may get more efficient at processing some kinds of information. But do we continue to make progress toward more advanced forms of reasoning or higher levels of rationality?

Philosophers since Plato and Aristotle have theorized about the nature of advanced reasoning and logic. In the early days of psychology, James Mark Baldwin (1895) postulated a "hyper-logical" stage of mental development marked by the emergence of pure thought, form without content. Piaget (1928/1972) took up the question of formal reasoning in some of his earliest work. By formal reasoning, Piaget (1928/1972) meant "formal deduction," which

> consists in drawing conclusions, not from a fact given in immediate observation, nor from a judgment which one holds to be true without any qualifications (and thus incorporates into reality such as one conceives it), but in a judgment which one simply assumes, i.e. which one admits without believing it, just to see what it will lead to.
>
> *(p. 69)*

Piaget's (1928/1972) research showed that formal or "hypothetico-deductive" (p. 69) reasoning begins to be seen at age 11 or 12 years. The deductions of younger children may be logical, but such deduction "bears only upon the beliefs which the child has adopted himself" (p. 67). Formal reasoning, in Piaget's conception, enables the adolescent to reason strictly about hypotheses in a constructed realm of possibility that is explicitly distinguished from empirical reality. "To be formal," he proposed, "deduction must detach itself from reality and take up its stand upon the plane of the purely possible, which is by definition the domain of hypothesis" (p. 71).

As Piaget subsequently developed his structural theory of developmental stages, his conception of *formal reasoning* became his theory of *formal operations*. Inhelder and Piaget (1955/1958) provided the definitive statement of that theory along with supporting evidence from a series of 15 studies in which over 1,500 children and adolescents, ranging in age from 4 through 16 years, were interviewed about their responses to a variety of scientific tasks, involving apparatus such as a pendulum or balance beam, that required logical reasoning about possibilities and hypotheses. The results showed isolated inferences in the preschool years and concrete operational reasoning reflecting the logic of classification and seriation beginning about age 7 or 8 years, consistent with earlier and later work (Inhelder and Piaget, 1959/1964). Also consistent with earlier work (Piaget, 1928/1972), formal reasoning began to be seen at about age 11 or 12 years.

Inhelder and Piaget (1955/1958) continued to define formal reasoning as *hypothetico-deductive reasoning*—that is, as reasoning that begins with at least one premise that is purely hypothetical, or even known to be false, and proceeds from there through strictly logical deductions to a conclusion that follows necessarily from the premises, with full awareness that if a premise is false the conclusion may be false as well. Children can deduce what follows from premises they accept. Hypothetico-deductive reasoning extends the range of deductive reasoning to the realm of possibility, enabling exploration of the logical consequences of premises one does not accept. Such ability is crucial to scientific hypothesis testing, which reserves judgment on the truth of theories even as it deduces their predictions. Hypothetico-deductive reasoning continues to be widely studied not only in the transition to adolescence (Markovits, 2014, 2020; Moshman 2011a) but also in the reasoning of adults (Evans, 2007).

More broadly, formal reasoning construes reality as a subset of possibilities. Hypothetico-deductive reasoning enables the rigorous and systematic elaboration of logical possibilities, which in turn enables one to reconsider reality within a larger hypothetical context. Even young children consider possibilities, as can be seen in the imaginative play of preschoolers. But children's possibilities are relatively direct extensions of reality. Formal operations transcend concrete operations in that possibilities are now formulated in such a way that reality can be understood and evaluated as the realization of a particular possibility. This enabled better hypothesis testing on the scientific tasks of Inhelder and Piaget (1955/1958), but the implications, they noted, extend far beyond that. With the attainment of formal operations, all sorts of accepted ideologies and conventions may be seen as open to critique and reconsideration on the basis of newly constructed possibilities.

Finally, formal operations are second-order operations in that they operate on concrete (first-order) operations, such as classification and seriation, to create logics that recognize classes of classes and relations of relations. Formal operations, in Piaget's theory, involve the "complete combinatorial system" of propositional logic, which represents a more advanced and stable form of equilibrium than the multiple concrete logics of classes and relations. Thus there is a metacognitive aspect to Piaget's conception of formal operations as second-order operations that derives from his metacognitive conception of development as a reflective process of constructing more equilibrated structures. We will return to these matters in addressing metalogical understanding as an aspect of epistemic cognition in Chapter 4 and reflection as a developmental process in Chapter 7.

Psychologists have been skeptical of the more technical aspects of Piaget's theoretical account of formal operations, which are widely seen as unclear and difficult to test. Nevertheless, developmental research has strongly supported Inhelder and Piaget's (1955/1958) empirical observation that hypothetico-deductive reasoning emerges at about age 11 or 12 years (Moshman, 1990, 2011a; Moshman & Franks, 1986). Recent research has been aimed at providing a more detailed picture of the transition from concrete to formal reasoning by investigating progress across the preadolescent years in the elaboration and manipulation of mental models of possible states of affairs (Markovits, 2014, 2020).

The major challenge to Piaget's theory of formal operations has come from research on adult reasoning, which seems to show much less rationality than does Piaget's research. The study of child development since the 1960s has consisted in large part of efforts to show that infants and children are more rational than Piaget claimed. The study of adult reasoning since the 1960s, in contrast, has focused largely on demonstrating systematic deviations from logical, statistical, and other norms. Such deviations have been interpreted by many to show that human irrationality is not just a matter of the occasional mistake but a matter of deep flaws in how we process information.

Logical Reasoning in Adulthood

I now consider the literature of adult logical reasoning, first historically and then in the context of the developmental literature on logical reasoning. Does the theory of formal operations overestimate human rationality? Does the literature of adult reasoning underestimate it? As we will see, a combination of dual process theory and a developmental perspective enables us to reconcile the seemingly divergent findings. I conclude that logical reasoning does indeed develop, but the adult reasoning literature helps put this into context by addressing the nature and limitations of advanced logical functioning.

The View from Cognitive Psychology

Psychological research on logical reasoning can be traced to a series of studies published in German by Störring beginning in 1908 (cited in Woodworth & Sells, 1935) and one in English by Wilkins (1928). Drawing on Aristotelian logic, these studies presented abstract categorical syllogisms, each consisting of two premises and a conclusion. Each premise and each conclusion was stated with letters in one of four possible forms: *All X are Y*, *No X are Y*, *Some X are Y*, and *Some X are not Y*. Some of the syllogisms were valid and others were not. For example, the syllogism *All A are C; All B are C; therefore, Some B are A* is not valid because the conclusion, although possible, does not follow necessarily from the premises. Results showed high rates of error in evaluating the validity of abstract syllogisms, including systematic errors associated with particular patterns.

Woodworth and Sells (1935) provided a theoretical analysis of results from these early studies, suggesting that, despite some evidence of logic, participants' identification of valid inferences was compromised by three factors. First, there was a tendency to interpret "some" as "some but not all" (which, depending on context, is often a reasonable interpretation in ordinary language) rather than as "at least some and perhaps all" (which is how the term is used in formal logic). Second, there is a tendency toward "caution" that rendered participants wary of conclusions involving "All" statements. Third, participants' judgments of validity were influenced by whether the conclusion matched the premises in "atmosphere," which involved being affirmative ("All") vs. negative ("No") and/or being universal ("All" or "No") vs. particular ("Some are" or "Some are not"). Four decades before the rise of the heuristics and biases literature (introduced in Chapter 1), the tendency toward "caution" may be regarded as a bias, and the "atmosphere effect" may be considered an early example of what would come to be called a *heuristic*. Woodworth and Sells (1935) also provided new evidence on syllogistic reasoning (later published in greater detail by Sells, 1936) in support of their analysis.

Chapman and Chapman (1959) questioned the evidence for the postulated "atmosphere effect" and provided new evidence from research in which they presented sets of premises; in each case, they asked participants to choose their own conclusion from a set of choices (rather than providing complete arguments, as in all the earlier research). They found that neither "atmosphere" nor a combined consideration of "atmosphere" and "caution" (proposed by Sells, 1936) could account for their pattern of results. They proposed that many or most of the seemingly erroneous responses could be accounted for on the basis of reasonable interpretations of language and reasonable construals of task expectations, consistent with the first explanation from Woodworth and Sells (1935).

Mary Henle (1962) provided a classic philosophical and empirical defense of the role of logic in thinking. After reviewing philosophical analyses and psychological research, she used examples from her own research to illustrate cases where apparent errors in logical reasoning were due not to errors in the reasoning process itself but to other factors. In some cases, the problem was "failure to grasp or accept the logical task" (p. 370) by focusing on the truth of conclusions rather than whether they follow from the premises. Other cases involved "restatement of a premise or conclusion so that the intended meaning is changed" (p. 371). Some involved omitting a premise or slipping in additional premises. Henle concluded that, if one considers the premises that participants were actually starting from and the task as they understood it, there was no evidence for faulty reasoning. On the contrary, "the laws of logic . . . are widely discernible in the thinking process" (p. 373). She noted that logical inference "need not be explicit" (p. 373) but may involve "an implicit logical process" (p. 374). Henle provided some examples of rapid automatic inferences in daily life, such as "I do not want to wear the same dress two days in succession. I wore this dress yesterday; so I do not want to wear this dress today" (p. 374). She added, "if people were unable to reason logically, so that each arrived at different conclusions from the same premises, it is difficult to see how they could understand each other, follow one another's thinking, reach common decisions, and work together" (p. 374).

The modern era of research on adult reasoning is commonly traced to the early work of Peter Wason in the 1960s (reviewed by Wason & Johnson-Laird, 1972). Wason expanded the focus of research beyond the categorical syllogisms of Aristotle to modern propositional logic, focusing particularly on conditional reasoning, which involves reasoning from a premise of the form "If X then Y." His "selection task" is likely the most famous task in the extensive literature of logical reasoning. In the standard version, you are presented with a set of four cards, each with a letter on one side and a number on the other, and a hypothesis about those cards. The hypothesis is to be tested by turning one or more of the four cards, but no more than necessary. For example, the hypothesis might be, "If a card has a vowel on one side, then it has an even number on the other side" and the corresponding cards would show E, K, 4, and 7 on the visible sides. Which of these cards must be turned to determine conclusively whether that hypothesis is true or false? The two most common responses are to choose just the E card or the E and the 4. The logically correct response, however, is E and 7. The E card, which has a vowel on the visible side, would falsify the hypothesis if it had an odd number on the other side. The 7 card, which has an odd number on the visible side, would falsify the hypothesis if it had a vowel on the other side. Both of these cards must be turned because either could falsify the hypothesis. No other card needs to be turned because no other card could falsify the hypothesis, regardless of what is on the other side. If the hypothesis is not falsified by what appears on the other side of the E and 7 cards, then it is true.

Research on logical tasks has continued actively ever since and has generated a variety of theories of logical reasoning aimed at explaining both successes and failures. Two major sorts of theories provide general accounts of basic logical processes: mental logic theories and mental model theories. Mental logic theories (Braine & O'Brien, 1998; Rips, 1994), which postulate rules of logic, were discussed earlier in relation to logical inference in preschool children. Mental model theories (Johnson-Laird, 1983, 2006; Johnson-Laird & Byrne, 1991) propose that logical reasoning involves the elaboration and manipulation of mental models of possible states of affairs, rather than the application of rules, a conception that (as noted earlier) has been applied to developmental research by Markovits (2014, 2020). There is substantial evidence for both sorts of theories, suggesting that both logical rules and mental models play a role in logical reasoning.

Beginning in the 1970s, the literature on errors in logical reasoning was increasingly supplemented by research on what came to be called "heuristics and biases" (Kahneman, 2011), as discussed in Chapter 1. This was initially a rather distinct literature that was seen by many as demonstrating that people do not just make logical mistakes but rely on a variety of heuristics and biases rather than engaging in logical reasoning at all. The trend in the last three decades of the 20th century was toward conceptions of human beings as deeply and fundamentally illogical and, more generally, irrational.

But the evidence for human logical abilities, including the developmental research reviewed earlier, is multifaceted and difficult to deny. The major resolution to this problem has been within the context of dual processing. Dual process theories, as discussed in Chapter 1, have been the dominant approach since the turn of the century in explaining human reasoning and rationality. The standard dual process view is that we can be logical and often are, but that we fall short so often because our logical processes are not our only processes. The usual assumption here is that logic is part of System 2 deliberation and reflection, which does not always override System 1 automatic processes and intuitions. But that assumption is contrary to the views of both Piaget and Henle, as discussed above, and has been seriously questioned within 21st century cognitive psychology.

Is Logic a System 2 Ability?

In recent years, dual process researchers have questioned the usual assumption that logic is a System 2 ability. Research methodologies that impose strict time limits or extraneous burdens on working memory, which have been shown to dampen System 2 responses, have been found not to have the expected dampening effect on logic. Results indicate instead that people commonly make System 1 logical inferences. A major challenge for current dual process theorizing is to explain the origin, nature, and role of what dual process researchers call "implicit logic" (Trippas & Handley, 2018), "fast logic" (De Neys, 2018), and "logical intuitions" (De Neys, 2012; Pennycook, 2018; Thompson & Newman, 2018).

As seen earlier in this chapter, developmental research shows automatic and intuitive forms of logic in the early years of life. This is fully consistent with the independent conclusions in 21st century cognitive psychology that logic is a System 1 ability. What distinguishes System 2 is not logic but reasoning, which is relatively general and requires intensive use of working memory. But development is not the replacement of System 1 with System 2. Rather, combining developmental and dual process insights, we should see System 2 as supplementing System 1. The development of reasoning is, at least in part, a matter of comprehending and gaining control over systems of logic that can be traced back to early childhood and, even before that, to basic modes of biological functioning.

From a Developmental Perspective

The study of adult reasoning has long been quite distinct from the study of the development of reasoning. Adult reasoning is studied by cognitive psychologists, whereas the development of reasoning is studied by developmental psychologists, who are generally most concerned with childhood and adolescence. The study of the development of reasoning is generally seen as part of the field of cognitive development, which could be seen as the overlap of cognitive psychology and developmental psychology but is more commonly understood as a subdivision of developmental psychology. Research on adult reasoning is generally published in journals of cognitive psychology, such as *Thinking & Reasoning*, where clear evidence of systematic deviation from logical, statistical, or other norms is deemed theoretically interesting. Research on the development of reasoning is generally published in developmental journals, where the focus is often on showing clear evidence of some competence at an earlier age than anyone has shown before. Research on adult reasoning generally ignores development (for a recent example, see Evans, 2017), and researchers who study the development of reasoning often fail to address the adult reasoning literature (with notable counterexamples in the study of adolescence, such as Klaczynski, 2000; Markovits, 2013). The result of the communication gap between cognitive and developmental psychology is an apparent counter-developmental trend from preschool logic, as demonstrated in the developmental literature since the 1970s, to adult irrationality, as demonstrated in the cognitive literature since the 1960s (Moshman, 2004b).

Considering the literature on adult logical reasoning from a developmental perspective yields at least four important insights. First, as already discussed, there is a strong basis in early childhood research and biological theorizing (Piaget, 1967/1971) for the sorts of implicit logic recently "discovered" in dual process research. Second, a developmental perspective shows the importance of logic, which has been doubted by theorists such as Mercier and Sperber (2017; for discussion, see Mercier & Sperber, 2019; Moshman, 2018; Noveck, 2019). Some of the logic tasks in the literature of adult reasoning may be artificial or peculiar, but logic is fundamental across the lifespan.

The third developmental insight involves standards for comparison. Lacking a developmental perspective, it is natural to look at adult rationality in comparison to normative ideals from philosophy or by comparing adults to each other, leading to the conclusion that adults fall far short of logical and other ideals and some are even more irrational than others. This is an important part of the picture, but a developmental perspective complements the view from cognitive psychology. Adult shortcomings and individual differences in rationality must be seen in the context of the developmental reality that all normal humans beyond the age of 12 or 13 years show forms of reasoning and levels of rationality virtually never seen in 8-year-olds, who in turn show forms of reasoning and levels of rationality never seen in 4-year-olds, who in turn show rational competencies far beyond the sensorimotor logic already seen in infancy.

Finally, even among adults, it is important to distinguish developmental differences from other individual differences. Not all individual differences are developmental, but some can only be understood by recognizing that some individuals are operating at a higher developmental level than others, and that developmental progress remains possible, though not inevitable, long beyond childhood. But development is not simply a matter of avoiding mistakes or learning particular rules or strategies. A clear understanding of what (potentially) develops in adolescence and adulthood and how such development takes place (the topic of Chapter 7) provides the basis for educational efforts to promote such development (Chapter 8).

Mathematical Reasoning

Mathematical reasoning is closely related to logical reasoning but forms a major category of its own. It ranges from basic conceptions of numbers to complex statistical reasoning.

The Concept of Number

We generally take numbers for granted and think of learning to count as a simple matter of repeating and memorizing a sequence of number names in whatever language is spoken by the adults around you. Epistemologically, however, there are complex questions to be asked about what a number actually is and how it is possible for the human mind to know whatever it is we know about numbers (McCulloch, 1961).

Piaget (1941/1965a, 1967/1971) proposed that a number is, both epistemologically and developmentally, a synthesis of classification and seriation. The number 5, for example, is the (abstract) class of all sets of 5 things. If I have 5 horses, 5 dogs, and 4 cats, the first two sets fall in the same numerical category (sets of 5) and the third does not, for reasons having nothing to do with the characteristics of horses, dogs, or cats. But 5 is not just a different category from 4 or 6. The number 5 is defined in part by its being simultaneously larger than 4 and smaller than 6 in the series of integers, with all that logically entails. Mathematical knowledge, like logical knowledge, involves necessary truths and a conception of justification as proof. Logico-mathematical knowledge thus differs from empirical knowledge of the physical world, which is contingent on what the world is like and subject to revision on the basis of new data. Only a synthesis of classification and seriation can account for the logical properties of number and the associated logic of elementary arithmetic.

Piaget (1941/1965a) conducted a detailed investigation of "the construction of number in relation to logical operations," hypothesizing "that the construction of number goes hand-in-hand with the development of logic" (p. viii). Over a series of ten studies, children ranging in age from 3 to 8 years (mostly 4 to 7) were interviewed about tasks assessing their comprehension of the logic of elementary mathematics, including their understanding of conservation of quantity, one-to-one correspondence, part–whole relations, cardinal and ordinal properties of number, multiplication of classes and numbers, equivalence, and reversibility. Piaget concluded:

> Our results do, in fact, show that number is organized, stage after stage, in close connection with the gradual elaboration of systems of inclusions (hierarchy of logical classes) and systems of asymmetrical relations (qualitative seriations), the sequence of numbers thus resulting from an operational synthesis of classification and seriation. In our view, logical and arithmetical operations therefore constitute a single system that is psychologically natural.
>
> *(p. viii)*

A major alternative to Piaget's account was provided by Gelman and Gallistel (1978), who proposed that understanding of number involves the coordinated application of five principles of counting: the one–one principle (tag each item with one and only one unique number name); the stable-order principle (don't change the order of the numbers); the cardinal principle (the last number in the count is the total number of items; the abstraction principle (any set of items, however diverse, can be counted); and the order-irrelevance principle (the order in which the items are tagged does not matter). Their research and that of many others provides a detailed picture of how children construct the logic of elementary mathematics in the preschool years, including evidence often interpreted as showing earlier understanding than Piaget indicated. There appears to be a consensus, however, that the logic of numbers is increasingly understood over the course of early childhood, and that children of any given age are at least as competent mathematically as Piaget indicated (Feiman, Hartshorne, & Barner, 2019).

Probabilistic and Statistical Reasoning

Mathematical reasoning of course extends far beyond numbers and counting (Cauley, 1992; Smith, 2002). Probabilistic reasoning, for example, enables us to be rigorous about our uncertainty by coordinating deduction and probability. Piaget and Inhelder (1951/1975) found developmental progress in conceptions of chance, with concrete forms of probabilistic reasoning emerging about age 7 or 8 years and formal elaboration of possibilities at age 11 or 12 years.

Not surprisingly, developmental researchers have sought and found evidence for statistical inferences at increasingly early ages, even in infancy (Sobel & Kirkham, 2007), whereas the adult cognition literature has shown systematic deviations from basic probabilistic and statistical norms in adults (Kahneman, 2011). Once again, we see Piaget's developmental account challenged by developmentalists as underestimating the rationality of young children and by researchers on adult reasoning as failing to acknowledge the irrationality of adults. Here too, a developmental dual process approach resolves the apparent developmental reversal by showing how statistical inference is increasingly supplemented over the course of development by statistical reasoning, but never replaced.

Even in matters of probability, mathematical reasoning is strictly deductive and thus remains within the logico-mathematic domain of necessary inference. Can logic go beyond that? Does reasoning go beyond logic? We will expand the account of reasoning in the next chapter.

Conclusion

Let us conclude with four questions about logic. Was logic invented by logicians? Is it a property or outcome of language? Is it how we think? Is it how we ought to think? The answers, I suggest, are No, No, Mostly Not, and Sometimes.

Starting with the first question, logicians at least since Aristotle have been constructing and reconstructing systems of logic, but even if we give a logician credit for inventing some system of logic, the invention is not a free creation. It is an explicit systematization of a logic that was already implicit in an earlier system. As we have seen, logic existed long before logicians discovered it.

With regard to the second question, logic is most visible in language and is commonly seen as a feature or property of language or as an ability that language makes possible. As we have seen, however, developmental research shows clear evidence of logic in prelinguistic children. Research with nonhuman species, moreover, shows what many take to be evidence of logical inference in a variety of mammals and birds, perhaps even in wasps. Language greatly facilitates the development and use of logic but is not the source of logic.

With regard to the third question, we sometimes think in accord with rules of logic, but our thinking does not inherently follow such rules and often deviates systematically from them. There is an important role for logic in thinking, and especially in reasoning, but neither thinking nor reasoning is simply a matter of following rules of logic.

Turning to the fourth question, maybe we ought to think in accord with rules of logic, at least when we are reasoning. We should indeed make logical inferences when they are relevant and avoid inferences contrary to relevant rules of logic. Reasoning, however, is more than logic. Beyond logical reasoning, as we will see in the next chapter, there are other types of reasoning that cannot be reduced to logic or to each other. At the very least, in addition to (1) logical reasoning, we must consider (2) scientific reasoning, which is crucial to understanding the world; (3) principled reasoning, which is crucial to morality; and (4) precedent-based reasoning, which is crucial to social systems.

3

REASONING BEYOND LOGIC

The prototypical example of logic is deduction. If we define logic strictly as deduction, then we can say a rational agent engages in logical reasoning when (or to the extent that) the agent makes a deliberate inference in accord with strict rules that are understood by the agent to generate a conclusion that follows necessarily from the premises. Such inferences are deductive; their deliberate and reflective application, as discussed in Chapter 2, is deductive reasoning.

Philosophers often distinguish induction from deduction, some distinguish abduction from induction, and some discuss informal logic. This raises questions about the scope of logic. Are there nondeductive systems of logic? What exactly is logic? Induction is generally defined as reaching a conclusion that goes beyond what the premises require. Is this logic? Are there rules of induction, even if the results are not logically necessary? Abduction is defined as inference to the best explanation. Is this logic? Are there rules of abduction? Informal logic may not follow formal rules. Are there other kinds of rules?

As we will see in this chapter, scientific interpretation and explanation require much more than following rules to reach necessary conclusions and, thus, go beyond anything like deductive logic. The same is true for various sorts of moral and social reasoning. For present purposes, I use the term *logic* to refer to strict norms of good reasoning, especially rules of deductive necessity. This definition acknowledges that logic in its broader sense may be more than strict deduction.

Even in this broader sense of logic, however, reasoning includes more than logic. I will propose in this chapter that scientific, principled, and precedent-based reasoning are epistemologically and psychologically distinct from logical reasoning and from each other. This suggests a much richer picture of human reasoning than the account of logical reasoning presented in Chapter 2, with a variety of ways people may achieve or fall short of rational norms.

Scientific Reasoning

We look first at scientific reasoning. As we will see, scientific reasoning is epistemologically distinct from logical reasoning in ways that children increasingly come to understand. The development of scientific reasoning is correspondingly distinct from the development of logical reasoning but shows a similar pattern of progress.

Scientific Reasoning as Empirical and Causal Reasoning

Outside of logical reasoning, perhaps the most-studied form of reasoning is scientific reasoning. But what exactly is scientific reasoning?

For a start, scientific reasoning has long been seen as including an ability to design unconfounded experiments (Inhelder & Piaget, 1955/1958). If I want to know which of three variables is responsible for some effect, I must manipulate the variables independently of each other. If I flip three switches and a light goes on, I don't know which switch (or switches) caused the light to go on. If I just wanted the light to go on, no problem. But if my goal is to understand what causes the light to go on, I must flip one switch at a time, holding everything else constant. The quest to understand, rather than just create some effect, is *empirical* in its concern for what the world is really like and *causal* in its concern for how things work. If this is all there is to scientific reasoning, however, scientific reasoning does not appear to be anything more than the application of logic to understanding the world. Even if it turns out that the effect of a given switch depends on the position of another, which complicates the causal logic, this remains a matter of logic, involving strict rules of inference and a single correct conclusion.

Somewhat more broadly, scientific reasoning is often presented as fundamentally a matter of testing hypotheses and evaluating evidence. This includes designing unconfounded experiments to test causal predictions, but it goes beyond that. The four-card "selection task" (Wason & Johnson-Laird, 1972) presented in the previous chapter can be seen as a study of hypothesis testing. Suppose we take the conditional *If X then Y* to represent a hypothesis that X causes Y. We can test this by getting further evidence about (1) a case where X is present; (2) a case where X is not present; (3) a case where Y is present; and (4) a case where Y is not present. The task is to determine which of these four sorts of research must be done to reach a definitive conclusion about the truth or falsity of the hypothesis. The solution requires (a) the insight that we must do any research that could turn up a case of X without Y, because any such case would disconfirm the hypothesis that X causes Y; and (b) the further insight that we need not do any other research, because no other case could disconfirm the hypothesis. Thus, we must do studies 1 and 4 because either of those could disconfirm the hypothesis. If either of these studies turns up a case of cause without effect, the hypothesis is false. If no such disconfirming case shows up, then the hypothesis is true regardless of what we might have found in studies 2 or 3, which need not be done because they could not disconfirm the hypothesis. As we saw in Chapter 2, this is a notoriously difficult task. However difficult such hypothesis testing may be psychologically, however, the task remains a matter of logic with clear right and wrong answers distinguished on the basis of formal rules without regard for what we mean by *X* or *Y*. Hypothesis testing with a simple hypothesis in a limited domain of potential data may be mostly or entirely a matter of logic.

Scientific reasoning, however, is not just controlling variables, testing hypotheses, and evaluating evidence in limited environments involving a few switches or a set of four cards. Science aims to explain the world, which requires an ongoing process of formulating, testing, and revising theories. Our theories influence what data we collect and guide our interpretations of the data. Scientific data do not "speak for themselves," and their relevance and import for various scientific theories may be a matter of reasonable disagreement. We coordinate theories and data in an ongoing effort to improve our knowledge (Kuhn, Amsel, & O'Loughlin, 1988). This includes broad use of relevant background information—in contrast to logic, which relies on isolating premises from the world to determine what follows from those premises alone. Scientific reasoning is rational in its coordination of theories and data to make progress in causal understanding, but psychologists and philosophers of science generally agree that such progress is not simply a matter of following rules of logic to a necessary conclusion (Carey & Smith, 1993; Koslowski, 1996, 2013; Koslowski, Marasia, Chelenza, & Dublin, 2008; Rosenberg & McIntyre, 2020).

Scientific reasoning is thus empirical and causal (Koslowski, 1996; 2013; Koslowski et al., 2008; Rosenberg & McIntyre, 2020; Sodian, 2018). It is empirical in that it posits a world outside itself and seeks to explain that world. This requires maintaining a distinction between theory and evidence and seeking evidence about what the world is really like. In addition, scientific reasoning is generally causal in that its explanations generally posit causal relations within the world. Science is not the accumulation of information. It is the formulation of causal theories and the seeking of evidence to test those theories as part of an effort to explain some aspect of reality. As Koslowski et al. (2008) put it in the title of an article: "Information becomes evidence when an explanation can incorporate it into a causal framework."

Science, then, may be defined as the empirical study and theoretical explanation of the world. Correspondingly, *scientific reasoning* is reasoning aimed at empirical justification and truth. This includes the reflective coordination of theories and data for the purpose of making progress in our causal understanding of the world.

Epistemologies of Science and Logic

The philosophy of science is in large part the epistemology of science in that its central concern is understanding the nature of scientific truth and the justification of scientific claims and methodologies. Philosophers of science generally agree that scientific knowledge is not a direct copy of the world, a logically necessary consequence of available data, or a collection of information. Nevertheless, science aims to understand a world outside itself and is in that sense fundamentally empirical. Data are not sufficient for science, but without data there is no science.

Logic, in contrast, makes no use of data except for premises accepted without question. It reaches conclusions that must be so regardless of any data beyond the accepted premises. If you claim there are more dogs than cats in a room, you should be able to justify that with evidence about the number of dogs and cats, whereas if you claim that there are more dogs than animals, you are clearly wrong regardless of evidence. There must be at least as many animals as dogs in any room. This conclusion is not based on long experience counting animals in a variety of rooms. It is based on understanding the necessary logic of hierarchical classification. More generally, logical necessities require no empirical evidence and cannot be contradicted by evidence because they are not about what the world happens to be like (Moshman, 1990, 2015; Smith, 1993). Thus, scientific reasoning is distinct from logical reasoning in its reliance on data.

In addition to being empirical, scientific reasoning is causal reasoning. Scientific theories are generally causal theories. This does not mean everything is reducible to physics. Our conceptions of causality must reflect the complexity of what we seek to understand. Biological systems show self-regulatory forms of causation not seen in physics. Psychological functioning and social organization further complicate causal explanation. Dynamic systems manifest complex and circular forms of causality in which the systems themselves are causal agents (Witherington, 2011). Whatever the complications of causality, however—and ignoring, for present purposes, the subatomic mysteries of quantum mechanics—science is fundamentally causal (Moshman, 2015).

Logic, in contrast, is implicative, not causal. In logic, the conditional *If p then q* can be understood as telling us that p *implies* q. In science, however, the major concern would be whether p *causes* q. Thus, scientific reasoning is distinct from logical reasoning in its postulation of a real world that can be understood through causal theorizing. Causality plays no role in logical reasoning but is crucial to scientific reasoning.

The epistemology of science is not just a concern of philosophers. On the contrary, we all have "intuitive epistemologies of science," which "include ideas about the sources and justification of scientific knowledge, its constructive and tentative character, its embeddedness into cultural and historical contexts, the role of theories, observation and experiments, and the role of rational argument in the construction of scientific knowledge" (Sodian, 2018, p. 234). Research in developmental psychology, educational psychology, and science education shows universal progress in understanding the "nature of science" over the course of childhood (Sodian, 2018), with progress possible but much less universal in adolescence and beyond (Moshman, 2015). Understanding the nature of science is in large part a matter of understanding its epistemology, which is crucial to engaging in scientific reasoning. We will look more generally at epistemic development in the next chapter.

Development of Scientific Reasoning

Piaget (1936/1963) discussed sensorimotor experimentation in connection with what he called "tertiary circular reactions." In primary circular reactions, first seen about the age of 1 month, the infant attempts to reproduce a favorable outcome centered on its own body, such as getting its thumb back in its mouth to recreate the experience of sucking on it. In secondary circular reactions, beginning about age 4 months, the infant attempts to reproduce an outcome involving an external object, but the object is so tied to the infant's actions that it is not yet seen as external. In tertiary circular reactions, in contrast, beginning at about 12 months, the focus shifts to the object itself and associated matters of causality and space, resulting in intentional variations in action to see what happens. In an example of the transition from secondary to tertiary circular reactions, Piaget (1936/1963) described how his son, Laurent (at 10 months, 2 days), discovered the possibility of throwing a case of soap and letting it fall. As expected in a secondary circular reaction, however, he was content simply to reproduce this result because what interested him "was not the objective phenomenon of the fall—that is to say, the object's trajectory—but the very act of letting go" (p. 268). But eight days later, Piaget saw evidence of a tertiary circular reaction when Laurent repeatedly dropped a small piece of bread, even breaking off fragments and letting them drop. In this case,

> he pays no attention to the act of letting go whereas he watches with great interest the body in motion; in particular, he looks at it for a long time when it has fallen, and picks it up when he can.
>
> *(pp. 268–269)*

The following day:

> Laurent is lying on his back but nevertheless resumes his experiments of the day before. He grasps in succession a celluloid swan, a box, etc., stretches out his arm and lets them fall. He distinctly varies the positions of the fall. Sometimes he stretches out his arm vertically, sometimes he holds it obliquely, in front of or behind his eyes, etc. When the object falls in a new position (for example on his pillow), he lets it fall two or three times more on the same place, as though to study the spatial relation; then he modifies the situation.
>
> *(p. 269)*

Sensorimotor causality shows a closely related developmental trend toward objectivity. Over the first year of life, infants construct causality in relation to the causal impact of their own actions (Piaget, 1937/1954). As they move into their second year, "causality will be really objectified and spatialized, thus becoming detached from the action itself to be externalized in the universe of perception, free to be applied in return to the visible aspects of the action itself" (Piaget, 1937/1954, p. 271). Thus, children in the second year of life engage what they have come to see as an objective world of causal interactions among objects in space and they actively conduct experiments on that world. In Piaget's (1936/1963) words: "The objectification of causality is the source of experimentation" (p. 278).

All of this, however, is a matter of practical intelligence at what Piaget called the sensorimotor level. Over the second year of life, infants construct a representational intelligence that enables them to mentally represent the world and act mentally on those representations. This enables them to represent and think about causal relations, with ongoing development in their causal reasoning over the course of childhood as children reconstruct their early sensorimotor insights at the level of representational intelligence. Research with children beyond infancy showed systematic progress in causal understanding corresponding to the more general construction of concrete operational structures at about age 7 or 8 years and formal structures at about 11 or 12 years (Piaget, 1971/1974), with related progress in scientific reasoning leading at the formal operational level to reflective hypothesis testing, including the ability to isolate variables in order to determine their effects (Inhelder & Piaget, 1955/1958).

Developmental research on children's scientific reasoning has focused mostly on providing evidence showing earlier competence than Piaget indicated with respect to causal inference and hypothesis testing (Gopnik, 2012; Sodian, 2018). As in the case of logical reasoning, there appears to be a consensus that children of any given age are at least as competent as Piaget claimed, if not more. Research with scientific reasoning in adults, however, shows major deviations from Piaget's conception of mature scientific reasoning, including strong tendencies to test hypotheses by seeking out supporting data rather than by seeking data that could falsify the hypothesis (Moshman, 2011a; Wason & Johnson-Laird, 1972). As in the case of logical reasoning, the scientific reasoning of adults not only falls far short of rational norms but even seems to fall short of the reasoning many developmentalists attribute to young children.

A solution to this apparent developmental paradox has been provided by Deanna Kuhn (1989, 2005; Kuhn et al., 1988), who highlighted the metacognitive nature of advanced scientific reasoning. Children engage in active exploration of the world, make causal inferences, and construct intuitive theories, but do not reflectively differentiate and coordinate theories and data. Progress in scientific reasoning consists of progress in "thinking about theories, rather than merely with them, and thinking about evidence, rather than merely being influenced by it. This development is thus metacognitive" (Kuhn, 1989, p. 688). In her later work, Kuhn

(2005) especially emphasized the epistemic basis for advanced reasoning, noting that adolescents and adults show substantial individual differences in epistemic cognition and scientific reasoning and that we all fall short of scientific ideals. We will address metacognition and epistemic cognition in more detail in the next chapter.

This metacognitive approach is fully consistent with a dual process model. People of all ages have many reasons to notice, seek, retain, and recall information supporting their views. There is no reason to expect this tendency to disappear at advanced levels of development. But we can complement, and sometimes override, our natural heuristics and biases with deliberate efforts to seek data systematically and to identify falsifying evidence, and with reflective coordination of theories with emerging data. In scientific reasoning, as we already saw in logical reasoning, a developmental dual process conception helps reconcile developmental research showing the rationality of young children with cognitive research documenting the limited rationality of adults.

Moral Reasoning

Moral reasoning is reasoning about matters of morality, which includes respect and concern for the rights and welfare of others. Some people construe morality more broadly to include respect for a variety of societal norms that vary across cultures. As we will see, however, there is good reason to distinguish morality from social convention and strong evidence that this distinction is understood by young children and increasingly respected over the course of development. I focus in this section on moral reasoning, which is rooted in principle, and then turn in the following section to social conventional reasoning, which is rooted in precedent.

Moral Reasoning as Principled Reasoning

Consider this simple case. You hire a group of three 8-year-olds to clear snow around your house for $15. They are equally competent, work equally hard, and contribute equally to getting the job done well. How much should each get paid? No, this is not a trick question. Each should get paid $5. Solving this moral problem is no more difficult than dividing 15 by 3, an objective matter of following mathematical rules. The children themselves would understand that. All three would likely object to differential pay unless it could be justified on the basis of some children working harder and/or accomplishing more.

Situations like this are common, and the basic principle of equality that applies in such a situation is elementary and universal. But the principle is not just mathematical. If we had 15 flowers and three vases, we would see the mathematical logic of putting 5 flowers in each vase, but we could decide, say, to put 7 in one and 4 in each of the others, or put 6 in each of two vases and just 3 in the other. Some people might deem some distributions esthetically objectionable, but there would be no question of any moral objection. Giving some children more or less than others for no good reason, however, is a different matter. People are not vases. People have rights of fair treatment that vases do not have. People have moral obligations to treat each other on a basis of mutual respect, which requires fair treatment for all. In the case of people, unlike the case of vases, the matter of distribution across three options is not just mathematical; it raises issues of individual rights and corresponding moral obligations.

But what if one of the children worked much harder than either of the others and accomplished much more? What if they worked equally hard but one was much more competent and ended up doing most of the work? All other things being equal, we should treat all persons equally, but at least some other things are often unequal. Situational factors, such as differential effort or ability, may or may not justify deviations from strict equality of treatment. Deviations from a mathematical rule of strict equality may be permitted or even required in some cases by the underlying moral principle of equal respect for all persons.

What is a principle, and what makes it morally obligatory? We may define a *principle* as an abstract norm whose application to cases requires rational judgment rather than strict imposition of a concrete rule. Moral principles apply fully and equally to all persons, consistent with the defining moral requirement of respect for persons (Dworkin, 1985). But a principle is not just a rule to be followed. Principles serve as guidelines and constraints, ruling out some possibilities and showing how some of the remaining possibilities are better justified than others, but there may not be a single objectively correct answer, even if some answers are better justified than others (Moshman, 1995, 2011a, 2015). In the case of the three snow shovelers, if one child is more competent than the others and shoveled more snow, a case might be made for that child being paid more, but a case might also be made for paying the children equally. All other things being equal, however, it would be clearly unfair for that child to be paid less. There does not appear to be any rule to tell us exactly what the three payments should be, but moral principles limit the range of legitimate possibilities and provide guidance in choosing among the remaining possibilities.

Perspective taking is intrinsic to principled reasoning. Moral principles arise from the coordination of multiple perspectives and ideally take all possible perspectives into account. This includes not only individual perspectives but the perspectives of social groups. Perspective taking, moreover, is not just cognitive but also emotional, including empathic responses that play crucial roles in moral judgment and action (Gibbs, 2019). Nevertheless, moral justifications must be principled (Bloom, 2016).

Moral Epistemology

"Everyone," proclaimed Piaget (1932/1965b), "is aware of the kinship between logical and ethical norms. Logic is the morality of thought just as morality is the logic of action" (p. 398).

If we construe logic narrowly as a matter of following strict rules that yield necessary conclusions, this conception misses the principled nature of morality. Principles are not rules; principled reasoning requires a more subtle epistemology allowing for rational diversity in interpretations and judgments. Some judgments are morally more justifiable than others, but in many cases there is no single demonstrably correct moral answer and little reason to believe that logic alone could supply one (Moshman, 2015). Moral reasoning is not simply the social application of logical reasoning.

On a somewhat broader interpretation, however, Piaget's statement expresses the view, central to his work on moral judgment, that there is a moral rationality intrinsic to human social interaction. This is a broadly Kantian view that is widely, but not universally, shared by moral philosophers. Although the rational basis for morality has been doubted in recent decades by many psychologists, there is strong psychological evidence for development toward moral rationality (Gibbs, 2019; Moshman, 1995, 2011a; more on this in the next subsection).

Moral reasoning thus resembles scientific reasoning in having a rational basis that cannot be reduced to logic (Bloom, 2016). But moral reasoning is not scientific reasoning. Scientific reasoning aims to determine what the world is really like and to provide causal explanations of what goes on within it. Moral reasoning, in contrast, aims to evaluate the world and to tell us what to do. Unlike science, morality (like logic) is normative rather than descriptive.

Moral justification and truth, then, are distinct from the justification and truth of both logical necessities and scientific explanations. Morality has an epistemology of its own, distinct from the epistemologies of both logic and science (Moshman, 2015). Moral reasoning, on the basis of moral epistemology, incorporates principled reasoning and perspective taking in ways that distinguish it from both logical and scientific reasoning.

The distinction is not just that morality is a social matter. Morality, which involves respect or concern for the rights or welfare of others, is also epistemologically distinct from matters of social convention and personal identity (Moshman, 2015; Nucci, 2001, 2014; Smetana, 2011; Smetana, Jambon, & Ball, 2014; Turiel, 1983, 2008; see below for more on social convention).

Development of Moral Reasoning

Extensive research since the 1960s has shown dramatic progress over the course of childhood in children's ability to see themselves from the perspective of other people. Selman (1980) proposed that development beyond childhood involves the emerging ability to engage in *third-party perspective taking*, which involves seeing one's reciprocal relation to another person from the (meta)perspective of a real or hypothetical third party. He also proposed a still more advanced, and perhaps less universal, level of perspective taking that involves taking the perspective of the social order.

Perspective taking is not itself moral. Understanding the perspectives of others may serve the immoral purpose of exploiting them more effectively by anticipating their reactions. Nevertheless, Kohlberg's (1981, 1984) Piagetian theory of moral development proposed that moral development beyond childhood involves recognizing the moral value of relationships, which requires third-party perspective taking. He also proposed that development may proceed beyond that to a reconsideration of human relations from the perspective of the social system, which requires Selman's societal level of perspective taking.

John Gibbs (2019) proposed a neo-Kohlbergian theory that posits four stages of moral development, drawing on increasingly advanced levels of perspective taking, which is construed as both cognitive and emotional. Children make progress in understanding and respecting reciprocity, but the reciprocity of Stage 2, typical of older children, is a pragmatic reciprocity of self-interested deals. In adolescence, developing individuals construct the ideal reciprocity and genuine mutuality of Stage 3, which requires third-party perspective taking. Some individuals in at least some societies proceed from there to the social system perspective of Stage 4, rooted in societal perspective taking.

Research on the development of moral reasoning has looked specifically at principled reasoning about matters including free speech, religious liberty, democratic decision-making, forms of government, and student rights (Helwig, Ruck, & Peterson-Badali, 2014). Participants across a range of ages and cultural contexts have been presented with a variety of moral and social dilemmas and have been asked to explain and justify their responses. Helwig (1995), for example, asked 12-year-olds, 16-year-olds, and college students to evaluate potential laws restricting freedoms of speech and religion. Participants were also asked to evaluate the exercise of intellectual and religious freedom in relatively straightforward cases and in more challenging cases involving, for example, harmful religious practices or the use of racial slurs. Regardless of age, students generally showed substantial support for freedoms of speech and religion, but also recognized limits on these rights in cases where they potentially conflicted with other rights or values. Students of all ages disagreed with each other about how best to resolve complex cases, but their justifications showed clear understanding of relevant civil liberties principles.

Related research (reviewed in Helwig et al., 2014) supports the conclusion that principled moral reasoning is common in adolescents and adults, who often show explicit understanding of principles implicit in the moral judgments of children. The development of principled reasoning is not so much the emergence of new principles as the increasing metacognitive awareness, understanding, and control of one's principles. Unlike children, adolescents and adults understand that principles, although morally obligatory, are not rigid rules.

A broader look at developmental and cognitive research on human morality shows the same pattern already observed in the study of logical and scientific reasoning. Developmental research on children has focused largely on showing empathy, perspective taking, and moral action earlier than expected by Piaget

(1932/1965b) and by Piagetian theorists such as Selman, Kohlberg, and Gibbs (Bloom, 2013). Research with adults, in contrast, has focused on showing systematic deviations from rational moral norms. Moral judgment has come to be seen as mostly the result of a variety of cognitive and moral heuristics and biases. Many researchers have concluded that our moral and immoral judgments and actions are largely driven by emotions and intuitions, with only a limited role for reasoning, not only in childhood but throughout our lives (Haidt, 2001).

In recent years, however, many researchers have provided new evidence for the important role of reasoning in moral judgment. Landy and Royzman (2018) reviewed much of the relevant literature and proposed a developmental dual process account of moral reasoning that they call the *moral myopia model*. By "moral myopia," Landy and Royzman (2018) mean "singularly attending to one salient aspect of a moral problem rather than thinking about multiple moral considerations . . . in a more complex, integrative way" (p. 71). Although children make developmental progress in their ability to decenter from one salient aspect of a problem and to coordinate multiple considerations, the moral myopia model acknowledges that adults still show moral myopia. Depending on circumstances, however, adults may show reasoning beyond the capacity of children, with some more likely than others to do so. Landy and Royzman (2018) argue that their model accounts for evidence that "reasoning can be applied to resolve situations in which moral concerns clash and . . . can promote differentiating between moral and conventional transgressions" (p. 71).

Integrating developmental research with dual process theory, it appears that principled moral reasoning and third-party perspective taking emerge at the transition to adolescence but that they supplement and sometimes shape emotional and intuitive reactions, rather than replacing them. A developmental dual process approach (Landy & Royzman, 2018) provides an integrative picture of moral reasoning that accounts for both developmental progress (Gibbs, 2019) and human limitations (Haidt, 2001).

Social Conventional Reasoning

Reasoning about social conventions, like reasoning about morality, is a matter of reasoning about social norms. As we will see, however, social conventional reasoning is precedent-based rather than principled and, thus, rests on a distinct epistemology.

Conventional Reasoning as Precedent-Based Reasoning

Consider the three young snow shovelers a couple of years later. Suppose they now have a history of getting jobs they can do together. Early on, one of them was arranging these jobs (in addition to doing a third of the work) and it was agreed that the arranger should get 40% of the pay and the others 30% each. Later, a second one took over the role of lining up jobs and got 40% of the pay. Now they have agreed that the third should take over this role. How should their income be distributed?

Once again this is not a trick question. The new arranger should receive 40%. But why? Perhaps the job of arranger is so challenging and time-consuming that the arranger should receive 50%. Perhaps it is so minimal, due to friendly neighbors, that the pay should be divided equally. Even with more information there may be no single correct answer to the question of how the income should be distributed. But having decided as a group to pay the arranger 40%, and especially after maintaining that division for a second arranger, the group established a social convention and a precedent for future pay allocations, leading to legitimate expectations on the part of individuals. It would not have been morally wrong at the start for the three children to agree that they would share job income equally regardless of who arranged the job. But having settled on a different division of income, to change the established practice requires justification. Even when multiple choices are legitimate, a group choice or practice sets up a precedent that may be a legitimate social constraint on future choices.

Social groups establish social conventions that are not required by general moral principles but nevertheless have normative force within that group. Ignoring precedent within a group undermines the mutual expectations between individuals that make the group a group. In the case of larger groups, up to and including societies and nations, there may be social conventions that define the group across generations, even as individual members are replaced, and historical precedents that serve as a basis for reasoning within the group. Precedents, like principles, require application and interpretation in particular cases and may not yield single correct results, but are nevertheless binding in that they must be considered and apparent deviations must be explained and justified. The difference is that moral principles are universally binding on all rational social agents, whereas precedents are only binding in specific social contexts.

Reasoning about matters of social convention routinely involves logical, empirical, and moral considerations. In the case of the young jobs group, the total of their individual earnings cannot be greater than the group's overall income (a logical necessity), it may be useful to consider evidence about their relative contributions (a matter of empirical truth), and they should be fair to each other (a matter of moral principle). Precedent, however, provides a basis for reasoning in specific social contexts that goes beyond logic, science, or morality.

Epistemology of Social Conventions

Social conventions are norms of behavior specific to particular social groups or systems that indicate what one should or should not do within those social contexts. Unlike moral norms, they do not have a universal rational basis that makes them obligatory for everyone. Every social system has its own history and, thus, its own conventions that are relative to that history. But social conventions are not just empirical generalizations concerning typical behavior in particular social systems. They are normative, like moral norms, but lack the universality of moral norms.

We must therefore consider an epistemology of social convention distinct from the epistemologies of logic, science, and morality already discussed (Moshman, 2015). Social conventions may sometimes consist of rules that can be rigorously applied, but they generally require judgment and interpretation that go beyond logic. Social conventions may be based on empirical knowledge of social phenomena, but they are neither empirical generalizations nor scientific theories. Finally, social conventions are normative, but their application lacks the universality of moral norms. Social convention is thus an epistemic domain with its own conceptions of justification and truth and its own prototypical form of reasoning: precedent-based reasoning.

Development of Precedent-Based Reasoning

Gibbs (2019), drawing on Kohlberg's (1984) stages, proposed a social system morality as the fourth and final stage of his theory of moral development. Evidence across several decades has shown that children generally construct a Stage 3 morality of mutual expectations, reciprocity, and third-party perspective taking around the transition to adolescence, and that Stage 4 social system morality is constructed after that and is less universal. Meanwhile, social cognitive domain theorists (Turiel, 1983, 2008; Smetana, Jambon, & Ball, 2014) have provided extensive evidence that children distinguish morality from social convention on epistemological grounds by the age of 4 or 5 years. Young children already understand, for example, that hitting is wrong because it hurts others regardless of whether there is a rule against it, whereas lining up in certain ways at certain times is only obligatory in particular social contexts where this is expected. Thus, there is evidence for both early competence and extended development in conceptions of social convention.

Central to the development of social conventional reasoning is the development of its prototypical form: precedent-based reasoning. Such reasoning has been much less studied than logical, scientific, or moral reasoning, but relevant evidence does exist. Paul Klaczynski (2011; see also Klaczynski & Felmban, 2019) interviewed individuals of ages 8, 11, 14, and 17–18 years about vignettes in which a rule was violated under conditions that did or did not present mitigating circumstances. For example, a principal must decide whether to enforce a rule against teasing. In one condition the violator was retaliating after a long history of being teased (mitigating circumstance). In another condition the violator was simply jealous of a student who got higher grades. Analysis of the responses showed systematic differences between the 14-year-olds (who responded much like the older teens) and the 11-year-olds (who responded much like the 8-year-olds). Participants of all ages recognized the legitimacy of rule enforcement by authorities and understood that a general or arbitrary failure to enforce rules tends to undermine both their deterrence value and the perceived legitimacy of the authority failing to enforce them. Unlike the preteens, however, the teens understood that declining to enforce a rule because of mitigating circumstances does not set the same sort of precedent as routine or unjustified failures to enforce. Failure to enforce a rule sets a precedent for future nonenforcement, but the general precedent for nonenforcement is limited if a special exception is justified on the basis of specific mitigating circumstances, thus creating a narrower precedent.

As with other forms of reasoning, a developmental dual process model best accommodates the data of developmental and cognitive psychology. Human inferential processes rely heavily on perceived analogies beginning in infancy and continuing throughout our lives (Goswami, 1992). The development of precedent-based reasoning does not supplant our ongoing reliance on automatic and intuitive analogical inferences, but supplements and regulates such inferences.

Social conventional reasoning is more than precedent-based reasoning and routinely makes use of logic, evidence, and moral principles. It appears, however, that conventional reasoning is epistemologically distinct from logical, scientific, and moral reasoning in its reliance on precedent-based reasoning. We will return to precedent-based reasoning in the discussion of constitutional reasoning and legal tradition in Chapter 6.

Reasoning as Epistemologically Self-Regulated Thinking

In Chapter 1 I defined reasoning as epistemologically self-regulated thinking. This definition was not crucial in Chapter 2 because logical reasoning is widely recognized as reasoning. In the present chapter, however, the question of what counts as reasoning arises. What does it mean for thinking to be epistemologically self-regulated? Having considered three additional forms of reasoning, we now look at reasoning more generally.

The Epistemic Basis of Reasoning

Scientific, moral, and social conventional reasoning differ from each other, as we have seen, but share one characteristic that distinguishes them all from logic. They are all subjective in a way that logic, arguably, is not. Of course, all reasoning, even logical reasoning, takes place from the (subjective) viewpoint of the reasoner. But logical reasoning conforms to rules so strict that they leave no room for any answer other than the correct one. Scientific, moral, and social conventional reasoning, in contrast, are subjective in a deeper sense. There are often rationally justifiable differences of opinion about such matters. But this doesn't mean that all opinions are equally justified. Some scientific, moral, and conventional claims or conclusions are better justified than others, and some are just plain false.

Research in cognitive and developmental psychology shows that people distinguish logic from other domains on epistemological grounds, with increasingly explicit understanding of this distinction as individuals construct increasingly reflective levels of metalogical understanding. In scientific, moral, and social conventional domains, extensive research has converged on an account of epistemic development as progress from (1) objectivist conceptions of knowledge in which everything is a matter of fact or logic, to (2) subjectivist conceptions in which everything is relative, to (3) rationalist conceptions that find a basis for objectivity despite inherent subjectivity and, thus, restore a role for justification and a meaningful conception of truth.

I have defined thinking as the deliberate application and coordination of one's inferences to serve one's purposes. Thinking is thus intrinsically metacognitive in that it involves knowledge and control of cognition. Reasoning is thinking regulated specifically for purposes of truth and justification and thus involves epistemological aspects of metacognition. In the next chapter we will look in much more detail at matters of metacognition, and especially epistemic cognition.

Reasoning as the Generation and Use of Reasons

Reasoning provides us with reasons for what we believe and what we do. Automatic inferences routinely modify our beliefs and cause us to act, but only reasoning, because it is deliberate and reflective, provides reasons. When we believe or act on the basis of reasoning we can say why we believe what we do or acted as we did. Consistent with the definition of reasoning as epistemologically self-regulated thinking, we may also define it as the generation and use of reasons.

But it is not just individuals who generate and use reasons. Groups of two or more individuals engaged in argumentation generate and use reasons and thus engage in collaborative reasoning. Collaborative reasoning, however, is not simply a collection of reasons. In collaborative reasoning, each of the collaborators is a rational agent—that is, an agent who believes or acts on the basis of reasons and who engages with other rational agents on this basis. To be a rational agent, moreover, is to be a *person*—that is, the sort of agent who can participate in argumentation and, more broadly, in deliberative democracy. We will return to these matters of reasoning in argumentation and deliberative democracy in Chapters 5 and 6, respectively.

Conclusion

We are faced throughout life with questions of what to believe and what to do. We should address such matters logically, to the extent that logic is relevant, but we should not expect logic to answer all our questions. As we have seen in this chapter, we supplement our logical reasoning with scientific, moral, and social conventional reasoning.

It might seem the account of multiple forms of reasoning in Chapters 2 and 3 provides the outline of a comprehensive theory of reasoning. What remains, it might seem, is to fill in the details concerning the development and functioning of the various forms of logical, scientific, moral, and social conventional reasoning, and perhaps consider whether there are any additional sorts of reasoning not reducible to any of these. As already noted, however, all such reasoning is rooted in metacognition, and especially in epistemic cognition. We cannot understand reasoning without understanding how people control their inferences and what people know about justification and truth. We now turn to these matters.

4

METACOGNITION AND EPISTEMIC COGNITION

In the previous chapters we defined (1) *thinking* as the deliberate application and coordination of one's inferences to serve one's purposes and (2) *reasoning* as epistemologically self-regulated thinking. Thinking (including reasoning) is thus metacognitive in its cognitive self-regulation of cognition. Reasoning, specifically, is epistemological in its concern with truth and justification.

In this chapter we look more directly and systematically at metacognition, focusing especially on epistemic cognition. Our conceptions of justification and truth are crucial to our reasoning. As we will see in Chapter 6, moreover, epistemic cognition is also crucial to democratic self-governance, which requires not only rational deliberation among peers but also appropriate respect for expertise. Thus, democracy requires widespread knowledge about the nature of knowledge. We will see in Chapter 8 that epistemic cognition is a crucial consideration in education aimed at the promotion of rationality and democracy.

The development of metacognition begins early and proceeds rapidly across childhood. Epistemic cognition shows a universal course of development across childhood with substantial potential for further development beyond that in our knowledge about justification and truth. A developmental sequence seen in childhood, beyond childhood, and in multiple epistemic domains is a transition from (1) a conception of knowledge as objective truth, to (2) a conception of knowledge as subjective opinion, to (3) a conception of knowledge as justified belief.

Metacognition

I begin in this section with metacognition, which is crucial to thinking. I focus especially on metacognition in child development and in the logical reasoning of adults. I then turn in the following two sections to epistemic cognition, the subset of metacognition most crucial to reasoning.

The Study of Metacognition

Metacognition is cognition about cognition. The study of metacognition dates at least to Plato, but the term "metacognition" originated in the late 1970s in developmental and educational psychology (Brown, 1978; Flavell, 1979). The psychological and educational literature on metacognition now includes thousands of publications using that term and many thousands more using related terminology. Overlapping concepts from a variety of academic fields over the past century include executive functioning, executive control, self-monitoring, self-regulation, self-knowledge, introspection, reflection, epistemic cognition, critical thinking, cognizance, consciousness, metarepresentation, attribution, perspective taking, and theory of mind (Campbell & Bickhard, 1986; Demetriou, Makris, Kazi, Spanoudis, & Shayer, 2018; Demetriou & Spanoudis, 2018; Dewey, 1910/1997; Miller, 2012; Piaget, 1977/2001; Pillow, 2012; Stanovich, 2011; Tarricone, 2011).

Research on metacognition generally distinguishes knowledge of cognition from regulation of cognition (Schraw & Moshman, 1995). Knowledge of cognition refers to what individuals know about their own cognition, the cognition of others, or cognition in general. Regulation of cognition involves metacognitive activities that help control one's inferential processes, including planful strategy selection, monitoring of comprehension and task performance, and evaluation of processes and outcomes. Beyond this basic distinction, however, the theoretical conceptualization of metacognition is a complex matter, complicated by the diversity of the terminology used. Researchers who use the term "metacognition," for example, generally focus on cognition about one's own cognition; researchers using the terms "attribution," "perspective taking," or "theory of mind" generally focus on cognition about other minds; and researchers referring to "epistemic cognition" are usually most concerned with knowledge about general issues of justification and truth. All of this is metacognitive in the broad sense of the term, but the diverse terminology accurately reflects the expansive and multifaceted nature of metacognition.

Metacognition in Development

Cognition about cognition is central to the developmental theory of intelligence formulated over the past several decades by Andreas Demetriou and colleagues (Demetriou et al., 2018; Demetriou & Spanoudis, 2018). In order to provide a differentiated picture of what might broadly be called the metacognitive realm, they highlight what they call "cognizance" as a crucial aspect of what they call "reflexive consciousness." *Consciousness* is defined as "awareness of one's own existence and current relation with the world" as in the statement, "I know I am here and that the object I see is blue." Consistent with dual process theories, it is acknowledged that much cognitive activity is unconscious. A basic level of consciousness includes "awareness of one's own current object of thought" as in "I know that I see a red apple." *Reflexive consciousness* is defined as "awareness of one's own mental processes (I know that I see by my eyes), knowledge (I know I saw apples before), and abilities (I am good in remembering what I saw before)." This includes *cognizance*, the portion of reflexive consciousness "involving awareness of cognitive processes" (Demetriou et al., 2018, all quotes from p. 1).

Cognizance draws on *self-monitoring*, defined as "the mind's eye turning to itself," as in "I try to balance on a seesaw" or "I try to learn how to add up numbers." It also draws on *reflection*, defined as "mentally re-enacting past experiences, memories, or thoughts to better understand events, actions, and thoughts and their relations." Finally, cognizance draws on *metarepresentation*, which is defined as "encoding of the results of self-monitoring and reflection and tagging or redescripting them into new representations for future use." Research indicates that cognizance plays a role in the emergence of executive control and in the relation of executive control and reasoning. Cognizance, executive control, and reasoning are seen together as the "developmental trinity of mind" (Demetriou et al., 2018, all quotes from p. 1).

In a cross-sectional and longitudinal study motivated by this metacognitive theory, Kazi, Kazali, Makris, Spanoudis, and Demetriou (2019) looked specifically at how cognizance mediates between executive control and reasoning over the age range of 4–10 years. A total of 113 children of ages 4, 6, or 8 years were assessed on a battery of cognitive and metacognitive tasks and were assessed again two years later (when the oldest were 10 years old). Cognizance was assessed via measures of (1) awareness of the perceptual and inferential origins of knowledge, involving the ability to differentiate vision, hearing, and inference as distinct sources of knowledge; (2) awareness of cognitive processes, involving the ability to evaluate the similarity and relative difficulty of multiple pairs of tasks; (3) first-order theory of mind, which requires understanding that a character would look for an object where she believed it to be, even if that belief was known to the child to be false; and (4) second-order theory of mind, which requires determining what one character would believe about what a second character believes under circumstances of incomplete information. Executive control was assessed via measures of (1) attention control, involving perceptual discrimination and response inhibition; (2) cognitive flexibility, involving the flexible pairing of labels with picture properties; and (3) working memory, involving the backward recall of between two and six words or digits. Reasoning was assessed via measures of (1) inductive reasoning, involving matrices of increasing complexity such that they required abstraction of one, two, or three dimensions; and (2) deductive reasoning, involving the ability to determine the implications of rules involving three simple logical forms.

Consistent with theoretical expectations and previous research, results indicated that even 4-year-olds have inferential and metacognitive abilities and that between ages 4 and 10 years children show systematic age-related progress in reasoning and in multiple aspects of metacognition, leading to what Kazi et al. (2019) described as "the highly organized cognitive attainment observed at the end of childhood." Even second-order theory of mind was within the competence of many (though not most) 8- and 10-year-olds. More detailed analyses supported theoretical predictions concerning the crucial role of cognizance in the development of executive control and reasoning. Kazi et al. (2019) concluded that the results "strongly suggested that there is a central core of cognizance underlying awareness of one's own and others' mental states" and that this core "develops systematically through the years, emerging from cognitive actions or experiences and contributing to their further development, in an ever-changing spiral of interactions with executive and reasoning process[es]."

Metacognition in Reasoning

Research on reasoning, as we saw in Chapters 2 and 3, provides extensive evidence for the crucial importance of metacognition. In recent reasoning research, metacognition is generally conceptualized within a dual process framework in which metacognition is associated with the deliberate and reflective processes of System 2 and/or with the resolution of conflicts emerging from the interplay of System 2 with the automatic inferences and intuitions of System 1 (Amsel, Klaczynski, Johnston, Bench, Close, Sadler, & Walker, 2008; Markovits, Brunet, Thompson, & Brisson, 2013; Markovits, Thomson, & Brisson, 2015). These studies generally use complex statistical techniques to test multiple predictions derived from the particular dual process model used by the study. For present purposes, I illustrate how such studies are conducted without detailing the specific models, predictions, analyses, and results.

Focusing on logical reasoning, Markovits et al. (2013) provided what they called in their title, "direct evidence for a dual process model of deductive inference." Across two studies, the authors presented college students with a series of seemingly reasonable simple inferences that enabled researchers to distinguish (a) a "statistical strategy," which intuitively accepts or rejects inferences on the basis of the estimated likelihood of counterexamples; from (b) a "counterexample strategy," which recognizes that a single counterexample undermines the validity of a deductive argument. Though previous researchers had provided evidence for both sorts of processes, the focus had been on showing that reasoners found to be generally more competent were more likely to use the counterexample strategy. The purpose of the present research was to show that most reasoners are capable of both strategies and to examine their interplay. It was hypothesized that the statistical strategy was a System 1 default strategy, whereas the counterexample strategy involved System 2 deliberation and reflection, and that reasoners exercised some degree of agency in choosing a strategy. Strategy use was manipulated through the imposition of strict time constraints, which interfered with System 2 functioning. Study 1 compared performance under time constraint with performance when allowed as much time as needed; it also compared participants who experienced the time constraints before getting unlimited time to those who experienced the time constraints after a period of unlimited time to respond. Study 2 added measures of reasoner confidence. Results were consistent with detailed predictions made on the basis of the dual process model.

In two additional studies, Markovits et al. (2015) presented college students with a series of conditional inference tasks systematically varying in content. Some tasks used familiar content that would easily enable students to think of counterexamples and thereby reject invalid arguments. Some tasks used content that, though also familiar, did not suggest obvious counterexamples. Finally, some tasks used "abstract" content with no meaning. Confidence in one's judgments was also assessed. The pattern of results was "consistent with a dual meta-representational model, which supposes that people have both a meta-representation of logical validity, preferentially used to evaluate abstract content, and one based on knowledge-based cues, which is preferentially activated with familiar content" (Markovits et al., 2015, p. 689). In the second study, half the students began with an experimental manipulation intended to orient their thinking toward counterexamples, which had previously been shown to improve logical performance, although it does not explicitly teach about logical principles such as necessity. Once again the pattern of results, albeit complex, suggested that people have logical conceptions of inferential validity, but these conceptions operate within the larger context of a dual process model and do not always prevail.

Metacognitive Development Beyond Childhood

Metacognitive development continues beyond age 10 years but rapidly becomes much less age-related and universal as children move into adolescence. As we have seen, metacognition is already apparent in young children, but even in adulthood no one ever becomes, in some general way, metacognitive. Our metacognition is always part of a larger cognitive system and is best construed within a developmental dual process model of cognition.

Much of the literature on metacognitive development beyond childhood focuses on what has come to be called epistemic cognition (Greene et al. 2016; Moshman, 2015), which is the aspect of metacognition of particular concern with respect to reasoning (Moshman, 2011a). As we will see in Chapters 6 and 8, epistemic development beyond childhood is also a matter of special concern for democracy and education. Before turning to epistemic development beyond childhood, however, we first consider its development across childhood.

Epistemic Development in Childhood

Epistemic cognition is the aspect or subdivision of metacognition concerned with knowledge about epistemology—that is, knowledge about the justification and truth of beliefs. Research on cognitive development in childhood has addressed the development of epistemic cognition using a variety of terminologies, usually without direct reference to epistemology. I consider in this section three relatively discrete metacognitive literatures that address important aspects of early epistemic development (Moshman, 2015).

Development of Metalogical Understanding

As we saw in Chapter 2, logic is initially implicit in biological self-regulation (Piaget, 1967/1971) and then in sensorimotor action beginning in the first year of life (Langer, 1980, 1986; Piaget, 1936/1963). The development of logical reasoning is not about the appearance of logic but about increasing control of our inferences and increasingly explicit knowledge about the logic implicit in them (Moshman, 1990, 2004b). The control of our inferences is metacognitive; the explicit knowledge about logical necessity and proof is, specifically, epistemic.

Developmental research on knowledge about logic suggests a sequence of four stages of metalogical understanding (Moshman, 1990, 2015). Stage 1 (Explicit Content/Implicit Inference) is typical of children under the age of 6 years. Children in this stage can tell you what they are thinking about (for example, toys, animals, colors, sizes) but they are not aware they are making inferences, though of course they are making inferences all the time (as we saw in Chapter 2). As a result, preschool children do not distinguish conclusions from premises, do not attribute inferences to others, and do not recognize inference as a potential source of knowledge (Miller, 2012; Pillow, 2012; Sodian & Wimmer, 1987). In Stage 2 (Explicit Inference/Implicit Logic), associated with later childhood, children are aware not only of what they are thinking about but also of their inferences. They recognize conclusions as the outcome of inferences, distinguish conclusions from premises, recognize that others also make inferences, and understand that, as a result of inference, people may come to know things they have not observed or been told. The explicit attention to inferences involves an implicit appreciation of their logical form and necessity.

Stage 3 (Explicit Logic/Implicit Metalogic) may be considered the adult level of metalogical understanding, involving what Markovits et al. (2015) call "a metacognitive representation of abstract validity" (p. 681). Stage 3 competencies begin to be seen about age 11 or 12 years and are routinely seen in adolescents and adults, though people of all ages (as we saw in Chapter 2) commonly fall short of logical norms. In Stage 3, explicit awareness of logical form and necessity makes it possible to distinguish the validity of an argument (does the conclusion follow necessarily from the premises?) from the truth of its individual premises and conclusion (Moshman & Franks, 1986). This enables hypothetico-deductive reasoning, central to Piaget's conception of formal reasoning (Chapter 2). The explicit attention to logic entails an implicit metalogical understanding of logic as a domain of necessity distinct from empirical science. Stage 4 (Explicit Metalogic) is the stage of logicians, who reflect on the nature and justification of formal logical systems, their interrelations with each other and with natural human languages, the nature and scope of logic, and the relation of logic to science and other domains.

The description of these stages provides an important insight into the process of development that accounts for them. In each stage transition, what was previously implicit becomes an explicit object of reflection. In Chapter 7, we will return to the development of metalogical understanding as part of a more general account of the processes that account for progress in reasoning and rationality.

Preschool Theory of Mind

Extensive research with young children has made it clear that they know much about cognitive and other aspects of the mind from very early ages. In fact, by the age of 4 years, knowledge of mind is sufficiently organized and has sufficient explanatory power that 4-year-olds are commonly said to have a "theory of mind" (Allen & Bickhard, 2018; Miller, 2012; Moshman, 2015; Pillow, 2012; Sodian & Kristen, 2016).

In contrast to research using the term "metacognition," which generally focuses on people's knowledge about and regulation of their own cognition, research using the term "theory of mind" generally focuses on knowledge about other minds, especially with regard to other people's knowledge and inferential processes. Despite the distinction in terminology and research traditions, most research on what is called "theory of mind" falls squarely within the broader realm of metacognition as cognition about cognition. Correspondingly, research on what is called "metacognition" is widely interpreted as showing that people, at least beyond the age of 4 years, organize their metacognitive knowledge into theories (Schraw and Moshman, 1995). As we saw in the previous section, the metacognitive theory of development proposed by Demetriou and colleagues (Demetriou & Spanoudis, 2018; Demetriou et al., 2018; Kazi et al., 2019) uses the term cognizance to include knowledge of both one's own and other minds.

The most popular measure of theory of mind has been the *false belief task*, which assesses the understanding that other people will act on the basis of their own beliefs, even if those beliefs are false. Extensive research has shown that most 4-year-olds, and virtually all 5-year-olds, understand this, whereas 3-year-olds generally do not (Allen & Bickhard, 2018; Miller, 2012; Moshman, 2015; O'Madagain & Tomasello, 2019; Pillow, 2012; Sodian & Kristen, 2016; Wellman, Cross, & Watson, 2001, Wimmer & Perner, 1983). In a typical study, a child sees a hidden object moved from one location to another and then must predict where another person, who was aware of its original location but did not see it moved, will look for it. Children of age 4 generally expect the other person to look for the object where the person saw it hidden, even though it is no longer there, whereas 3-year-olds generally expect the other person to look for the object where the child knows it to be, apparently unable to conceive that the other person could have a different, and false, belief.

Understanding that people may have different beliefs and that beliefs may be false raises questions of truth and justification. Such questions initially arise with respect to particular beliefs but ultimately lead to questions about knowledge in general. Thus, in the 4-year-old's theory of mind we have what may be seen as the beginnings of epistemic cognition (Allen & Bickhard, 2018; Iordanou, 2016; Moshman, 2015; Sodian & Kristen, 2016).

Many developmental researchers have provided evidence they interpret as showing that theory of mind, or at least important aspects of it, can be seen in children under 4 years (Miller, 2012; Moshman, 2015; Sodian & Kristen, 2016). Some have argued for theory of mind in infancy (for reviews, see Sodian, 2011; Sodian & Kristen, 2016). The term apparently originated in the study of nonhuman species (Premack & Woodruff, 1978), and there is ongoing disagreement about how to interpret evidence in very young children and in other species. But there is a strong theoretical consensus that human children by the age of 4 years have important insight into the minds of others, including the knowledge that people may have, and act on, false beliefs.

Constructivist Theory of Mind

Bucking the trend to find theories of mind in younger and younger children, some developmentalists have provided evidence for further development of theory of mind in later childhood. In particular, the insights of older children suggest that they, unlike younger children, recognize the active, interpretive nature of the mind as a constructor of knowledge. Research on epistemic development beyond age 4 years provides a picture of progress toward constructivist theories of mind. The minds of very young children are already active, interpretive, and constructive, but only as they get older do children increasingly recognize and theorize about this, thus constructing a constructivist theory of mind (Carpendale & Chandler, 1996; Chandler, Hallett, & Sokol, 2002; Lalonde & Chandler, 2002; Miller, 2012; Moshman, 2015; Pillow, 2012).

Michael Chandler and colleagues (Carpendale & Chandler, 1996; Chandler, Hallett, & Sokol, 2002; Lalonde & Chandler, 2002) have studied the development of knowledge about subjectivity and interpretive diversity beyond the recognition of false belief at age 4. Carpendale and Chandler, for example, presented children ranging from 5 through 8 years with a variety of tasks in which two puppets disagreed with each other about matters of interpretation involving ambiguous figures (such as the classic duck-rabbit, which can be seen as a duck or a rabbit), lexical ambiguity (such as "wait for a ring," which could refer to the ring of a telephone or a ring to wear), and ambiguous referential communication (leaving two possibilities). The children also encountered deviant interpretations (such as perceiving the duck-rabbit as an elephant) and disagreements about matters of taste (such as whether a soup tasted good or bad). Younger children showed some ability to recognize and explain differences in taste but were mostly unable to recognize the legitimacy of different interpretations. The 7- and 8-year-olds showed substantially greater understanding that two interpretations may both be legitimate in cases of ambiguity. They usually recognized, however, that the deviant interpretations could not be justified. The explanations of the older children showed an emerging insight that legitimate interpretations, unlike matters of taste, are grounded in evidence and reasons concerning the object to be interpreted.

Related research has shown similar developmental trends across childhood (Chandler et al., 2002; Miller, 2012; Moshman, 2015; Pillow, 2012; Wainryb, Shaw, Langley, Cottam, & Lewis, 2004). Epistemic development beyond basic theory of mind appears to involve two steps. The first is the recognition that differences in belief are not only a matter of someone not knowing what someone else knows and thereby having a false belief. Two people may have different perspectives on the same thing and therefore perceive or interpret it differently. Thus, children increasingly understand the relativity of perspective. But development is not simply progress toward epistemological relativism. Older children come to recognize that, in some cases, despite legitimate diversity of interpretation, there may be a rational basis for judgment. The duck-rabbit may reasonably be seen as either a duck or a rabbit, but there is no justification for calling it an elephant.

Epistemic development in childhood is thus, in large part, progress in knowledge about the constructive powers of the mind. As we will see in Chapter 7, the constructive powers of the mind are the basis for a constructivist account of development in which the actions of organisms are seen as playing a major role, along with heredity and environment, in developmental progress. The emergence of a constructivist theory of mind, which recognizes the constructive powers of the mind, thus enables increasing control of one's own development.

Epistemic Development Beyond Childhood

As we have seen, older children know far more about knowledge than younger children, who already know enough by age 4 years to be said to have a theory of mind. What remains to develop? As we will now see, there is extensive evidence that epistemic development beyond childhood proceeds from (1) simplistic notions of truth and falsity, to (2) increasing recognition of the subjectivity and relativity of knowledge, to (3) increasing appreciation of the possibility of rational judgment despite subjectivity. But wait. Isn't that the developmental trend we just observed in childhood? Indeed it is, and this is no small issue (Iordanou, 2016). Before we turn to specific theories and research concerning later epistemic development, we need to look in a more general way at the life-span pattern.

Epistemology Across the Lifespan

Epistemic cognition has generally been seen as an advanced and late-developing form of cognition and has generally been studied in adolescents and college students. Young adolescents are assumed in this literature to be epistemologically naïve. The focus is on describing this epistemic starting point and successive levels of epistemic development. But research on children makes it clear that the epistemic cognition of young adolescents, far from being a starting point, is the sophisticated outcome of an ongoing developmental process.

Chandler et al. (2002) provided an elegant and convincing resolution to the problem of coordinating these two literatures. Epistemic development, they argued, occurs in two cycles, each proceeding through three corresponding stages to create a developmental spiral. The developmental trend is recursive, with precisely two iterations, one in childhood and one beyond. Child development is at the "retail" level, and development beyond childhood is at the "wholesale" level. Epistemic development in childhood moves from a naïve objectivism to a "retail" subjectivism that acknowledges genuine differences in interpretation and disagreements that cannot be rationally resolved, but only in particular cases that come to one's attention. The subsequent understanding that some interpretations are better justified than others and that some beliefs are just plain wrong is also achieved by children only at a "retail" level, thus completing the first cycle of development in late childhood.

Adolescents retain the hard-won epistemic insights of childhood but recognize "wholesale" questions of knowledge, including abstract issues of truth, justification, objectivity, and subjectivity. At this higher level they begin with simplistic conceptions of truth and objectivity but often come to recognize "the dangerous prospect that diversity of opinion is somehow intrinsic to the knowing process" (Chandler et al., 2002, p. 162). Adolescent subjectivism, unlike that of childhood, threatens the very basis for knowledge. But some people, at least some of the time, show evidence of development beyond radical subjectivism to a rationalist theory of knowledge, the third stage of the second cycle.

Theories of Epistemic Development Beyond Childhood

There are a variety of theories and research traditions in the study of epistemic development beyond childhood (Moshman, 2015). Although they differ substantially in methodology, they all posit a sequence of steps, each of which represents progress over the previous one. The number of steps varies across theories but can readily be reduced, for each of the major theories, to the three basic stages that Chandler et al. (2002) proposed for both child development and (at a higher level) later development. However, even if adolescents and adults cycle through the same issues as children at a more abstract level, research shows an important difference between the two cycles. In contrast to epistemic development in childhood, which is universal and strongly tied to age, epistemic development beyond childhood varies greatly across individuals in its rate and extent.

The study of epistemic cognition is generally traced back to a longitudinal study by William Perry (1970/1999) of "intellectual and ethical development" in college. Students were interviewed annually across their four years of college about their educational experiences. Except for this general focus, the interviews were unstructured and open-ended. The results were interpreted as illustrating nine "positions" that emerge in a natural progression, though some students develop more rapidly than others and some fail to develop beyond the second or third position. The first three positions represent increasingly complex forms of *dualism*, involving a sharp distinction between right and wrong. Diversity of opinion and cognitive uncertainty are increasingly seen as possible and legitimate across the three positions but are attributed to confusion (position 2) or temporary ignorance in cases where authorities have not yet determined the truth (position 3). Some students move beyond this to posit, outside the realm of authority, a distinct epistemic realm in which diversity of opinion is expected and legitimate (position 4), but that realm often expands to swallow the dualistic realm of truth and falsity, leading (in position 5) to a "radical reperception of all knowledge as contextual and relativistic" (p. 121). Development beyond this (positions 6–9) is seen by Perry as a matter of commitment, responsibility, and personal identity.

Patricia King and Karen Kitchener (1994) provided a developmental theory of "reflective judgment" that drew on the work of Perry (1970/1999) but was also rooted in philosopher John Dewey's (1910/1997) conception of "reflective thinking" and motivated by educational concerns with "critical thinking." They too relied on interviews, but their interviews were specifically structured to focus on matters of intellectual diversity, justification, certainty, and truth. Thousands of adolescents and adults in dozens of studies have participated in such interviews, including some who were interviewed multiple times over periods of up to ten years. The results are generally consistent with a sequence of seven stages, though most people provide judgments associated with two or three adjacent stages, and progress through the stages (as with Perry's positions) is highly variable in rate and extent. The first three stages, labeled "pre-reflective," proceed from simplistic conceptions of absolute truth (stage 1), to increasing recognition that knowledge may not be immediately available (stage 2), to acknowledgment that personal opinions must sometimes be respected until certainty can be attained (stage 3). The next two stages, designated "quasi-reflective," involve increasing recognition of the uncertainties and ambiguities of knowledge (stage 4), leading to a conception of knowledge (stage 5) as "contextual and subjective" due to being "filtered through a person's perceptions and criteria for judgment" (p. 14).

Thus far, King and Kitchener's (1994) theory is generally consistent with that of Perry (1970/1999), but it diverges beyond stage 5. Perry took the radical subjectivism, contextualism, and relativism of his fifth position as the outcome of epistemic development and presented his remaining four positions as matters of personal choice and the development of identity. King and Kitchener, in contrast, proposed that some individuals achieve "reflective thinking," which acknowledges that knowledge is constructed but seeks justifications and better interpretations through the coordination of multiple perspectives and contexts (stage 6) and, in its most advanced form (stage 7), construes knowledge as "the outcome of a process of reasonable inquiry," which generates conclusions that may be "defended as representing the most complete, plausible, or compelling understanding of an issue on the basis of the available evidence" (p. 14). Thus, King and Kitchener's seven stages, like Perry's nine positions, can be divided into three levels, with the difference that King and Kitchener, unlike Perry, posited a post-subjectivist level that recognizes the possibility of rational judgment despite subjectivity.

Annick Mansfield and Blythe Clinchy (2002) assessed the epistemic cognition of children at about 10 years and then followed them longitudinally with further assessments three years later and again three years after that, when they were about 16. Participants were presented with vignettes in which protagonists disagreed with each other and were then asked a series of questions about the disagreement, their own view, whether certainty could be achieved, and whether both protagonists could be right. Despite substantial differences across individuals and vignettes, they found a general age trend in "epistemological positions" from an "objective" concern with facts, to a "subjective" respect for opinions, to an "integrated" appreciation of both. Although Mansfield and Clinchy's criteria for attributing advanced epistemologies were less stringent than those of King and Kitchener (1994), leading to what appears to be somewhat earlier development, their three positions correspond well with the three general levels into which King and Kitchener divide their seven stages, indicating theoretical agreement about the basic course of epistemic development.

Michael Chandler, in addition to his work reported earlier on the emergence of a constructivist theory of mind in middle childhood, also studied epistemic development in adolescence (Chandler, 1975, 1987; Boyes & Chandler, 1992; Chandler, Boyes, & Ball, 1990), including its role in identity formation. Children beyond age 4 years often doubt the truth of particular claims, but such doubts are "retail" because they are "case-specific." Adolescents, in contrast, may face "that wholesale brand of unassuageable doubt that ultimately poisons the whole well of certainty, by calling into radical question the very prospects for any kind of trustworthy knowledge whatsoever" (Chandler et al., 1990, p. 378). This may lead to "skepticism," an "epistemic posture" similar to the subjectivist intermediate level proposed by previous theorists. Some proceed beyond this to "postskeptical rationalism," which rejects "unbridled relativism" in favor of acknowledging "rationally based truth claims" and "arguably good reasons for choosing one course of action over another" (Chandler et al., 1990, p. 380). Chandler's account of epistemic development beyond childhood is thus broadly consistent with those of King and Kitchener (1994) and Mansfield and Clinchy (2002). Research independently assessing epistemic cognition and personal identity suggested that identity formation is a distinct process partly accounted for by progress in epistemic cognition (Boyes & Chandler, 1992; Chandler et al., 1990), rather than a substitute for a post-subjectivist epistemology (as in Perry, 1970/1999).

Deanna Kuhn, known for her research on both scientific reasoning (as discussed in Chapter 3) and argumentation (to be discussed in Chapters 5 and 8), has long seen "epistemological understanding" as crucial to both (Kuhn, 2005; Kuhn, Cheney, & Weinstock, 2000; Kuhn & Weinstock, 2002). In contrast to the extensive interviews and complex coding schemes of other theorists, Kuhn et al. (2000) simply presented scenarios in which two characters disagreed and asked participants whether only one was right or whether both "could have some rightness," and, if the latter, whether one view could be better or more right than the other. Responses that only one character could be right were coded as "absolutist." Responses that neither view could be better or more right than the other were coded as "multiplist." Finally, responses that one view could be better even if neither is absolutely right or wrong were coded as "evaluativist." Although responses differed systematically across topics, Kuhn (2005; Kuhn et al., 2000; Kuhn & Weinstock, 2002) proposed a post-childhood developmental sequence that proceeds in different domains at different rates and to different extents but always from absolutism to multiplism to evaluativism.

Absolutists, in Kuhn's (2005) developmental analysis, have already moved beyond the naïve "realism" of early childhood in which beliefs are assumed to be "faithful copies of reality . . . received directly from the external world" (p. 30). Acknowledging the possibility of false belief, absolutists nevertheless assume that such beliefs can only result from "inadequate or incorrect information" and "are easily correctable by reference to an external reality" (Kuhn, 2005, p. 31). In a case of disagreement, someone must be wrong. But some adolescents come to question this, at least in some domains, and move to a multiplist epistemology in which knowledge is a subjective function of the knower rather than a causal outcome of the known. Mind enters the picture. But now, everyone is right. Some individuals, however, at least in some domains, show further progress in the "extended task of coordinating the subjective and the objective elements of knowing" (Kuhn, 2005, p. 32), thus achieving a post-relativist epistemology of evaluativism, which recognizes that "some opinions are in fact more right than others, to the extent they are better supported by argument and evidence" (Kuhn, 2005, p. 32). Development thus proceeds, as in other theories of epistemic progress beyond childhood, from an objectivist conception of knowledge as facts, to a subjectivist conception of knowledge as opinions, to a rationalist conception of knowledge as "judgments, which require support in a framework of alternatives, evidence, and argument" (Kuhn, 2005, p. 32).

The major theories of epistemic development beyond childhood, as we have just seen, postulate a sequence that can readily be seen as a transition from objectivism to subjectivism to rationalism. Objectivism is an epistemology (theory of knowledge) that holds there to be ultimate truths that are directly observable, provable, or known to infallible authorities. Subjectivism is an epistemology in which knowledge is seen as constructed from, and thus determined by, one's point of view. Rationalism is an epistemology in which reasons short of proof provide bases for belief and action. A closer look at relevant theories and evidence, however, complicates the picture of epistemic cognition in multiple ways.

Complexities of Epistemic Cognition

Epistemic cognition cannot be understood simply as a three-stage developmental sequence proceeding from objectivism to subjectivism to rationalism. In this section I note several ways in which this picture is too simple (Greene et al., 2016; Moshman, 2015). I conclude, however, that the three-stage model remains fundamental not only to understanding epistemic cognition but more generally to understanding the nature of rationality and development.

Complications and More Complications

One major complication of the three-stage model of epistemic development is the fact that the three-stage sequence can be seen both in childhood and in development beyond childhood. As discussed, Chandler et al. (2002) proposed that epistemic development is best understood as a developmental spiral in which the transition from objectivism to subjectivism to rationalism occurs twice, first at a "retail" level of particular cases and then at a "wholesale" level of knowledge in general. But the complexities of epistemic cognition and development go beyond this.

A second complication is that there are substantial individual differences in the rate and extent of development, especially with respect to the second cycle. Even in childhood, development proceeds more rapidly in some children and less rapidly in others. Nevertheless, virtually all children achieve a basic theory of mind by their fifth birthday and then proceed beyond that toward an increasingly constructivist theory of mind, with age-related milestones along the way in their understanding of viewpoint diversity, relativity of perspective, and the possibility of rational judgment. Development beyond childhood, in contrast, is much less age-related and universal. Whether and at what rate it proceeds varies greatly across individuals, depending in large part on social contexts that may promote or hinder epistemic development (a matter to which we return in Chapters 7 and 8).

To further complicate matters, general stages of development cannot account for the evidence that epistemic cognition is to a large extent domain-specific. As discussed earlier in this chapter, epistemic development in the domain of logic is a matter of increasing comprehension of the logical necessity of deductive inferences. Although the three-stage model accounts for the development of causal, principled, and precedent-based reasoning, which are central to the domains of science, morality, and social convention, respectively (see Chapter 3), it does not seem applicable to the development of metalogical understanding (Moshman, 2015). Even where the three-stage model applies, moreover, development may proceed at different rates in different domains and for different topics within domains, and may cease at different stages. The transition from objectivism to subjectivism, for example, may occur earlier with respect to matters of sociology, morality, or history than with respect to matters of physics or chemistry because the role of subjectivity is more obvious in the former cases. But subjectivism may persist longer in the former cases than the latter and may never be overcome, whereas subjectivism in the physical sciences, if achieved at all, may be more quickly replaced by a post-subjectivist rationalism. Such differences, and their educational implications, have been explored in many studies (Greene et al., 2016).

Finally, as dual process theories remind us, individual judgments and behavior in any particular context reflect a variety of automatic processes and intuitions, with results that may or may not reflect the individual's most sophisticated epistemic insights. Optimal reasoning based on one's best epistemic understanding is possible, but reasoning is in large part a function of heuristics and biases automatically activated by subtle features of context and task demands. Epistemic development enhances the quality of our best reasoning, but regardless of epistemic level, we do not always function at our epistemic best.

Recognizing Subjectivity and Transcending Subjectivism

Despite all the complexities of epistemic cognition, the three-stage sequence from objectivism to subjectivism to rationalism shows up in study after study, plays a major role in reasoning, and seems crucial to understanding human rationality and development. Following objectivism, the sequence consists of two transitions. The first transition involves the recognition of inherent subjectivity, with the subjectivist implication that what appeared to be the truth is simply our point of view, which is one of many points of view. The second transition recognizes the possibility of rational judgment despite subjectivity, thus transcending subjectivism to restore a role for objectivity.

With respect to reasoning, the recognition of subjectivity has the potential to undermine our motivation (Kuhn, 2005). Why think hard when all ideas are just subjective opinions, no better or worse than any other opinions? In transcending subjectivism, we see that there is reason after all to pursue the truth, even if it is not so readily and permanently achieved as we once thought. Advanced epistemic cognition is important not only in directing our reasoning but also in motivating it.

The three-stage sequence is consistent with a general conception of rationality as metasubjective objectivity (Moshman, 2011a). Objectivity is achieved not by overcoming all subjectivity but rather by reflecting on and compensating for particular subjectivities. New subjectivities, and associated limits on our objectivity, are always waiting to be discovered, and then to be overcome, leading to greater objectivity. But even when we transcend a particular subjective perspective, we do so from some meta-perspective, which is itself subjective. Transcending subjectivity is an ongoing developmental process, not a final achievement. We will address this in more detail in Chapter 7.

Conclusion

In this chapter we have supplemented the earlier consideration of various forms of reasoning (Chapters 2 and 3) with a direct look at metacognition, the basis for thinking, and especially the subset of metacognition known as epistemic cognition, the basis for reasoning. We have seen that metacognition, including epistemic cognition, develops rapidly over the first 11 or 12 years of life, with the potential for further development, especially in epistemic cognition, long beyond that. This is fully consistent with the pattern seen in the development of various forms of reasoning. As we will discuss further in Chapter 7, cognitive development can be seen as progress toward rationality, thus distinguishing it from other cognitive changes. A distinction can be made between basic development, referring to the universal progress in rationality across the first 12 years of life, and advanced development, referring to further progress that is highly variable across individuals.

But there remains something missing in this picture. As is typical in the literatures of cognitive and developmental psychology, we have been looking almost exclusively at the reasoning and epistemic cognition of individuals. We now turn to argumentation, which I construe as collaborative reasoning.

5

ARGUMENTATION AS COLLABORATIVE REASONING

We have seen in Chapters 2 through 4 that, over the course of childhood, we all construct multiple forms of reasoning—including logical, scientific, principled, and precedent-based reasoning—and the metacognitive abilities and epistemic insights that support such reasoning. By the age of 12 or 13 years, all normal humans have rational abilities and understandings at a level beyond that of any child of 8 or 9 years, though such children are themselves functioning at a level beyond any 4-year-old, who in turn is the product of four years of ongoing development.

It is equally clear, however, that teenagers and adults, regardless of age, often fall far short of optimal reasoning. There are substantial individual differences in the levels of rational competence achieved, but even those most capable of advanced reasoning and epistemic understanding often reach conclusions guided largely by automatic inferences and biases. Dual process theory has been presented as a theoretical framework that accounts for both human rational competence and the routine and systematic failures in actual human reasoning.

In recent years, many psychologists and philosophers have argued for reconceptualizing reasoning as a fundamentally social process of argumentation (Laden, 2012; Mercier & Sperber, 2017). Hugo Mercier and Dan Sperber (2017), in particular, have proposed that reasoning evolved to serve social purposes, thus explaining the well-documented failures of individual reasoning. Mercier and Sperber go too far, in my view, in downgrading individual rationality and the role of logic (Moshman, 2018; see Chapter 7). But they are right that argumentation is crucial to reasoning in ways that the study of reasoning has largely failed to address. In considering argumentation in this chapter, I am not just moving to a new topic but expanding the discussion to a whole new dimension of reasoning.

Argumentation is a rational social process of generating and responding to reasons. That is, it is a process of reciprocal justification. Argumentation often takes the form of debate, in which each side attempts to prevail by showing the other to be wrong. Even then, argumentation is a rational process in that it relies on reasons (Aikin & Talisse, 2019).

But argumentation is not only, or even primarily, a matter of debate. My concern in this chapter is with what I deem the ideal form of argumentation, a process of collaborative reasoning aimed at achieving the truth, or at least the most justified conclusion, which may differ from any of the initial positions.

I begin with a case of collaborative logical reasoning, in which groups turn out to be more logical than individuals. I then review research showing that groups commonly show better reasoning than individuals. But group reasoning, obviously, can also go wrong. The final portion of the chapter considers the circumstances under which collaborative reasoning is most likely to be productive and the ways we can enhance its rationality.

Collaborative Reasoning in a Logic Task

In this section I report a study of logical reasoning in which groups performed more rationally than individuals. The study involved the *selection task* (presented briefly in Chapter 2 and again in more detail below), which was introduced in the 1960s and quickly came to be seen as a major challenge to usual conceptions of human rationality (Wason & Johnson-Laird, 1972). The task requires participants to select the card or cards (out of a set of four) that must be turned to test a simple hypothesis. The solution is to turn the two cards that could falsify the hypothesis (one of which is a less obvious choice than the other) and not turn either of the other two cards (though one of those is tempting). Multiple studies showed that only about 10% of college students selected the correct two cards (Wason & Johnson-Laird, 1972). Performance was better on some variations of the task, leading to theoretical controversy about how to account for the complex pattern of results that accumulated over the 1970s and 1980s (Moshman, 2011a).

The Selection Task and Me

My personal connection to the selection task goes back to the 1970s when I was a graduate student in developmental psychology doing research on the development of logical and scientific reasoning in adolescence. Research on the selection task seemed to suggest that most adults did not understand the basic logic of hypothesis testing that was central to Piaget's conception of formal operations, the stage of cognitive development attained in early adolescence. My dissertation research (Moshman, 1979) used a variation of the selection task to show that there was developmental progress in hypothesis testing over the course of adolescence but that failures of logic remained common even among college students.

I also worked the selection task into my teaching and for decades routinely introduced it by having students come up with individual answers and then challenging them to discuss the task with each other to reach a consensus solution (with the threat that no one could leave until they did). My only intervention was to record all initially selected card combinations on the blackboard, tally the number of students selecting each, and occasionally survey the class to document shifts of opinion on the blackboard. Although the vast majority of students initially showed the same incorrect selection patterns routinely seen in research, most classes converged on the correct selection pattern well before the end of the class period. Peer pressure was obviously not prevailing given that initially popular response patterns were ultimately rejected. What I observed instead was a rational social process in which individuals presented differing views about which cards should or should not be turned and a variety of arguments for or against these views, with the strongest arguments, in most cases, ultimately prevailing.

In the early 1990s I sought to document the remarkable success of group reasoning on the selection task in collaboration with Molly Geil, a student who conducted the research described below and wrote up the quantitative part of the results for her master's thesis. We presented the study at the 1994 meeting of the Jean Piaget Society in Chicago but had difficulty getting it published. It was rejected by an education journal and then by a journal focusing specifically on science education, in large part because it did not provide evidence of student learning.

By the time of the second rejection, however, I had become aware of a new journal entitled *Thinking and Reasoning* that seemed an ideal outlet for the study, which, we had tried to be clear, was about group reasoning, not individual learning. The two initial reviewers identified themselves as Henry Markovits and David O'Brien, both major contributors to the study of logical reasoning. Both appreciated the quantitative documentation of rational group performance on the notoriously difficult selection task but wanted to see more qualitative analysis of the actual processes of argumentation that led to group success. A revised version of the manuscript was finally accepted for publication in 1997 and published the following year.

The increasing interest in group reasoning in recent years is reflected in the citation rate of Moshman and Geil (1998), as shown by Google Scholar (as of February 2020). In each of the 10 years following its publication (1998–2007), the article was cited between one and seven times, with an average rate under four citations per year and no reason to expect that figure to increase. In each of the next 7 years (2008–2014), however, the article was cited between 5 and 17 times, averaging about 13 citations per year. Over the subsequent 5 years (2015–2019), citation rates ranged from 18 to 30, with an average over 23 citations per year, reaching 30 in 2019.

A Study of Group Reasoning

The Moshman and Geil (1998) study engaged 143 college students, mostly education majors, in reasoning about the original version of the selection task. Each student was presented with a sheet of paper picturing four cards that showed, from left to right, E, K, 4, and 7. Each card, they were informed, had a letter on one side and a number on the other. Below the cards was this hypothesis: "If a card has a vowel on one side then it has an even number on the other side." Students were asked to select the card or cards they would need to turn to determine conclusively whether the hypothesis was true or false for the set of four cards, and to justify their response in writing.

The correct response is to select E (a vowel) and 7 (an odd number). The vowel must be turned because an odd number on the other side would falsify the hypothesis; the odd number must be turned because a vowel on the other side would falsify the hypothesis. Neither of the other cards needs to be turned because neither could falsify the hypothesis. If the hypothesis is not falsified by turning the E and 7 cards, then it is true regardless of further evidence.

The challenge of this task is that it requires insight and effort to recognize the crucial importance of falsification and consider each card with that in mind. In the absence of sufficient metalogical understanding and self-regulation, we succumb to a natural verification bias, seeking to support the hypothesis (if vowel, then even) by turning the E (a vowel) to look for an even number, and perhaps also the 4 (an even number) to look for a vowel. Thus, the most common responses to the selection task are to select only the E or only E and 4. The challenge is to recognize that the 7 must also be turned because it could falsify the hypothesis, and the 4 need not be turned because it could not falsify the hypothesis.

Of the 143 participants, 32 were asked to solve the task individually. The remaining 111 were assigned to 20 groups of 5 or 6 students, with each group asked to reach a consensus. In half of those groups, each student was asked to solve the task individually prior to group discussion. All sessions were videotaped.

Evidence for Collective Rationality

Results for the 32 students who only solved the task individually were consistent with the literature. Although they were told to take as much time as necessary and understood that they needed to remain for the allotted 50 minutes to earn class credit and would be expected to justify their response in writing, only three selected the correct response of E and 7. The most common responses were E and 4 (selected by 14) and E only (selected by 5), with no other response pattern selected by more than two individuals.

For the 20 groups, on the other hand, the results were dramatically different. All 20 reached a consensus within 45 minutes. The correct response of E and 7 was selected by 15 groups, with 3 selecting E only; 1 selecting E, 4, and 7; and 1 selecting all four cards. Whether students provided individual responses prior to group discussion turned out to make no difference; correct responses were provided by eight of the ten groups in which individuals first responded individually, and seven of the ten in which they did not.

Further analysis focused on the ten groups for which individual responses were provided prior to discussion. In no case did all students in a group make the same initial selections. In seven groups there was at least one person who initially selected the correct combination of E and 7. This was never the most common initial response, but it nevertheless prevailed in five of these seven cases. Even more interesting, the correct response also prevailed in all three of the remaining groups despite the fact that not a single individual in those groups initially selected that combination of cards.

Examination of the videotapes showed that students routinely challenged each other to justify their selections and encouraged each other to consider consequences and alternatives. Final selections reflected voluntary agreement based on emerging logical insights rather than passive conformity to views favored by the most peers or by someone deemed more expert than others. To illustrate the rational and constructive quality of discussion, we summarized and quoted at length from the discussions in two of the three groups (out of the ten that made initial individual selections) that reached the correct conclusion despite no individual initially doing so.

Collaborative Reasoning: Group 1

Group 1 consisted of Alice, Ben, Carol, Dan, and Earl (these are not their real names, but Alice and Carol were female and the others male). Alice initially selected the E, 4, and 7 cards to be turned; the others all selected just E and 4. As discussion began, everyone agreed that E should be turned to see if there was an even number on the other side, 4 should be turned to see if there was a vowel, and the other two cards need not be turned. Alice laughed off her original selection of the 7 as a mistake and joined Ben, Carol, and Dan in reinforcing each other's statements as to the relevance of E and 4 to the hypothesis and the irrelevance of K and 7. But then Alice reconsidered:

Alice: Maybe 7 has a vowel on the other side.
Ben: It could, but as far as this hypothesis here, it just doesn't matter.
Alice: But if it has . . .
Dan: It just says if it has a vowel on one side.
Alice: Yeah, but it says if it has a vowel on one side, then it has an even number on the other side.
Dan: So maybe we're wrong.
Carol: [surprised and excited] Oh, that's *true*!

Everyone agreed that this complicated the issue, leading Ben to propose that turning the E and 4 would "test" the hypothesis, and finding an even number and a vowel, respectively, on the other sides would "support it as opposed to proving it," because "we couldn't prove it unless we turned over all of them." But after some discussion of the mechanics of turning and keeping track of four cards, Dan suddenly questioned the need to turn K, and Alice agreed it was unnecessary because the hypothesis was only "concerned with vowels." Then:

Carol: But what if it has an even number on the other side?
Dan: It doesn't say anything about . . .
Alice: It doesn't say that if it's a consonant . . .
Dan: It just says if it has a vowel. It doesn't say if it has a consonant it can't have any of them.
Carol: That's true
Dan: I don't think we have to turn over K.

Apparently convinced, Carol now wondered whether 4 is also unnecessary, noting, "it doesn't say that if it has an even number on one side it has a vowel on the other," and then concluding, "really we don't need to turn over 4." Ben joined her in explaining that the conditional hypothesis is not reversible:

Carol: You don't have to turn over 4 because it [the hypothesis] says if it has a vowel on one side it has an even number on the other side.
Ben: It doesn't say if it has an even number on one side it has a vowel on the other.

Alice and Dan continued to insist that the 4 must be turned, however, and when Carol tried to explain that the 4 "could have a consonant on the other side and it still wouldn't . . .," Alice interjected, "Yeah, but we need to check it because it *is* an even number, so we have to find out if it *has* a vowel on the other side." Carol responded, "Yeah, I guess," and Alice, defending the choice of E, 4, and 7, went on to explain that the E must be turned because "we have to find out if it's an even number," and the 7 must be turned because "we need to find out if it's a consonant or a vowel because if it's a vowel then it's false."

In the literature of the selection task, the response of E, 4, and 7 has long been seen as showing a partial insight into the crucial importance of falsification (Wason & Johnson-Laird, 1972). Alice's explanation illustrates this nicely. On one hand, she still explains the selection of E and 4 on the basis of a search for cards combining a vowel with an even number (which seemingly verify the hypothesis *If vowel, then even*): we turn the vowel to look for an even number and we turn the even number to look for a vowel. But she has recognized, and convinced the others, that the 7 must also be turned, even though it could not turn out to be a vowel with an even number, because it could turn out to be a vowel with an odd number, which would falsify the hypothesis. The partial insight is recognizing that any card that could falsify the hypothesis must be turned. What remains is the full insight of recognizing that *only* cards that could falsify the hypothesis need to be turned.

But Ben and Carol now had at least an inkling of this, enough so they continued to question the need to turn the 4. When Ben wondered about the implications of it having a consonant on the reverse side, Carol suggested that turning the 4 would "prove" the hypothesis if there were a vowel on the reverse side and "wouldn't do anything" if there were a consonant. "It would either prove it or it wouldn't do anything," she concluded. "The 7 and the E are the only ones that can disprove it." There was a very long pause at this point, during which Alice looked back at the instructions, murmuring "to determine conclusively." Then:

Dan: Okay, we have to turn over E for sure, right?
Carol: Yeah.
Dan: Because it has a vowel on one side and we need to find out if it has an even number on the other. K we don't have to worry about, because it doesn't say anything about . . .
Ben: . . . consonants . . .
Dan: . . . having a consonant.
Alice: It doesn't say if it has a consonant it's odd, or whatever.
Dan: And 4 . . .
Ben: I think we need to turn 4.
Dan: I think we have to turn over 4 because . . .
Earl: It's the same as E, really.
Alice: It's the same as E, yeah, we know it's an even number so we have to find out if it has . . .
Dan: Well, maybe we don't. [He pauses, then proceeds slowly, with Carol nodding and murmuring assent.] If it has a consonant on one side it doesn't matter if it has an odd or an even number. So it really doesn't matter if we look at 4. Does it? Do you see that?
Alice and Ben [simultaneously]: I see what you're saying.
Dan: It can tell us where that's right, but it can't tell us it's wrong.
Carol: Yeah.
Dan: And 7 I think we have to turn over. 'Cause we need to find out if that has a vowel.
Carol: Because it can prove right or wrong.
Dan: Because it can prove it wrong.

The group then confirmed that agreement had been reached and reflected on the process that had generated this consensus:

Ben: So, are we narrowing it down to E and 7 this time?
Dan: I think so.
Carol: I think it should be E and 7 now.
Dan. I do too.
Ben: That's pretty interesting to watch us all concur.

Alice: I wouldn't have come up with this if we hadn't, you know, talked about it.
Carol: I know, I was totally set on E and 4.
Ben: We *all* were.

Recall that Alice originally selected 7 in addition to E and 4. With respect to 7, one person eventually succeeded in convincing the group that it must be turned. But everyone fully agreed at the start that of course the 4 must be turned, just as surely as the E must be turned and for the same reason: to verify the hypothesis. With respect to the 4, then, the group managed to talk itself out of a unanimous misconception. Each of the five students independently wrote on the final task sheet that only E and 7 should be turned and provided a written explanation consistent with the group's final arguments.

Who was responsible for the final selection of E and 7? Four of the five students (everyone but Earl) fully shared responsibility for the group response. Alice was the only student who initially proposed turning 7 and was the first to point out that it could have a vowel on the reverse side. Ben was the first to distinguish "supporting" a hypothesis from "proving" it, though he mistakenly argued that proof required turning all four cards. Dan then took the lead in showing that K need not be turned. Carol expanded on Dan's argument to make the case that 4 also need not be turned, initially convincing Ben but not Alice or Dan. Alice then noted that 7 could falsify the hypothesis. Carol noted later that 4 could not disprove the hypothesis whereas E and 7 could. Finally, Dan established that the group had agreed to turn 7 (in addition to E) and provided what turned out to be the decisive argument for not turning 4. Through collaborative reasoning, the four students generated a higher level of understanding than any of them alone achieved.

Collaborative Reasoning: Group 2

Group 2 consisted of Frank, Gwen, Hal, Ike, and Jay (again the names are fictitious, but Gwen was female and the others male). Hal initially proposed to turn only the E; Frank proposed E, 4, and 7; and the other three proposed E and 4. Jay began the discussion by proposing to turn just E and 4; Gwen agreed. Frank agreed on turning E and 4 but noted his selection of 7 as well. He argued that E must be turned because it is a vowel, and K need not be turned "because we're not concerned with a consonant having an odd or even; we're talking about just the vowel card." With respect to the other side of the 4, he started to explain, "if that's a vowel, then . . .," but Hal interrupted, "see, that doesn't have to be a vowel, though." "Yeah, it does," responded Gwen, but Hal continued to explain his view, noting the irreversibility of the hypothesis: "All that that's saying is that all the vowels have to have even numbers on the other side. But it's not saying that, like, the number 4 has to have a vowel on the other side." Frank and Gwen now agreed, and Hal continued:

> The only thing that you have to turn over is E, but by turning over E you're just supporting the hypothesis, you're not proving. The only way you can prove that thing right is if you have all the vowels facing up and then you turn all of them over. You know what I'm saying? That's the only way you can prove that hypothesis correct.

Frank now asserted, "you'd have to turn over 7." Hal responded, "you'd have to turn over all of the vowels and they'd have to be facing up too. You couldn't have one facing the other way because you wouldn't know." Gwen and Jay agreed, and the discussion moved on to the requirements of the task and then returned to the need to turn E and the irrelevance of K and 4. Frank was not done, however, and finally got his point across:

Frank: But we would have to turn over the 7, then. Because a vowel, like an I or an O, would throw us off.
Gwen: You're right, we wouldn't be sure of the 7.
Frank: So, the E and the 7?
Gwen: Yeah.
Hal: Yeah, that's a good point.
Gwen: It *is* a good point. [Pause.] So we've decided E and 7 because we want to know if E has an even number under it and if 7 has a vowel under it or a consonant.
Frank: That would disprove it.
Gwen: Right. That's interesting.

Frank and Gwen concluded the session by clarifying that if the 7 has a vowel under it, then the hypothesis is false, which is why the 7 must be turned. Each of the five students then indicated the choice of E and 7 on the final task sheet and provided an explanation consistent with the group's final argument. Three of the five played major roles in the discussion. Frank was a persistent advocate for turning the 7, finally convincing the others. Hal made the case that the 4 need not be turned, though initially as part of an argument for just turning E. Gwen insisted at first on turning 4 but was convinced by Hal's argument against this. Later, she was the first to appreciate the significance of Frank's argument for turning 7 and helped him clarify it and convince the others (Moshman & Geil, 1998).

Additional Evidence for Collective Rationality

Extensive research in cognitive, developmental, social, and educational psychology demonstrates the rational advantages of collaborative reasoning—that is, argumentation in collaborative contexts. I begin this section with a brief overview of theory and research concerning the value of collaborative cognition and then turn specifically to studies that, like Moshman and Geil (1998), show the rationality of group reasoning in comparison to individual reasoning, including some that look specifically at the conditions favoring collective rationality.

Rational Advantages of Collaborative Cognition

Research on collaborative learning, memory, judgment, problem solving, decision-making, and reasoning provides extensive evidence for the cognitive value of collaborative cognition, including peer argumentation (Baillon, Bleichrodt, Liu, & Wakker, 2016; Bearison & Dorval, 2002; Curşeu, Mesiec, Pluut, & Lucas, 2015; Doise & Mugny, 1984; Laughlin, 2011; Mercier, Boudry, Paglieri, & Trouche, 2017; Mercier & Sperber, 2017; Moshman & Geil, 1998; Piaget, 1932/1965b; Tomasello, 2014; Zillmer & Kuhn, 2018). With respect to the Wason selection task, for example, research with individuals has generally shown that cues about the importance of falsification are less helpful than one might expect, but it appears that groups profit more from such cues than do individuals (Augustinova, 2008). Although the selection task is likely beyond young children (more below), there is no doubt that children engage in meaningful argumentation beginning in the preschool years and show rapid progress in collaborative reasoning (Domberg, Köymen, & Tomasello, 2018).

Much of the research on peer argumentation has focused especially on showing that collaborative reasoning promotes the learning and development of those who engage in it (Baillon et al., 2016; Doise & Mugny, 1984; Laughlin, 2011, Chapter 7; Piaget, 1932/1965b). Part of what develops, moreover, is the ability to engage more productively in collaborative cognition of various sorts. This has important implications for both development and education, to be addressed in Chapters 7 and 8 respectively.

Group Rationality

I turn now to the more specific question of the rationality of groups engaged in collaborative reasoning as compared to the rationality of individuals reasoning on their own. It is well established that under the right circumstances group performance is more competent than that of the average individual. Patrick Laughlin (2011) reviewed and organized the literature on group problem solving, broadly defined to include decision-making, reasoning, and related cognitive processes, including decades of his own research. He concluded (Laughlin 2011, pp. 141–142) that group tasks can be ordered on a continuum from "intellective" (involving matters of logic and/or clear facts) to "judgmental" (where there is no "generally accepted demonstrably correct answer"). In judgmental tasks a consensus may suffice; in intellective tasks the objective is truth. The intellective/judgmental continuum reflects an underlying continuum of "demonstrability." High demonstrability requires not only a shared logic and sufficient information, but also the ability and opportunity of correct group members to convince others and the ability of the others to recognize correct solutions. The greater the demonstrability of a particular solution, the smaller the proportion of group members needed to convince the group to adopt that solution. Demonstrability makes it possible for a minority to convince a majority, and high demonstrability makes it possible for a single correct individual to convince everyone else. Thus for highly intellective tasks, groups perform as rationally as their most rational member.

In the most intellective tasks, Laughlin (2011) noted, groups may even outperform the best of an equivalent number of individuals, using more complex and insightful strategies that enable them to succeed on fewer trials. This is consistent with Moshman and Geil's (1998) finding that groups may identify the correct solution to the selection task even if none of their members were able to do so individually. Here we see the strongest evidence for the constructive power of peer argumentation.

How could a group construct a better answer than any individual within it? The final resolution may be a combination of the best ideas produced by individuals, even if only one person originally comes up with some of those ideas. In Moshman and Geil (1998), for example, Group 2 ultimately accepted Frank's argument for turning the 7 and Hal's argument against turning the 4, though each was initially alone in his view. Similarly, Group 1 concluded that the 7 must be turned, although only Alice initially made this selection.

It is noteworthy, however, that Group 1 also reached a consensus against turning 4, despite the fact that its five members unanimously agreed at the start that the 4 must be selected. No single individual, moreover, was responsible for this new understanding. Carol was the first to propose that the 4 should not be turned, but her arguments drew on Dan's case against turning K, Ben's earlier distinction between "supporting" and "proving" the hypothesis, and Alice's insight with respect to 7 about the crucial importance of falsification. It was Dan, moreover, who ultimately convinced the others, with Carol's assistance, that 4 need not be turned. The group decision not to turn 4 was not a choice among conflicting individual ideas. It was a novel insight co-constructed by four members of the group. At its most creative and powerful, the rationality of groups is not just a matter of selecting and combining the best ideas. It also involves the social construction of new ideas.

Conditions of Collective Rationality

Research looking specifically at the conditions of collective rationality has shown that the value of collaborative reasoning is due not just to the pooling of ideas but to the process of argumentation (Baillon et al., 2016). Curşeu, Jansen, and Chappin (2013), for example, divided 617 college students into 176 small groups—91 of them "collaborative" and 85 "consultative." Each group was presented with the same set of ten decision-making tasks adapted from tasks commonly used in the literature on human heuristics and biases (introduced in Chapter 1). In the present versions, the logically or statistically normative solution in each case was presented as one of several options. Collaborative groups were instructed to reach a consensus choice for each task. In the consultative groups, a group leader was randomly selected to make the group choice on each task after getting input from each of the other group members, who were not permitted to discuss the task with each other.

Analysis focused on the extent to which groups achieved "synergy," defined as "an objective gain in group performance as compared to summed individual performances" (Curşeu et al., 2013, p. 2). A group process can be said to show weak synergy if the group performs better than its average member, and strong synergy if it performs better than its best member. Curşeu et al. (2013) predicted that the collaborative groups would show greater synergy than consultative groups because the opportunity to engage in discussion would enhance rational decision-making. This prediction was confirmed. The collaborative groups generally achieved at least weak synergy and were significantly more likely than the consultative groups to do so. Moreover, the collaborative groups, on average, came significantly closer than the consultative groups to strong synergy, though most did not achieve it.

This research provides specific evidence for the role of collaborative reasoning in the rationality of groups. With a slight shift in terminology, we can say that, at least under some circumstances, microdemocracies outreason microdictatorships, raising the question of whether and how we might extend the present analysis to the societal level. We take up that question in Chapter 6.

Researchers have also addressed the question of access to relevant information by designing studies that systematically manipulated such access. Laughlin (2011) reviewed research in which information favoring a suboptimal decision was distributed to all group members, whereas information favoring an optimal decision was provided only to individuals. He found a clear pattern: Such groups generally made suboptimal decisions because they focused on the shared information and failed to integrate the additional information known only to particular individuals. But the research showed two ways of enhancing rationality. First, groups were more likely to make the optimal decision if the task was presented as a problem to be solved rather than a judgment to be made. Second, groups also did better if individuals were appointed as "experts" on the unique information each possessed, thus "providing social validation for information known only to one person" (Laughlin, 2011, p. 142). This research also raises questions for Chapter 6. How can we enhance the ability of democratic institutions to function in a problem-solving mode and take relevant expertise into account?

The Rational Social Ideal

Despite the evidence for group rationality, groups can also be irrational, sometimes less rational than their average member, sometimes even doing terrible things that most or all of their members wish they hadn't (Moshman, 2007b, 2011b). This raises a series of questions, some of them addressed in part by the research just reviewed: What aspects of group functioning promote rationality? How can we arrange and support rational groups? How can we extend this to rational social systems?

In this section I consider five features of the two groups from Moshman and Geil (1998), and other such groups, that seem important for the rational outcomes observed in that study. These features are mostly obvious things that would usually go without saying, but this is the place to make them explicit. The discussion in each case notes extensions to democratic social systems, to be considered further in the next chapter and beyond. The focus for now, however, is the nature of these groups as rational social ideals.

Small Group

For a start, the two groups were small enough that everyone could get repeated opportunities to speak to the group, everyone could hear from everyone else, and individuals with differing views could engage in sustained argument that others were free to join. No one was required to speak, but everyone was free to do so multiple times, and most actively participated.

Obviously, the opportunity for this sort of free discussion declines as the size of the group increases. Group discussion procedures, such as Robert's Rules of Order, enable groups of several dozen to approximate the ideal of free discussion. For a group of several hundred, however, it is inevitable that opportunities to speak will be strictly limited, even if everyone ultimately gets a turn; moreover, sustained argumentation among a small number of individuals will be impossible due to the number of people waiting their turn to speak.

For a larger social system, face-to-face discussion among all persons is obviously impossible. This raises serious questions about the possibility of scaling up the benefits of group rationality to social systems. Can the members of a society be said to be engaged in collaborative reasoning? How can a social system operate rationally?

Individual Competence

A second characteristic of the two groups is that all participants were college students. How would younger individuals have done? Based on research on the development of logical reasoning in individuals, it seems likely that rational group performance on the selection task could be found even if the members of the group were young teens, but not if they were children under 11 or 12 years. The problem is not just that none of the children would initially have the correct solution. The problem is that the children would lack the hypothetico-deductive reasoning necessary to grasp the logic of the task even if (as with the adult groups in Augustinova, 2008) they were provided with helpful insights.

In addition to developing competence in logical and other forms of reasoning, children also show substantial and predictable development in argumentation ability over the first 11 or 12 years of life. Argumentation competence, it should be clear, is social as well as cognitive. To argue well, one must (1) recognize the need to provide reasons for one's ideas, which includes understanding what counts as a reason and what others will find convincing; (2) recognize the need to refute alternative ideas, which requires attending to others and understanding their ideas; and (3) recognize the possibility of higher-order argumentation, which includes responding to refutations of one's own ideas, anticipating such refutations, acknowledging strengths and weaknesses in a variety of ideas, including one's own, and working with others to construct better ideas. Children make substantial progress in the first set of competencies beginning in the preschool years, with ongoing development across childhood in the first two sets, and show some capacity for higher-order argumentation by the age of 11 or 12 years. People of all ages fall far short of ideal argumentation, however, with substantial differences across individuals in the rationality of their argumentation, due in large part to differences in epistemic cognition. Beyond the age of about 12 years, individual differences in rational argumentation are more related to education and experience than to age (Kuhn, 1991, 2005).

Group rationality, as we have seen, is not just the sum of the rationality of the individuals composing the group (Baillon et al., 2016; Curşeu et al., 2013; Curşeu et al., 2015; Laughlin, 2011). Nevertheless, even in collaborative reasoning, individual competence matters. For social systems concerned with argumentation, education aimed at the promotion of individual rationality is important, though part of a larger picture.

Respect for Reasons

A third characteristic of both groups is respect for reasons, which was seen throughout and created an ideal process of argumentation. Participants provided reasons for their selections, attended to the reasons provided by others, responded to those reasons, and considered objections to their own reasons. They attempted to convince others to change their selections and were open to being convinced to change their own, but no one was pressured or forced to conform to a majority view just to create a unanimous group conclusion. Aiming for a correct solution, the consensus they sought to achieve was a justified consensus, not just an end to the argument. Outside the realm of logic, it may be more difficult for groups to approximate ideal rational functioning, but small groups may nevertheless encourage greater respect for reasons than would be seen in individuals on their own.

At the level of social systems, respect for reasons is complicated not only by group size but by considerations of ideology, identity, and expertise. When argument turns to complex social issues, ideologies and identities may commit us to favor or oppose particular proposals without adequate consideration of relevant reasons. There are also complex issues concerning the role of experts and the democratic use of expertise. We return to all of these matters in the next chapter.

Respect for Persons

Reasons are, of course, provided by persons. Respect for reasons requires respect for persons, which is also manifested in the present two groups. Argumentation in each was conducted in such a way that everyone had ample opportunity to speak, though no one was required to do so; everyone's ideas were taken seriously, which is not to say they were supported; and participants disagreed with each other's ideas without attacking each other personally. As we have seen, there is evidence that groups operating on a basis of equal respect for all participants may operate more rationally, on average, than those set up with a single authority receiving input from others (Curşeu et al., 2013).

Liberal democracies are founded on a moral basis of equal respect for all persons. The case for equal respect, however, is not just moral or governmental. There is an epistemic case for equal respect for persons based on its contribution to rational argumentation and the progress of knowledge. In the next chapter we consider the extension of this insight to social systems.

Intellectual Freedom

Finally, the two groups that have been the focus of this chapter were characterized by intellectual freedom, not as an ideology but as a natural condition of rational argumentation. Nobody needed to condemn censorship because it was taken for granted that all persons were free to express all views about the cards to be selected.

But the implicit commitment to intellectual freedom was more subtle than just a commitment to free speech. Participants did not feel free to talk about anything they pleased. Without anyone setting any limit, the conversation naturally remained on topic, focused on the logic of the task at hand. The participants shared a common goal of determining the pattern of cards to be selected and understood that to maximize their chances of identifying the logically correct solution they should limit their speech to the topic at hand but set no limits on viewpoints regarding the logic of the task or the cards to be turned. Incorrect views of which cards to turn disappeared not because those who held them were silenced or intimidated but because those who held them were convinced to change their views.

There remains the question of intellectual freedom in social systems, where, in multiple forums and institutions, we face the interplay of ideologies and identities, often with respect to complex issues requiring special expertise. Over the next three chapters, we will return to intellectual freedom repeatedly as we examine its role at a societal level (Chapter 6) and consider its special importance for development (Chapter 7) and education (Chapter 8). As we will see, outside the realm of an open forum for free expression, there are many social contexts where speech can legitimately be restricted on the basis of topic but not viewpoint. We will also see that intellectual freedom, beyond freedom of expression, also includes access to information and ideas.

Conclusion

Despite the focus of reasoning research on individuals, theorists such as Habermas (1990) and Piaget (1995, 1932/1965b) have long argued for the importance of collaborative reasoning. Even at his most biological, Piaget (1967/1971) was always clear that logical operations, far from being just the property of individual organisms, are no less a property of social interaction:

> In the realm of knowledge, it seems obvious that individual operations of the intelligence and operations making for exchanges in cognitive cooperation are one and the same thing, the "general coordination of actions" to which we have continually referred being an interindividual as well as an intraindividual coordination because such "actions" can be collective as well as executed by individuals.
>
> *(p. 360)*

Research has strongly supported these theoretical positions.

But argumentation among individuals becomes increasingly difficult as the number of individuals increases. In small groups, under the right circumstances, people naturally work together in what may be called microdemocracies, collaborating to determine the truth and make the most justifiable choices. But democratic social systems on a larger scale are more complex because individuals cannot all speak to each other directly. Even where argumentation is possible, it may be undermined by considerations of ideology and identity and by lack of access to relevant expertise. We take up these matters in the next chapter, as we extend the discussion of social rationality to the societal level.

6

DEMOCRACY AS COLLABORATIVE RATIONALITY

In this chapter I consider democracy as a social system in which individuals collaborate in rational social action. Such a system requires deliberation, and many theorists of democracy have argued that deliberative democracy is the ideal form of democracy. But democracy, especially in its deliberative versions, requires rational agents. If people are less rational than is commonly assumed, democracy may not be possible. And there is plenty of reason for doubt about human rationality.

I begin this chapter with a definition of deliberative democracy as a form of democracy. Next, drawing on research and theory reviewed in Chapters 2–5, I argue that people are indeed sufficiently rational for democracy to work, and that psychological research on group rationality (Chapter 5) specifically supports deliberative democracy as the ideal form of governance. I then look at issues of ideology, identity, expertise, and intellectual freedom. I conclude that deliberative democracy is an ongoing challenge, but not an impossibility, and there is no better alternative.

For psychologists concerned with human reasoning and rationality, this chapter extends the discussion beyond the study of individual cognition (Chapters 2–4) and reasoning in small groups (Chapter 5) to the rationality of social systems. As we will see in Chapters 7 and 8, rational social systems not only reflect the rationality of the individuals within them but play important roles in the development and promotion of individual rationality.

For theorists of democracy, and anyone else concerned with democracy, this chapter presents a psychologically-based vision of deliberative democracy. This picture is generally consistent with the literature of deliberative democracy that has flourished in philosophy, law, political science, and related disciplines since the 1980s, rooted in neo-Kantian political moralities, such as those of Habermas

(1996) and Rawls (1971, 2001). The present approach, however, is rooted more directly in the psychological realities of cognition, development, and peer interaction.

Deliberative Democracy

Deliberative democracy is a form of liberal democracy that takes as its ideal the achievement of consensus through rational processes of argumentation. Deliberative democracy, as we will now see, is founded on respect for persons and respect for reasons. It is generally seen as an ideal but, at least in small peer groups, it is also a social fact.

Democracy: Respect for Persons

Democracy is commonly seen as a system in which individuals vote and the majority rules. But majorities may vote to ban minority religious and political views or to act against minority ethnic, racial, sexual, or other groups. Rule of the majority is a threat to minorities. If rule of the majority is all there is to democracy, then democracy is a danger to minorities of all sorts, and ultimately to everyone.

Liberal democracy may be defined as a social system based on equal respect for all persons. Equal respect for all persons entails a right of each to participate in democratic decision-making. This includes a right to have your vote count equally to others, which is the basis for the democratic principle of majority rule. But equal respect for all persons also entails respect for the fundamental rights of each individual, which constrains what democratic majorities may legitimately do (Rawls, 1971, 2001). These fundamental rights are typically specified in democratic constitutions protecting freedoms of belief and expression, legal equality, and rights to privacy and due process (Dworkin, 1985, 1996, 2011; Fallon, 2018; Nino, 1996; West Virginia v. Barnette, 1943).

At a societal level, respect for persons requires respect in the abstract for persons one has never met and will never meet, with the expectation that one's respect will be reciprocated. Thus, liberal democracy assumes equal and mutual respect as abstract principles (Gutmann & Thompson, 2004). Principles of equal and mutual respect do not require that people be identical or experience identical circumstances, but many have argued that democracy is undermined by radical economic inequality (Taylor, 2019).

Deliberative Democracy: Respect for Reasons

Many theorists of democracy have argued for some version of what has been called deliberative democracy (Aikin & Talisse, 2019; Bächtiger et al., 2018b; Elstub & McLaverty, 2014; Gutmann & Thompson, 2004, 2018; Nino, 1996). A *deliberative democracy* is a form of liberal democracy that takes as its ideal the achievement of consensus through rational processes of argumentation. As a form of liberal democracy, deliberative democracy is rooted in respect for persons. What distinguishes deliberative democracy is that it is equally rooted in respect for reasons. Respect for reasons, and associated processes of argumentation, serve to generate better understanding and better decisions. Such respect is thus in the best interest of the social system (Estlund & Landemore, 2018; Landemore, 2013). By recognizing persons as rational agents, moreover, respect for reasons furthers respect for persons. To respect persons is not just to allow them to vote. Full respect for persons requires serious consideration of their beliefs and reasons.

Ideally, deliberation leads to consensus in cases where consensus can be reached. When it fails to do so, majority rule remains the basis for making decisions that must be made. Even when a decision must be made by majority vote, however, it should be clear to all that the majority could be wrong and that dissent may remain justified.

Deliberative Democracy as an Ideal

Deliberative democracy is generally seen as an ideal to which societies should aspire. No actual society fully conforms to the ideal of deliberative democracy, so a description of any society as a deliberative democracy is, at best, an idealization of its actual functioning. Some societies come closer to the ideal than others but, even for those that fall far short, the ideal of deliberative democracy provides useful guidance in identifying shortcomings and enhancing deliberation and democracy.

Deliberative democracy rests on a conception of persons as rational agents. This conception is also an ideal. Individuals, like societies, routinely fall far short of rational norms. To refer to people as rational agents is an idealization that highlights an important feature of human psychology but ignores others. Even if the idealization misses part of reality, however, it can serve as an ideal in identifying irrationality and promoting human development.

Idealizations and ideals serve important roles (Appiah, 2017). In chemistry, the ideal gas law has long played a central role in understanding and predicting the motion of gases, despite the fact that no real gas precisely conforms to its fundamental assumptions. Similarly, at higher levels of complexity, idealizations of persons as rational agents and of social systems as deliberative democracies are important in understanding human behavior and social functioning. In addition, at the psychological and social levels, ideals serve a normative function. Ideals of rational agency and deliberative democracy guide us in recognizing where we fall short in matters of both truth and morality and in promoting developmental progress.

Deliberative Democracy as a Social Fact

Deliberative democracy is not just an ideal, however. It is also a social fact. As we saw in Chapter 5, research on group functioning shows that, under the right circumstances, small groups often function as microdemocracies in which individuals collaborate through processes of argumentation that fully respect both persons and reasons. Democratic deliberation at this level is not just a normative ideal but a very close approximation to actual human behavior. The problem of deliberative democracy, then, is not whether it is possible at all but whether and how we can scale up from the microdemocracies observed in cognitive, developmental, and social psychology to the political democracies postulated as theoretical or moral ideals for large social systems (Bächtiger & Wegmann, 2014; Parkinson, 2018).

Historically, there are many intermediate cases of deliberative democracy in small societies. The most famous example may be ancient Athens (Saxonhouse, 2006). Athens was not a liberal democracy, in that women and slaves were excluded from the deliberative Assembly, but for those Athenians recognized as full citizens, the Assembly was a democratic site for free and equal deliberation. Many small European societies for centuries after that relied on deliberative democratic gatherings of free men. Similarly, deliberative democracy was historically central to governance within many indigenous groups of the Americas (Taylor, 2019). To this day in the United States, many New England towns rely on town meetings for local governance.

But what about groups too large for face-to-face meetings? Deliberation is increasingly compromised as group size increases from dozens to hundreds to thousands to tens of thousands (as in ancient Athens). For a nation with a population in the millions, there is substantial basis for questioning even the possibility of achieving anything that approximates a deliberative democracy. But even at very large scales, some social systems do better than others. As we will see, psychological research provides good reason for retaining deliberative democracy as a normative ideal and useful guidance in our efforts to approximate it better.

Is Democracy Psychologically Possible?

There is plenty of reason for pessimism about the future of deliberative democracy. Many have questioned whether human beings are capable of deliberative democracy, or any form of democracy at all. The editors of the *Oxford Handbook of Deliberative Democracy* began their introductory chapter (Bächtiger et al., 2018a), as might be expected, by noting that deliberative democracy has become "a flourishing field" characterized by theoretical advances, innovative practice, empirical study, and "robust and productive" criticism. But they acknowledged immediately that "all is not rosy":

> As we bring this *Handbook* to fruition, the world at large appears to be moving in some disconcerting anti-deliberative and anti-democratic directions. Post-truth politics is the antithesis of deliberative democracy. Resurgent authoritarian and populist leaders in many countries have little interest in deliberation—except to suppress it. Even where deliberation is

> not repressed, we too often see levels of political polarization that signal inabilities to listen to the other side and reflect upon what they may have to say.
>
> *(p. 1)*

The rise of deliberative democracy as a theoretical ideal has not been accompanied by a rise in deliberative democracy. Some have worried, looking at current trends, that democracy, deliberative or otherwise, is simply on the way out (Taylor, 2019). Deliberative democracy may be the ideal social system for ideal rational agents, but perhaps humans fall so far short of rational ideals that they cannot sustain deliberative democratic social systems. Rosenberg (2014), reviewing relevant psychological research in social, cognitive, and developmental psychology, concluded:

> [P]eople tend to think in simple terms. They prefer homogeneous categories and look for single concrete causes and effects. Moreover, people construct these categorical and causal linkages in a typically flawed way. They tend: (a) to focus on what is apparent, concrete or more cognitively available; (b) to process this information either by utilising cognitive short cuts or by uncritically applying prior personal experience or culturally available explanations; and (c) unconsciously to skew final judgements so as to maintain their self-esteem or prior evaluations of persons or groups. In sum, individuals' thinking appears to lack the objectivity, complication, integration and abstraction to enable them to appreciate the complexity of social problems and to imagine effective, novel ways of addressing them.
>
> *(p. 112)*

Similarly, Karpowitz and Mendelberg (2018), reviewing the literature of political psychology, concluded that people express "high levels of confidence" in their own false beliefs and are highly resistant to correction. Failing to judge new information objectively, "they are strongly influenced by biases, such as the characteristics of the messenger" and subject to "motivated reasoning—the biased processing of information based on pre-existing emotions and attitudinal predispositions." Specifically, people "tend to be forgiving and uncritical of information or arguments that fit their predispositions and unforgiving and hypercritical of information that contradicts their beliefs." Exposure to "a balanced set of arguments" may lead those with "strong pre-existing attitudes" to "double down on their prior opinions." In general, "political judgments are made quickly, emotionally, and outside of conscious awareness, then rationalized with reasons afterwards." That is, "judgment typically comes *before* reasons—the exact reverse of the decision-making processes anticipated by deliberative theory" (p. 539, emphasis in original).

Neither Rosenberg (2014) nor Karpowitz and Mendelberg (2018), however, advocated giving up on deliberative democracy, nor do I (see also De Brasi, 2018). I argue in this section, based on evidence reviewed in Chapters 2 through 5, that people are sufficiently rational for deliberative democracy to be the ideal form of collective governance. Without denying the evidence for systematic and pervasive human irrationality, I suggest three reasons for cautious optimism. First, as seen in Chapters 2–4, people are not as utterly irrational as some have claimed. On the contrary, adults at their best are rational in ways beyond the competence of children, and even children show increasing rationality over the course of childhood. Second, as seen in Chapter 5, argumentation under the right circumstances enhances reasoning. Deliberative democracies draw in multiple ways on the rational powers of argumentation to operate more rationally than the individuals who compose them. Finally, as discussed in Chapter 8, there are many ways democratic societies can promote rationality, and thus democracy, through education. Human rationality, then, is a psychological fact, a social fact, and a reality that can be substantially enhanced through education.

Human Rationality as a Psychological Fact

Human irrationality is an obvious and well-documented fact of life, but human rationality is no less a fact, as shown by extensive research in cognitive and developmental psychology. Rationality can be seen in the logic intrinsic to biological self-regulation, in the sensorimotor functioning of infants, and in the justifiable logical and causal inferences of preschool children. Progress in rational agency over the first 12 years of life shows a universal and predictable trajectory. By the age of about 4 years, children's knowledge of mind is sufficiently organized and useful that theorists credit them with a theory of mind, including an understanding that beliefs can be false and that people act on the basis of their own beliefs even when those beliefs are false. Young children recognize direct observation and testimony from others as sources of knowledge. Beginning about age 6 years, they also recognize that they and others make inferences, which can also be a source of knowledge. By the age of 8 or 9 years, they show rigorous conceptual knowledge about the logic of classes, relations, and numbers and a constructivist theory of mind that recognizes and reflects on interpretive diversity. And beginning about age 11 or 12 years, they bring their deductive abilities to the realm of hypothetical possibilities, enabling advanced forms of logical, scientific, moral, and social conventional reasoning, and serious reflection on the justification of beliefs and the nature of knowledge and truth.

Nothing in the developmental evidence, however, negates the extensive evidence for adult irrationality. The most systematic theoretical effort to coordinate the evidence for both rationality and irrationality has been the development since the 1970s of dual process theories. In a basic version of dual processing, System 1 is automatic and intuitive whereas System 2 is deliberate and reflective. The heuristics and biases of System 1 are often adaptive, but they may lead us astray.

System 2 deliberation and reflection may overcome our biases and unjustified assumptions but may also introduce alternative biases and assumptions that serve to maintain our theoretical beliefs and personal identities. Thus, rationality is not simply a reflective override of our automatic processes and intuitions. Dual process theories help us see how rationality is possible, how it develops, and why it remains an ongoing challenge for everyone.

The complexities of dual processing, however, should not obscure the underlying developmental reality: All normal human beings beyond the age of about 12 years are capable of functioning at a level of rational agency beyond what would be possible for virtually any child under about 10 years, for any member of any other known species, or for any artifact known to humans or likely to be created in the near future (but for the far future, see the discussion of *Star Trek*'s Mr. Data in Chapter 9). Human reasoning falls far short of rational perfection in multiple ways, but the rational agency of human minds, as we saw in Chapters 2-4, is a well-documented psychological fact.

Human Rationality as a Social Fact

Karpowitz and Mendelberg (2018) wrote: "If nothing else, political psychologists are likely to agree on one conclusion: deliberation is an unnatural state of affairs for most citizens" (p. 538). But what they mean by deliberation is political argumentation about abstract social issues. Deliberation in the broader sense of serious argumentation within a group about matters at hand is a natural and common state of affairs for all normal human beings beyond early childhood, and often leads to more justifiable beliefs and actions. Research on group cognition has shown that groups often perform better than individuals, and that rational processes of argumentation play a central role in group rationality. Under ideal circumstances, groups may reason better than even the most rational individual within them.

Of course, not all groups function well even under favorable circumstances, and actual circumstances are often far from ideal. Nevertheless, social interaction under the right circumstances can greatly promote good reasoning, often better than what most individuals could muster on their own. Those circumstances include respect for reasons, respect for persons, and intellectual freedom. The potential for rationality, which is real but limited in individuals, can be greatly enhanced through argumentation (as discussed in detail in Chapter 5). This provides a second reason for cautious optimism about the possibility of democracy, and a psychological basis for specifically advocating deliberative democracy.

Education for Rationality

Dual process theories of reasoning and research on argumentation as collaborative reasoning provide bases for some degree of optimism about human rationality. There is no guarantee, however, that human beings naturally tend to be sufficiently rational, even in groups, for deliberative democracy. On the contrary, there is plenty of reason to worry that human rationality is not up to the task of democratic self-governance. Fortunately, rationality is not simply a fixed ability beyond our control that may turn out to be insufficient for our needs. If we need greater rationality for democracy to work, as it appears we do, there is much we can do to promote rationality. The single most important thing we can do, I suggest, is to make rationality the central goal of education.

The promotion of rationality, however, is not just the teaching and learning of some assortment of discrete facts or skills. To be rational is to be a rational agent, and rational agency is the outcome of developmental processes. Education for rationality, then, requires promoting the development of rational agency. The development of rational agency has already been addressed in Chapters 2–3 with respect to multiple forms of reasoning and in Chapter 4 with respect to metacognition and epistemic cognition, but the developmental portions of those chapters focused primarily on describing the pattern of developmental progress. In Chapter 7, I provide a more systematic lifespan account of the development of rational agency that cuts across multiple epistemic domains and forms of reasoning and focuses on the process of developmental change. Chapter 8 then presents a conception of education for rationality that recognizes the constructive and social aspects of the developmental processes responsible for progress in rational agency.

Education for rationality must also promote the rationality of group functioning both within small groups and within democratic society. This includes a variety of social and civic competencies and values that are also the outcome of developmental processes (more in Chapter 7) and can be promoted through education aimed at fostering development (Chapter 8).

Actual educational systems fall far short of what they could and should accomplish. Indeed, much of what passes for education in most societies, especially at elementary and secondary levels, is a process of indoctrination that undermines rationality and civic engagement. But as we will see in Chapter 8, there is good reason to believe that education, properly conceived and conducted, can enhance both the rational agency of individuals and the rationality of argumentation within democratic and deliberative systems.

Rationality and Identity

To say deliberative democracy is humanly possible is not to say it is easily achieved or readily sustained. On the contrary, deliberative democracy faces many formidable challenges, perhaps the most daunting and crucial of which is the urgent need "to tame the wild beast of identity" (Maalouf, 2001, p. 157).

Identity as a Theory of Oneself

Kwame Anthony Appiah, a philosopher who specializes in ethics and identity, tells the story of a Jewish man who is marooned on a desert island (2018, p. 41). When rescuers arrive after many years, they observe that he has put up three structures. "What are these buildings?" they ask. "This one is my house," he responds, "and this one is the synagogue I go to." "And that one," he adds, "is the synagogue I *don't* go to."

We see here the social nature of identity, its psychological centrality, and its potential to divide (Killen & Rutland, 2011; Moshman, 2011a). Identity brings us together in ways crucial to how we define ourselves individually, but often at the cost of setting us in opposition to others, sometimes so strongly that our opposition becomes increasingly central to our identities.

In the humanities and social sciences, as well as in ordinary discourse, the term "identity" is typically used to refer to one's affiliation with some social group, including national, ethnic, racial, sexual, political, and religious groups (Appiah, 2005, 2018; Moshman, 2007a). Within developmental psychology, however, the term typically refers to a relatively mature form of self-conception and personal commitment first seen in adolescence (Erikson, 1968; Moshman, 2011a; for related philosophical conceptions, see Korsgaard, 2009; Parfit, 1984). The two uses of the term are sometimes distinguished by referring respectively to "social identity" and "personal identity." Further analysis, however, undermines any sharp distinction. Our social identities are in large part a matter of identification—a psychological process involving personal interpretations, choices, and commitments with regard to our multiple overlapping group affiliations; correspondingly, our personal identities are constructed in social contexts and in large part oriented toward prioritizing and coordinating our multiple group connections (Moshman, 2007a, 2011a).

With this in mind, we may define *identity* as an explicit theory of oneself as a person (Moshman, 2011a). Let me elaborate on that definition to show how it coordinates the personal and social aspects of identity. This will help clarify both the psychological importance of identity and its danger to deliberative democracy.

To begin, an identity is a self-conception—that is, a conception of oneself. But people have many self-conceptions. The challenge of identity is to unify those self-conceptions, or at least identify and coordinate the most important, in a way that enables you to make sense of yourself. Thus, an identity is not just any conception of yourself, nor is it simply a collection of self-conceptions. Rather, your identity is a *theory* of yourself.

What does it mean to construe identity as a theory? A *theory* is a structure of knowledge that organizes and explains some domain or set of facts. A theory of yourself is a relatively coherent self-conception that explains your behavior and experiences. But even young children have structures of knowledge sufficiently organized and explanatory to qualify as theories, including theories of themselves. For example, children's understanding of false belief is widely taken to show a theory of mind as early as age 4 years (as discussed in Chapter 4). But this is not an identity. To have an identity in the developmental sense associated with Erik Erikson (1968; see Moshman, 2011a), it is not sufficient to have a theory of yourself posited by psychologists as implicit in your behavior. An identity is an *explicit* theory of oneself.

But not just any explicit theory of oneself is an identity. A theory of one's anatomy and physiology may be biologically insightful and medically useful, but it is not an identity. A theory of the external forces that cause you to behave in particular ways may be psychologically insightful and personally useful, but it is not an identity. An identity is, specifically, an explicit theory whereby you see yourself as a person. To see yourself as a person is, at minimum, to see yourself as a rational agent—that is, as having reasons for your actions. Even if your reasons are not good reasons you are still a rational agent (qualitatively), though less rational (quantitatively) than if you had good reasons. Some identities are more rational than others, but identity always involves an effort to see yourself as a rational agent.

To see yourself as a rational agent, moreover, is largely a matter of seeing yourself as a rational agent among other rational agents, which includes seeing yourself as a moral agent among other moral agents. It is largely in social interactions within communities of rational and moral agents that we provide reasons for our beliefs and actions in efforts to explain and justify them. Our theories of self are constructed and become increasingly explicit in social contexts. They enable us to explain and justify ourselves to ourselves and others.

But in large societies there are far too many rational agents for us to have direct relations with each as an individual. We address the complexity of the social world by categorizing people along a variety of dimensions for a variety of purposes and theorizing about the resulting social categories. We see ourselves and others as affiliated in a variety of ways with a variety of groups, and we see some of these affiliations as defining who we are in relation to others, who they are in relation to us, and what moral responsibilities we have to whom.

Dangers of Identity

Strong identities may enhance our rational agency by providing reasons for action based on our reflective theories of ourselves as persons. Identity is also, however, a threat to rationality. Evidence threatening your identity threatens your fundamental explanation and justification of who you are as a person. We naturally tend to ignore, deny, critique, or reinterpret evidence contrary to our theories, preferring to seek and focus on evidence that shows we are right, which we accept with much less scrutiny. This verification bias is routine even for theories that don't matter much to us (as in the Wason selection task discussed in Chapters 2 and 5). It is greatly exacerbated when the theories in question are the ideologies that define our identities—our deepest theories of who we are as persons and as groups.

And that's just the start of the problem. To the extent that identity is social, not just individual, societies are subject to a process of *dichotomization* in which, at the extreme, a single identity dimension, such as race, religion, or political ideology, comes to be seen by all as the primary basis for identity (Klein, 2020). As a result, people see themselves and others as fitting into a small number of primary categories within that single dimension—in the extreme just two, so that everyone is either one of "us" (whoever "we" may be) or one of "them." This can lead to processes of *dehumanization* in which "they" come to be seen as less than fully human, sometimes leading to violence, ethnic cleansing, and genocide in cases where those seen as subhuman are also seen as posing a threat to us (Maynard, forthcoming; Moshman, 2004a, 2007b, 2011b).

Even in cases that do not generate violence, identity-related processes of dichotomization and dehumanization seriously undermine deliberative democracy. Dichotomization reduces argumentation from an effort of multiple individuals to determine the truth and agree on a course of action to what is perceived instead as a contest between two ideologies and/or identities. This undermines the effort to address pluralism in a rational manner, a central concern of deliberative democracy (Cinalli & O'Flynn, 2014). Dehumanization of the other further undermines deliberation. Although we are usually well aware that our own groups are internally diverse, we see other groups as relatively homogeneous, thus underestimating the rational agency of individuals within them and downgrading their personhood. If "they" are mostly automatons driven by hatred, propaganda, and peer pressure, then there is no basis for them to participate as individuals in democratic deliberation. That leaves argumentation to take place mostly within ideological groups that don't talk to each other, likely leading to greater polarization of ideological belief.

Dehumanization, which denies the personhood of the other, is part of a more general phenomenon of *denial* (Bardon, 2020), often driven by our need to maintain our conceptions of ourselves and our groups as moral agents regardless of how we actually treat others. The verification bias in hypothesis testing may be an automatic response, but when denial serves to maintain our moral identities it is often active and strategic, albeit less than fully conscious. In dual process terms, we cannot rely on System 2 to make us rational by overruling System 1 because System 2 is itself engaged in processes of denial necessary to preserve our moral identities—our conceptions of ourselves as moral agents. The result is that we often have, to varying extents, *false* moral identities—that is, conceptions of ourselves and our groups as much more moral than we actually are (Moshman, 2004a, 2011a).

Rationalist Identity

There will always be identities, and with them processes of dichotomization, dehumanization, and denial that undermine our efforts to create deliberative democracies. One part of our response, to be explored in the next section, must be to create and maintain rational social institutions that engage us in collaborative reasoning to overcome our individual limitations. But we should also consider the rationality of identity and the possibility that some identities are more rational and/or more supportive of societal rationality. The challenge is to identify and encourage better identities without undermining the very concept of identity by specifying what identities everyone must have.

One characteristic of a good identity is that it is relatively rational. Drawing on the usual criteria for evaluating a theory, a theory of self might be considered more rational than some alternative theory of self if it is more coherent or more consistent with evidence. But these are difficult things to judge. All human identities likely fall far short of theoretical ideals, and none of us is in a good position to rate the relative rationality of our diverse identities.

Rather than focus on whether or to what extent an identity is *rational*, I suggest we focus instead on whether it is *rationalist*—that is, whether commitment to rationality is among the core commitments of the identity in question. A *rationalist identity* is an explicit theory of oneself that highlights and values one's rationality. To the extent that you are committed to rationality, you may be more willing to consider disconfirming evidence and critical arguments because, whatever other commitments you may have, determining the truth and doing the right thing are no less important to how you conceive who you are. Changing your mind on the basis of evidence or logic confirms your theory of yourself as the rational agent you want to be. We will address rationalist identity further in Chapter 7 as a potential outcome of advanced development and will consider the promotion of rationalist identity in Chapter 8 as an important part of educational efforts to promote rational agency without dictating or manipulating identity commitments.

We can't simply eliminate the wild beast of identity because our identities, however savage, are our best visions of who we are. The challenge is to regulate ourselves on the basis of the epistemic aim to seek and acknowledge the truth, however much we wish to evade or deny it, including truths about ourselves and about our moral obligations to others.

Rational Institutions

Even with progress in rationality and greater commitment to it, individual people will always fall woefully short of rational ideals. Deliberative democracy requires rational institutions. At the very least, such institutions must allow for democratic deliberation in order to achieve the epistemic benefits of argumentation. In a large society, however, deliberative democracy cannot consist of a single open forum in which every individual participates fully and equally in every decision. Thus, we must recognize deliberative democracies as deliberative systems coordinating the ongoing operations of rational institutions within them (Parkinson, 2018).

One issue of particular importance and concern is that rational deliberation on various topics requires various sorts of expertise (Post, 2012). But to gain the benefits of expertise we must rely on experts, which seems to require vesting authority in an elite group, contrary to basic norms of democracy (Brown, 2014; Rosenfeld, 2019; Taylor, 2019). If it could be shown that a system of rule by experts would be more rational than a deliberative democracy, we would indeed be faced with a difficult choice between expertise and democracy. But experts are only experts on particular topics, and expertise itself is the outcome of democratic deliberation among experts. As we will see, the challenge is to incorporate expertise into democratic functioning. What we need are (a) rational institutions committed to democratic deliberation and (b) a deliberative system that respects and maintains such institutions. In this section, I consider some rational institutions crucial to any large-scale deliberative democracy.

Legislatures

It is often said that we need more politicians willing and able to "reach across the aisle." In the United States Senate, there is literally an aisle separating the seats of Democrats and Republicans, the two major political parties. In many other legislative bodies around the world, the aisle is metaphorical but the ideological divide between the major political parties is no less real. To reach across the aisle is to seek some common ground or basis for collaboration, or at least meaningful discussion.

In legislatures dominated by two political parties composed of party loyalists who vote the party line, reaching across the aisle may be the best anyone can do. But an occasional breach of the aisle is not good enough for deliberative democracy. In the deliberative ideal, every member of the society speaks to and hears everyone else. In societies too large for this, representatives are chosen to meet as members of legislative institutions small enough for all members to meet together for deliberation. Organizing a legislature to operate as an ongoing battle between two political parties or ideological factions undermines democratic deliberation among the legislators and thus undermines deliberative democracy. We need to eliminate both the literal aisle and the ideological dichotomization it represents.

But is that possible? In the United States, the House of Representatives has no literal aisle but is divided no less sharply than the Senate between Democrats and Republicans. In both the House and the Senate (which together make up Congress, the legislative branch of the federal government), the two parties meet separately in party caucuses to decide on plans, select party leaders, and engage party solidarity. Turning to the states, we find the same pattern of a bicameral legislature that operates largely as an ongoing battle between the same two major parties.

But there is one notable exception. The Nebraska state legislature is the only unicameral state legislature in the U.S. It was specifically designed in the 1930s with multiple features to foster deliberative democracy by enhancing transparency and downplaying party politics. Nebraska senators operate somewhat more rationally than other state legislators not because of their individual qualities but because they operate within a system set up to encourage genuine deliberation, which is good for everyone.

The unicameral legislature (informally known as the Unicam) was conceived and promoted by George Norris, who represented Nebraska in the U.S. Congress from 1903 to 1943, first in the House of Representatives and later in the Senate. Nebraskans voted in 1934 to replace their traditional bicameral legislature with a unicameral legislature, which began operation in 1937. The Unicam has a single chamber consisting of 49 senators representing 49 legislative districts. Every bill is assigned to a committee of senators, who hold a public hearing at which anyone may speak. Bills approved by committee may be scheduled to be heard on the floor, where all 49 senators may participate at each stage of deliberation. In contrast to bicameral legislatures, there are no secret processes or reconciliation committees to resolve differences in bills passed by two chambers. To prevent quick passage of laws without adequate discussion and debate, legislation must be approved three times over an extended period, usually weeks or months, with deliberation prior to each vote. In addition, although bills can be amended by a majority of those present, approval at each of the three stages of debate requires 25 votes (or more in the case of a filibuster), even if some of the 49 senators are absent or abstain.

State senators are elected on a nonpartisan basis. All candidates run in a single primary; the top two go forward to the general election. These are often a Republican and a Democrat, but they are often two Republicans and can be (at least in Lincoln or Omaha) two Democrats. The operation of the Unicam is also, ideally, nonpartisan. There are no party caucuses. It is common for senators to work closely with each other on potential bills without regard to party affiliation and to find creative ways to get 25 or more votes from the 49 senators.

How does this work in practice? Of course, there is party politics. But sometimes the system enables senators to go beyond that. I present here one notable recent example.

In March 2017, as president-elect of the Academic Freedom Coalition of Nebraska (AFCON), I provided the Unicam's Education Committee with written testimony concerning AFCON's opposition to a bill designed to activate the Americanism committee of every school district across Nebraska. These committees were established by a 1949 Nebraska law driven by the rising anti-communist hysteria that a few years later came to be called McCarthyism. I testified that AFCON saw the Americanism law as an infringement on the academic freedom of teachers and students and on the academic integrity of Nebraska schools. Specifically, I argued that for a state legislature to determine curriculum and set methods of instruction, as this law did, is micromanagement, which in the present academic context is indoctrination. Compulsory Americanism is, paradoxically, just plain un-American; genuine patriotism, I insisted, cannot be compelled or coerced and does not require Americanism committees. Quoting from a historic decision of the U.S. Supreme Court striking down mandatory flag ceremonies (West Virginia v. Barnette, 1943), I argued that we should not underestimate "the appeal of our institutions to free minds" (p. 641).

The bill had strong support from the most conservative Republicans who, together with relatively moderate Republicans, had a substantial majority of the legislative seats. Nevertheless, like similar bills in previous years, it failed to pass due to liberal opposition and the absence of party discipline in the nonpartisan Unicam.

When I heard in January 2019 that a Republican state senator was once again dusting off Nebraska's Americanism law, I expected the worst, but was pleasantly surprised to find that the new bill had some noteworthy positive features. The bill was subsequently improved, moreover, by several amendments responding to liberal objections. In fact, in its final version, the bill essentially repealed the Americanism law and replaced it with a civics education law. The new law would eliminate the Americanism committees and require instead that the school board of each school district appoint a "committee on American civics." The difference was not just linguistic. The new committees were responsible for assuring that civics education is taken seriously, but their mandate showed considerable respect for the autonomy of students, faculty, and school systems.

The final version of the bill was supported by senators spanning the political spectrum. It passed 44-2, with one senator abstaining and two absent, and was signed by the governor. By the standards of academic freedom to be discussed in Chapter 8, the new law still micromanages curriculum, instruction, and assessment. But compared to the law it replaced, it is far more flexible in its requirements, far less indoctrinative in its language, and overall much more respectful of intellectual freedom. In an age of intense dispute over matters of history, government, and social responsibility, the nonpartisan structure and deliberative requirements of the Nebraska Unicam enabled it to reach near-consensus on a conception of civics education far more academically and morally justifiable than the compulsory Americanism it replaced.

Courts of Law

Legislatures pass laws, but the judicial system is generally responsible for determining whether someone has broken the law. In legal systems following English common law (including the United States and Canada), a criminal trial generally involves both a judge and a jury of peers. The judge is responsible for conducting a fair trial in accord with applicable legal procedures and instructing the jurors about applicable laws and legal standards. The exercise of such responsibility requires legal expertise.

The rationale for the jury system is that democratic standards of liberty and equality will be compromised if people can be convicted of crimes and sentenced in secret processes controlled by a legal elite. Instead, trials are generally public and the determination of guilt, in particular, is made by a group of jurors (generally 12) who can be considered peers of the accused in that they are selected from the public at large. The jurors generally do not have, and do not need, legal expertise, because the judge instructs them regarding legal considerations. The role of the jury is to attend to trial testimony, determine the facts of the matter, and reach a conclusion as to whether those facts show a violation of the law, as interpreted and explained by the judge.

Although jurors do not need legal expertise, the legal system relies on their rationality. One might reasonably wonder, then, given that people are not equally rational, why we need a jury of 12 people. Why not select the most rational and fair person from the pool of potential jurors and let that person serve alone as the jury? The jury selection process already begins with a pool of potential jurors and eliminates those who appear unable to understand the relevant facts or law or likely to have a conflict of interest. Even if we can't always tell who will be the very best juror, surely we could extend the jury selection process to settle on someone better than average.

The problem is that we know from extensive research that even the most rational people routinely fall far short of rational standards (Chapters 2–4) and that groups often show higher levels of rational performance than individuals (Chapter 5). The system of multiple jurors dates back centuries before this psychological research but seems entirely consistent with its basic findings.

Even groups do not always function rationally, of course. If a few members of the jury confidently assert some interpretation and conclusion, others may go along because it sounds plausible, then others because of peer pressure or a desire to reach closure, leading to a perfunctory hearing of alternative and dissenting views followed by a vote for the majority conclusion. But English common law generally requires a unanimous decision for the jury to reach a verdict (otherwise there is a "hung jury," which may lead to a new trial). The requirement of unanimity means dissenters cannot simply be outvoted; they must be convinced. Thus, deliberation is enhanced, which may lead to a fuller recall and consideration of the facts than any juror alone could muster and more comprehensive and justified interpretations than those initially reached by most or all of the individual jurors. Research on juries indicates that, as expected, "group discussion helps jurors individually and collectively to clarify their positions and conclusions, and increases their certainty that they are reaching the right verdict" (Hans, 2007, p. 586). Juries required to reach a unanimous verdict have been found more likely to begin with a "general discussion of the evidence" and to "pay more attention to those who hold minority views" (Hans, 2007, p. 587). Dissenters have been found to "participate more in the discussion and have more influence" when consensus must be achieved (Hans, 2007, p. 587).

Thus, the jury system (1) relies on peer decisions for moral reasons related to the nature of democracy; (2) relies on argumentation among multiple peers for epistemic reasons related to group rationality; and (3) generally requires consensus in order to maximize the epistemic advantages of collaborative reasoning. The jury is a small deliberative democracy operating within a court system that provides the legal expertise to connect the work of the jury to the larger social system of deliberative democracy of which the judicial system is a part. The court is not itself a deliberative democracy. Those present do not all have an equal right to speak or make decisions. But the operation of the court system provides the legal expertise that enables deliberative democracy to work across multiple levels within a deliberative and democratic system.

But why only one judge? In most cases it is presumed that the requirements of law are clear to anyone sufficiently expert in the law. But sometimes the state of the law is itself uncertain. Even legal experts may disagree about the most justifiable interpretation of a vague law, the applicability of a particular law to the case at hand, or the best way to resolve apparent inconsistencies between applicable laws. Experts may also disagree about whether particular laws or government actions are consistent with constitutional requirements, which may themselves be vague enough to justify multiple interpretations. In such cases, our best hope for rational legal judgment is deliberation among experts, which is generally achieved through a process of appeal to higher courts, up to a supreme court with multiple members.

Thus, the state of the law, in cases of controversy, is itself determined through a process of deliberation, but in this case the deliberation takes place among experts. Cases decided by a high court may be controversial, and some decisions may be denounced as political, rather than legal, and thus illegitimate (Fallon, 2018). Nevertheless, there are rational grounds for favoring some decisions over others (Amar, 2012; Dworkin, 1985, 1996, 2011; Fallon, 1987, 2018). As a result, judges from diverse backgrounds with diverse political views often reach consensus on legal matters (Fallon, 2018). Even when they don't, the expectation of written justification and the effort to find a rationale convincing to a majority encourage rational judgment.

In a legal system that maintains itself over many generations, a key consideration in settling any case is consistency with past cases. Even the highest court takes its own previous decisions as an important constraint on present decisions. Precedents may be overruled if they are deemed clearly wrong, but the default expectation is to rule in accord with them or provide specific reasons for new exceptions or new limits on their applicability. Thus, although precedents are not the only basis for legal reasoning, precedent-based reasoning (as discussed in Chapter 3) plays a key role in law. In relying on precedent, law establishes itself as a rational multigenerational social system where previous decisions become social conventions that play a role in present deliberations (Amar, 2012; Moshman, 2015).

Epistemic Institutions and Professions

Epistemic institutions and professions are those centrally concerned with truth and justification. These include science, education, and journalism. Epistemic institutions may be part of the government, supported by government, or independent of it; regardless, they are crucial to democracy (Rosenfeld, 2019).

It is important that scientists, educators, journalists, and others in knowledge-oriented professions understand their role in the larger deliberative and democratic system. It is equally important that everyone understand the reliance of democracy on truth and the epistemic nature of institutions claiming to provide such truth. I address these matters in Chapter 8, in which I consider the many ways in which academic institutions serve democracy and the means by which they do so.

Intellectual Freedom in Society

Free speech was widely deemed central to democracy in ancient Athens (Saxonhouse, 2006) because it served equal participation in governance among those permitted to participate in discussion at the Assembly (women and slaves were excluded). But what about states too large for direct democracy? In such states, governing—a process engaged in by citizens—becomes government—an abstract entity that may be a threat to individuals. In large-scale indirect democracies, then, guarantees of free speech serve as a protection of individual rights against government power. Nevertheless, free speech remains a right to participate, as emphasized in deliberative democracy. Beyond democratic participation and individual rights, free speech is also critical to the progress of knowledge, as discussed in Chapter 5 with respect to group discussion.

Thus, free speech is important for reasons of democracy, individual rights, and the pursuit of truth (Ash, 2016; Moshman, 2017, 2020). But free speech is not sufficient. Deliberative democracy requires *intellectual freedom*, which includes freedoms of belief, expression, discussion, inquiry, and access to information and ideas. I will return to intellectual freedom in Chapter 7 with respect to its role in the development of rationality and will address it most systematically in Chapter 8 with regard to the centrality of intellectual freedom for education. As we will see, the regulation of speech by educational, governmental, and other authorities is often necessary and justified, but authorities of all sorts routinely infringe without justification on the intellectual freedom necessary for education, democracy, and intellectual development. A central principle for addressing the legitimacy of restrictions on free expression is that restrictions on speech should generally not be based on the content of what is said and especially not on objections to the speaker's point of view (Strossen, 2018).

Conclusion

Deliberative democracy extends the benefits of argumentation to entire societies, at least in principle. Real societies, however, fall far short of deliberative and democratic ideals. That may always be the case, but we could do much better if education were aimed more directly and effectively at the promotion of rational agency and civic responsibility. In Chapter 8, I consider how education at all levels could be more effective in this regard.

Central to my conception of education for rationality and democracy is that such education must focus on enabling and encouraging developmental progress. Before we turn to education, then, we look first, in Chapter 7, at processes and patterns of development.

7

THE RATIONAL CONSTRUCTION OF RATIONAL AGENCY

In this chapter we consider the development of rationality. We have already addressed this in earlier chapters, which considered the development of logical reasoning (Chapter 2); of causal/scientific, principled/moral, and precedent-based reasoning (Chapter 3); and of metacognition, including epistemic cognition concerning the nature of justification and truth (Chapter 4). The present chapter goes beyond the earlier treatment in three major ways.

First, the aim here is to provide an account of development that goes beyond description to explanation. Chapters 2–4 focused mostly on describing developmental sequences. The present focus (especially in the second section) is on the rational and constructive process of change that explains developmental progress. This focus on process is critical not only for explaining development but also for educational efforts to promote the development of rationality (the topic of Chapter 8).

Second, the earlier accounts of stages or levels of development were each specific to particular forms or aspects of reasoning and rationality (such as logical reasoning, causal reasoning, and epistemic cognition). The aim here (especially in the third section) is to look more broadly at general patterns in the emergence and progress of rational agency. This suggests a distinction between basic development in childhood, leading to a universal level of maturity achieved about age 12 years, and advanced development in adolescence and beyond, which is much more individualized.

Finally, Chapters 2–4 focused on individual development. Following up on Chapters 5 and 6, we now consider the role of argumentation and democratic institutions in development (with more on education to follow in Chapter 8). In addition, I propose in the final section that groups and societies may themselves show developmental progress.

I begin with an evolutionary theory of human reasoning. The critique of this theory leads directly to the more developmental and constructivist account that undergirds the rest of the chapter.

"The Enigma of Reason"

The most important and influential book on reasoning since Daniel Kahneman's (2011) *Thinking: Fast and Slow* has probably been Hugo Mercier and Dan Sperber's (2017) *The Enigma of Reason*. In reviewing it for the journal *Human Development*, I praised it for directing attention to the social aspects of reasoning typically ignored in the cognitive and developmental literatures but argued that the proposed theory ignored extensive developmental research and, as a result, misconstrued the nature and role of both logic and reflection (Moshman, 2018; see also, Noveck, 2019; Mercier & Sperber, 2019). After providing a summary and critique of Mercier and Sperber's theory in this section, I then provide in the next section a constructivist developmental account of human reasoning and rationality that is more consistent with dual process theories and, I argue, with available evidence from cognitive and developmental psychology.

Mercier and Sperber's Theory

Mercier and Sperber (2017) provided an evolutionary account of human reasoning, crediting Charles Darwin with "the realization that whatever traits humans share as a species are not gifts of the gods but outcomes of biological evolution. Reason, being such a trait, must have evolved" (p. 1). Specifically, they argued, reasoning evolved to serve the social purpose of argumentation.

In elaborating their evolutionary account, Mercier and Sperber (2017) questioned the distinction made by dual process theories "between intuition and reasoning as if these were two quite different forms of inference," proposing instead that "reasoning is itself a kind of intuitive inference" (p. 7). They maintained that logicians, philosophers, and psychologists have greatly overemphasized the role of reflection in human inference because they themselves "commonly resort to higher-order arguments as part of their trade," which is "hardly typical of the population at large" (Mercier & Sperber, 2017, p. 152). Reflection is dismissed as a "professional twist of mind" rather than "a basic human trait" (Mercier & Sperber, 2017, p. 152).

Reasoning, Mercier and Sperber (2017) argued, is a matter of argumentation, rather than individual thinking, which leads them to discount the role of logic:

> Whereas reason is commonly viewed as a superior means to think better on one's own, we argue that it is mainly used in our interactions with others. We produce reasons in order to justify our thoughts and actions to others and to produce arguments to convince others to think and act as we suggest.

> We also use reason to evaluate not so much our own thought as the reasons others produce to justify themselves or to convince us.
>
> Whereas reasoning is commonly viewed as the use of logic, or at least some system of rules to expand and improve our knowledge and our decisions, we argue that reason is much more opportunistic and eclectic and is not bound to formal norms.
>
> *(p. 7)*

The role of logic in reasoning continues to be disparaged throughout the book. "Logic," the authors maintain, "tells us neither how we reason nor how we should reason" (Mercier & Sperber, 2017, p. 174). Logic is deemed pragmatic and contextual, sometimes helpful to reasoning, but playing no special role. As one subtitle insists, "In Reasoning, Logic Is a Heuristic Tool" (Mercier & Sperber, 2017, p. 158).

Critique

No serious developmentalist doubts the value of an evolutionary perspective, but nearly all reject simplistic evolutionary models that explain reasoning and other psychological phenomena on the basis of a direct causal link from evolution to genes to behavior. What is missing is development (Lerner & Overton, 2017; Lickliter & Witherington, 2017).

> The human species is indeed a product of evolution and can only be understood in light of its evolution. But it is no less true that a person is a product of development and can only be understood in light of that development. This makes little difference if development is driven by evolutionary instructions encoded in our genes. But research over the past half-century has made it increasingly clear that development can only be understood as a constructive process that coordinates emerging structural relations across genetic, physiological, behavioral, environmental, social, and cultural levels. Development is not determined by, and cannot be reduced to, genes or evolution.
>
> *(Moshman, 2018, p. 61)*

As discussed in Chapters 2 and 4, research on the development of logical reasoning and metalogical understanding shows that logic is implicit in norms of biological self-regulation and can be seen, long before the emergence of language, in the increasingly coordinated sensorimotor cognition of infants. We also saw that preschool children routinely make logical inferences and that, beginning about age 6 years, children recognize inference as a potential sources of knowledge and make systematic progress as they go on to construct increasingly reflective understandings of the difference between logical and empirical knowledge. As we will see in the next section, the development of metalogical understanding appears to be an ongoing constructive process in which knowledge implicit in inference at any level becomes an object of reflection, which generates more explicit knowledge about logic, which guides higher levels of reasoning. Reflection is not just a "professional twist of mind." On the contrary it is a universal feature of human cognition and, in its strongest form, a fundamental process of developmental change, especially with respect to logic.

The problem goes even deeper. The dismissal of logic is rooted in a general skepticism about the epistemic basis of reasoning:

> Mercier and Sperber (2017) see reasoning as metacognitive in some ways, but they do not see it as epistemic. In their view, reasoning evolved as a pragmatic instrument to serve particular social purposes, not to determine the truth, so any truth that results is mostly incidental. Justification is crucial to argumentation, but justification, in the proposed theory, is neither based on logic nor aimed at truth.
>
> This view is in sharp contrast to that of most philosophers, and especially epistemologists, who see truth as a necessary condition of knowledge. But Mercier and Sperber understand that they are challenging standard philosophical views. What they don't seem to realize is that they are also challenging the epistemic cognition of ordinary people (Moshman, 2015). By the age of 4 years, children recognize that beliefs can be false; for many years after that they construct increasingly sophisticated conceptions of truth, justification, and knowledge. This epistemic development is reflected in increasingly sophisticated argumentation. It is not clear how the proposed theory can account for this. Why would evolution generate a universal course of individual development toward false and useless ideas about logic and truth?
>
> *(Moshman, 2018, p. 63)*

I concluded that the proposed theory offers much of value but is best viewed as complementary to standard views, rather than as an alternative theory:

> With regard to the emphasis on argumentation, reasoning is both social *and* individual, with reciprocal influences across multiple levels. Perhaps we have underestimated the social aspect of reasoning as a collaborative activity, a claim worth considering, but there is no need to disparage the epistemic agency and development of individuals and much evidence to remind us not to do so.
>
> With regard to development, evolutionary accounts must acknowledge and explain developmental processes, sequences, and outcomes. People are not collections of evolved traits. The conceptualization of reason as a trait draws our attention away from its development and thus undermines our understanding of its nature, including its relation to logic.

> Finally, reasoning is indeed much more than logic, and the present work helps us see better the many ways in which this is so. But reasoning sometimes properly relies on strict deduction and its associated possibilities, impossibilities, and necessities. Logic is crucial to much of our reasoning whether we know it or not, and we're better off if we know it.
>
> *(Moshman, 2018, p. 64)*

Constructivist Accounts of Development

A comprehensive account of rational agency must explain its development. Nativist accounts highlight the genes, which are seen as having a direct causal role. In the extreme (as in Mercier & Sperber, 2017), genes are so strongly predictive of mature outcomes that development is essentially ignored. Behavior is assumed to be shaped directly by the evolutionary history of the species and explained on that basis.

The standard alternative to *nativism* is *empiricism*, which highlights learning from the environment. In the extreme, evolution is essentially ignored on the assumption that it provides nothing more than a blank slate for learning. Development, in turn, is reduced to nothing more than a process of learning whatever the physical or social environment presents or teaches.

Going beyond both nativism and empiricism, and even the sum of both, is *interactionism*, which recognizes that development usually or always involves an interaction of nativist and empiricist factors. At the very least, the interaction is statistical. The effects of heredity depend on one's environment, and the effects of any given environment depend on the genome of the species and/or individual differences in genes. Beyond such statistical interactions, moreover, interactionists often note that development involves an ongoing interaction of organism with environment, and thus (one might assume) of genes with environment.

But here we run into a whole new complication. Organisms are not simply collections of genes. The organism that interacts with its environment is itself the outcome of a developmental process involving, at the least, complex interactions of hereditary and environmental factors. A mature organism, and even a maturing one, cannot be reduced to its genes any more than to its environmental history. It is an emergent entity. And as the emerging organism achieves the ability to act, its behavior increasingly plays a role in development that cannot be reduced to genes, environments, or even in interaction of both.

Psychologists who emphasize the constructive role of the organism in its own development are *constructivists*. Nearly all developmentalists acknowledge the role of constructivist factors in development, along with nativist and empiricist factors, and in that sense all developmentalists are constructivists as well as nativists and empiricists. But many see the role of the organism as central and are thus constructivist in a stronger sense.

Constructivism is a theoretical perspective emphasizing the active role of the organism in the construction of knowledge. Constructivist theories take a variety of forms (Moshman, 1982). *Rational constructivism* (Moshman, 2011a) construes the constructive process of development as a rational process directed by an increasingly rational agent. Rational constructivism is rooted in the developmental epistemology of Jean Piaget (1975/1985, 1977/2001) and has been highly influential in subsequent research and theory on cognitive and moral development (Demetriou & Spanoudis, 2018; Gibbs, 2019; Kazi et al., 2019; Kohlberg, 1981, 1984; Kuhn, 2005; Kuhn et al., 1988; Moshman, 2004b, 2015; Nucci, 2001, 2014; O'Madagain & Tomasello, 2019; Tomasello, 2014; Turiel, 1983, 2008). In rational constructivism, the developing organism (at least in some species) increasingly approximates a rational agent, acting on the basis of reasons of its own, not simply doing what it is caused to do by forces beyond its control. The rational agent that emerges from development is, moreover, increasingly responsible for its own further development.

Rational constructivism is an idealized view of development corresponding to rational agency as an idealized view of personhood, rational agents as idealized persons, and deliberative democracy as an idealized social system. We are all subject to forces beyond our control; organisms and social systems change in a variety of ways due to a variety of nonrational and irrational forces. As we saw in Chapters 2–4, however, there is clear evidence for developmental progress in rationality. The most convincing explanation for this is that development, at its normative core, is a rational process directed by rational agents.

Reflection and Coordination as Developmental Processes

Piaget (1967/1971, 1977/2001) provided an account of cognitive development as an ongoing process of coordination and reflection by an increasingly rational agent.

> [L]ogico-mathematical structures owe their origin neither to physical experiment nor to instinctive or hereditary transmission but are derived by reflective abstractions from the general coordinations of action and, farther back still, from nervous coordinations, and so on back to the most widely generalized of the organizing functions in life.
>
> *(Piaget, 1967/1971, p. 342)*

Many theorists have highlighted and examined the role of reflection in development (Allen & Bickhard, 2018; Campbell & Bickhard, 1986; Karmiloff-Smith, 1992; Piaget, 1977/2001). A good example is the role of reflection in the development of metalogical understanding. I present here once again the four stages of metalogical understanding originally presented in Chapter 4, focusing now on the role of reflection in explaining the transition from each stage to the next.

As we saw in Chapter 2, logic is initially implicit in biological self-regulation (Piaget, 1967/1971) and then in infants' sensorimotor actions (Langer, 1980, 1986; Piaget, 1936/1963). The development of logical reasoning does not culminate in logic. On the contrary, logic can be found as far back as we look. What develops is our metacognitive control of our inferences and our explicit knowledge about the logic implicit in them (Moshman, 1990, 2004b; 2015). Stage 1 of metalogical development is the stage of explicit content and implicit inference (typical in children under 6 years). Stage 1 thinkers can tell you what they are thinking about but they are not aware of the inferences intrinsic to their cognitive processes and use of language. They do not distinguish conclusions from premises, do not attribute inferences to others, and do not recognize inference as a potential source of knowledge (Miller, 2012; Pillow, 2012; Sodian & Wimmer, 1987).

The transition to Stage 2 (beginning about age 6 years) involves a process of reflection on inference, rendering explicit what was earlier implicit in action. But we can only reflect on inferences from the standpoint of an implicit logic that addresses their normative properties. To attain Stage 2 metalogical understanding we must construct an implicit logic that enables us to assess our increasingly explicit inferences. Stage 2 thinkers recognize conclusions as the outcome of inferences, distinguish conclusions from premises, recognize that others also make inferences, and understand that, as a result of inference, people may come to know things they have not observed or been told. The explicit attention to inferences involves an implicit appreciation of their logical form and necessity.

The transition to Stage 3 begins about age 11 or 12 years and remains a work in progress for most people. It involves a process of reflection on logic itself. Explicit awareness of logical form makes it possible to distinguish (a) the abstract issue of whether a conclusion follows necessarily from some set of premises from (b) the more concrete challenge of evaluating the truth of individual premises and conclusions. This enables hypothetico-deductive reasoning, which greatly extends the scope of our rationality. The explicit attention to logic entails an implicit metalogical understanding of logic as a domain of necessity distinct from empirical science.

Given the challenges of Stage 3, most people probably leave their most advanced metalogical understandings implicit. The transition to Stage 4, which may be limited largely to logicians, involves reflections on (a) the nature and justification of formal logical systems, (b) their interrelations with each other and with natural human languages, (c) the nature and scope of logic, and (d) the relation of logic to science and other domains. Logicians are experts on logic, but this does not mean they invented it. What they are expert at is something we all use and, to varying extents, understand. Logicians have simply achieved a higher level of reflection on logic, which enhances understanding but raises whole new sets of questions to be addressed through further reflection.

The development of metalogical understanding is thus explained as a process of reflection through multiple levels (Campbell & Bickhard, 1986; Moshman, 1990).

In each stage transition, what was previously implicit becomes an explicit object of reflection.

Consider another example, which illustrates the interrelated roles of reflection and coordination as developmental processes. The development of epistemic cognition in domains such as science and morality, as we saw in Chapter 4, shows a recurring pattern of three basic stages. The first, objectivist, stage involves explicit knowledge about the world. Implicit in any act of knowing is the subjective perspective of the knower, but objectivist knowers construe the known as a given without recognizing that it is a function of their subjective perspective.

The transition to the subjectivist stage involves a process of reflection on subjectivity. Explicit awareness of one's subjectivity undermines one's earlier conception of the objectivity of knowledge, which represents an advance in understanding. Taken to a subjectivist extreme, however, the commitment to subjectivity undermines the possibility of objectivity and thus of knowledge.

The transition to the rationalist stage can be seen as a coordination of objectivity and subjectivity at a higher level of reflection that acknowledges both sufficiently to consider their relations. Regardless of the details, it seems clear that developmental progress in epistemic cognition is a constructive process. It may be influenced by genes and environments but is not driven by either, or even by an interaction of both.

Developmental progress through reflection and coordination is not a gradual accumulation of knowledge but the generation of a series of discrete and increasingly equilibrated stages (Piaget, 1975/1985). The philosopher Thomas Nagel (1986) put it this way:

> We can add to our knowledge of the world by accumulating information at a given level—by extensive observation from one standpoint. But we can raise our understanding to a new level only if we examine that relation between the world and ourselves which is responsible for our prior understanding, and form a new conception that includes a more detached understanding of ourselves, of the world, and of the interaction between them.
>
> *(p. 5)*

Peer Interaction as a Developmental Context

Children obviously learn from their peers, and much of what they learn is useful and important. But children also learn from adults, including their parents and teachers, who may often be a source of better information and guidance because they are more mature and experienced. What is special about peer interaction as a context for developmental progress is not that children can learn from their peers but that they can develop by interacting with peers (Piaget, 1932/1965b, 1995). Of course, children also develop in the course of interacting with adults (O'Madagain

& Tomasello, 2019; Tomasello, 2014), but there is reason to believe that interaction with peers plays a unique and crucial developmental role.

The role of peer interaction in development was central to Piaget's (1932/1965b) classic early work on moral development. Children routinely learn rules of behavior from parents and other authorities with the ability to enforce such rules. But genuine morality requires more than following rules enforced by those in power. Genuine morality requires respect for persons, including the ability to engage in reciprocal relations among rational agents who recognize each other as social equals. The development of what Piaget called an "autonomous" morality is a constructive process of coordination with others and reflection on one's relations with them, which can only take place in the context of peer interaction.

Piaget and many theorists since have extended this conception of the crucial importance of peer interaction for moral development into a more general conception of the special role of peer interaction, including argumentation, in the development of reasoning and rationality (Kuhn, 2005; Kuhn et al., 2016; Moshman, 2011a; Piaget, 1995). Respect for others as persons and peers requires respect for reasons. Respect for reasons and persons includes both paying attention to the reasons others have for their beliefs and actions and providing others with reasons for one's own beliefs and actions.

The development of epistemic cognition, for example, is surely enhanced by, and arguably requires, peer interaction. It is natural to construe what we perceive as the objective truth. We recognize our perceptions as subjective when we engage seriously with peers who have different perceptions. Peer interaction also enables us to coordinate our subjectivities to obtain a greater objectivity, and to reflect on this process in ways that promote our epistemic cognition. Peer interaction is also crucial preparation for participation in deliberative democracy in part because it promotes development of the social skills and understandings necessary for deliberative democracy, including those associated with argumentation.

Peer interaction is not just interaction with others one's own age. Strictly speaking, peer interaction is the reciprocal social interaction of rational agents who are, and perceive themselves to be, equal in authority, status, and power. Such interaction ideally takes place under conditions in which all are, and perceive themselves to be, equally free to express their views, hear from others, and fully engage in discussion. We have already seen that intellectual freedom is crucial for good reasoning (Chapter 5) and deliberative democracy (Chapter 6). In creating genuine peer interactions, intellectual freedom also enables and promotes developmental progress. There is much more to be said about this, but I will defer further discussion of intellectual freedom to Chapter 8, in which I address its role in education, including the development of rationality.

Development Across and Beyond Childhood

In Chapters 2–4 I discussed, in much more detail than some readers may have deemed necessary, developmental changes in multiple domains of reasoning and rationality, including logical reasoning, scientific reasoning, principled reasoning, precedent-based reasoning, and epistemic cognition. In this section I aim instead to propose a general pattern of development that we see in all domains (Moshman, 2009b, 2011a). There appears to be a period of basic development over the first 12 years in which natural human competencies are constructed in predictable, age-related sequences by all normal persons, followed by a period of advanced development in which the direction and extent of development are much more individualized, not inevitable, and no longer tied to age.

Basic Development

Cognitive development has long been seen as an age-related sequence of cognitive competencies. Piaget provided the best-known theoretical account of that sequence but there were important theories of cognitive development before him and there have been many since (Demetriou & Spanoudis, 2018; Kazi et al., 2019). Based on extensive empirical evidence, virtually all theories posit qualitative transformations in a consistent age-related sequence over the first 12 years of life. Most theorists of cognitive development since Piaget share his rational constructivist conception of the developmental process but differ in the precise processes and developmental contexts they emphasize and in their conceptualization of cognitive competence. For present purposes, we need not dwell on these theoretical differences. Our focus here is on the basic empirical picture of emerging competencies, about which there is greater consensus. In what follows I summarize evidence reviewed in Chapters 2–4.

A major trend in cognitive development since the 1960s has been the rapidly expanding literature on infant cognition, which can readily be interpreted as showing unexpected logical, causal, and moral competencies implicit in the behavior of pre-linguistic children. As language develops, children's logical, causal, and moral inferences become increasingly observable. Their behavior also begins to show evidence that they have metacognitive knowledge about minds and cognitive processes.

Beginning about age 4 years, children's knowledge of mind is sufficiently organized and explanatory that theorists routinely credit them with a "theory of mind" (Miller, 2012; Moshman, 2015; Pillow, 2012; Sodian & Kristen, 2016). This includes an explicit understanding that beliefs may be false and that people act on the basis of their own beliefs even when they are false (O'Madagain & Tomasello, 2019). Of course there are individual differences in the rate of development. The basic theory of mind typical of 4-year-olds does not appear suddenly on each child's fourth birthday. It is sometimes seen in 3-year-olds, especially those within a few months of turning 4, and sometimes not yet seen in 4-year-olds, especially those who have turned 4 recently. But basic theory of mind is virtually never seen in 2-year-olds and is virtually universal in 5-year-olds. Despite some developmental variation, virtually all 5-year-olds have attained a level of rationality virtually never seen before the age of 3 years.

Beginning about age 6 years, children show awareness that they are making inferences, attribute inferences to others, and recognize inference as a source of knowledge for themselves and others. Their explicit attention to inferences enables them to distinguish conclusions, the outcomes of inference, from premises. Implicit in their reasoning is a new appreciation of logical form and necessity (Moshman, 1990, 2015). Here again, development does not happen in an instant or always at the exact same age, but biologically normal children in normal human social environments construct the same basic rational competencies in the same sequence at about the same age.

By the age of 8 or 9 years, children have constructed a constructivist theory of mind, which recognizes the active and interpretative nature of the mind as a constructor of knowledge. This includes understandings of subjectivity that would have been literally unthinkable just a few years earlier (Miller, 2012; Moshman, 2015; Pillow, 2012).

Finally, around the age of 11 or 12 years children begin to demonstrate forms and levels of reasoning and rationality virtually never seen before the age of 10 years. These include hypothetico-deductive reasoning, explicit conceptions of inferential validity, reflective coordination of theories and evidence, third-party perspective taking, principled forms of moral reasoning, and reflective epistemologies (Moshman, 2011a, 2013). Most young adolescents become somewhat more consistent over the next few years in applying their most advanced reasoning and insights, but no one ever achieves anything close to consistently rational cognition. As we have seen in coordinating developmental research with dual process theories, advanced competencies often supplement earlier ones without replacing them. Young teens at their best far surpass the rationality of 9-year-old children, but people of all ages often show behavior that falls far short of this standard.

Advanced Development

Development generally continues beyond the age of 12 years but further development is much more specific to particular individuals and circumstances and much less related to age. Some adults sometimes show forms of logical, scientific, or moral reasoning beyond what would ever be seen in a 13-year-old. Some adults understand the relation of social systems to interpersonal morality in ways that would rarely be seen in a young teen. Some achieve advanced levels of metacognitive self-regulation or make progress in epistemic cognition toward reflective understandings of the subjectivity of knowledge, and some go beyond that in coordinating subjectivity and objectivity in ways that would mystify almost any young teen (and most older individuals as well). Some people construct rationalist identities that highlight and value rationality, justification, and truth.

In the extensive literature on advanced forms of human cognition and rational agency, however, I have never seen any evidence for any form or level of reasoning or rationality that is achieved by all normal adults but rarely seen in young teens.

This is in sharp contrast to the pattern of basic development in childhood just reviewed, where it is easy to show multiple examples of rational competencies routine at some given age that are rarely or never seen just a few years earlier. Thus, in understanding the development of rational agency, it seems important to make a distinction between the basic development of the first 12 or so years of life, which is universal and age-related, and advanced development in adolescence and beyond, which is much less predictable.

Adults generally share stereotypes of adolescents as subject to egocentrism, peer pressure, and irrational risks; failing to give appropriate weight to future consequences; and commonly operating on the basis of impulse and intuition rather than reflective reasoning. With respect to all of these cognitive crimes, adolescents are guilty as charged. What is routinely overlooked, however, is that adults are guilty of all the same crimes. Some people are more rational than others, but beyond age 12 we cannot predict rationality from age.

In the absence of psychological evidence, it is sometimes assumed on the basis of brain research that, because human brains arguably continue to develop at least until the age of 25 years, 25-year-olds have attained levels of rational agency not seen in older teens, who in turn have attained levels not seen in young teens. But our brains change throughout our lives, in large part as a result of our individual actions and environments. There is no evidence to support the assumption of general progress in rational agency during adolescence and beyond due to brain maturation or the corresponding assumption that there is some age at which adults have generally attained a level of rationality beyond the capacity of adolescent brains (Moshman, 2011a, 2013).

Nevertheless, as already noted, there is clear evidence for development in adolescence and beyond. Some people achieve advanced levels of epistemic cognition, for example, that are rarely or never seen in young teens. Some adults coordinate moral and social perspectives, principles, and precedents in reflective ways unseen in young teens. Adult groups sometimes coordinate their arguments and perspectives in reflective forms of argumentation not seen in a middle school class. Development beyond the age of 12 or 13 years is best seen as advanced development, differing from the basic development of childhood in that it is no longer universal and closely tied to age. Basic development can be expected for any normal individual in any normal human environment. The nature and extent of advanced development is much more dependent on specific individual and social circumstances, such as formal education.

All of this requires some rethinking of what we mean by psychological maturity and of the natural tendency of adults to perceive adolescents as immature.

> Immaturity is a meaningful and important biological concept, . . . not just a label for those not yet like us. It is not sufficient to assume we know it when we see it. To say an organism is immature implies there is something still to develop. But there is no evidence for a universally achieved state of maturity

> yet to be reached beyond adolescence. What we perceive as immaturity is the possibility of further development. Development often continues long beyond childhood and arguably remains possible throughout adulthood, but development beyond childhood, unlike child development, is not the attainment of a natural and universal state of maturity.
>
> *(Moshman, 2013, p. 169)*

Understanding the distinction between basic and advanced development leads to a somewhat counterintuitive conclusion about education, which will play an important role in the next chapter. Basic development will take place in any normal human environment, so to ensure basic development it may suffice to see that children develop in supportive environments in which they receive adequate nourishment, attention, cognitive challenges, social opportunities, etc. But advanced development requires something more; it can only be expected, or at least is far more likely, in environments that specifically promote it. Education for rationality should of course begin early and be a serious consideration in elementary education, but it is arguably most important in middle school and beyond, where progress in rationality can no longer be taken for granted.

Development of Rational Self-Governance

To be a rational agent is to believe and act on the basis of reasons, rather than being driven by external causes. To be a rational agent, then, is to be self-governing. Development can thus be construed as progress in rational self-governance. In individuals, the development of rational self-governance may be seen as the development of personhood. In interpersonal groups and social systems, the development of rational self-governance is the development of deliberative democracy.

Personhood

Who counts as a person? Psychologically, a person is at minimum a rational agent, so one criterion for personhood is rational agency. Even a grasshopper is a biological agent. But although the grasshopper acts, it does not have reasons for what it does. We may ask why the grasshopper jumps, but the expected response is a causal theory of elementary behavior, not an account of the grasshopper's beliefs and values. The grasshopper is an agent, but presumably not a rational agent.

What about a lizard? A parrot? A dog? A chimpanzee? A 9-month-old human infant? A 2-year-old child? Whether some or all of these are rational agents is not clear, depending on how we define rational agency and on empirical facts about various species and developmental milestones. What does seem clear, especially from research on young children's metacognition and theories of mind (Chapter 4), is that human beings attain rational agency by the age of 4 years. More plausibly, I think, children are rational agents in some minimal sense long before that, and attain a higher level of rational agency at about age 4 years.

But democracy requires equal respect for all persons, which entails legal equality in fundamental rights and liberties, including the right to vote. If the criterion for personhood is nothing more than rational agency, it seems to follow that we must accord full rights to all human beings who have reached the age of 4 years and arguably also to even younger children and some animals. The more defensible alternative is to distinguish levels of rationality, and thus levels of personhood, and set a threshold of full personhood. We must avoid setting the threshold too high, however. Based on the developmental research reviewed in this book, it seems reasonable to set the criterion of full personhood at the basic level of rational agency attained by all normal human beings in all human cultural contexts about the age of 12 or 13 years. We must of course promote development beyond that, but a more stringent criterion of full personhood would exclude many people of all ages and thus undermine democracy.

We must of course respect the personhood of all rational agents. For human children, such respect enables further development of rational agency to the point of full personhood. Even where it doesn't, however, there is a strong case to be made that at least some mammals, and probably some birds, are entitled to some degree of respect for their own choices.

We must also recognize our moral obligations to all who can suffer, even if they are not rational agents. At the very least, we have an obligation not to cause suffering needlessly, and arguably we have a moral obligation to relieve suffering in some cases. Rational agents have a moral responsibility to treat each other as rational agents, but there are moral obligations that extend beyond that.

Nevertheless, rational agency is central to personhood. Democracy requires a criterion of full personhood carrying full entitlement to fundamental rights and liberties. Developmental research suggests a criterion that distinguishes persons beyond the age of 12 or 13 years from children. Many have proposed that the voting age be lowered to 16 years (Hart & Youniss, 2018). Psychological research, I suggest, justifies the more radical step of lowering not just the voting age but the age of majority, and lowering it not just to 16 years but rather to 14 years. This is not to say 14-year-olds should be expected to function on their own without social support. We all need social support. But even young teens are much more like adults than children, and many young teens are more rational, by any measure, than many adults. What modern societies take to be the problems of adolescence, it appears, are largely due not to biologically immature brains but to the paradoxical social status of being psychologically an adult in a culture that treats you as a child (Moshman, 2011a, 2013).

Interpersonal and Societal Development

What about groups? Like individuals, groups often grow and change. But do groups develop? Neither growth nor change is necessarily a good thing, but if groups potentially develop, there may be reason to promote the development of groups, not just of the individuals who compose them.

Development may be defined as a type or pattern of change that is extended over time, self-regulated, qualitative, and progressive (Moshman, 2011a). In order to think more rigorously about developmental change we must consider each of these four criteria.

First, and perhaps most obvious, developmental change takes place over an extended period of time. In the case of individual development, that means developmental change takes place over some portion of the lifespan. In the case of very young infants, that may be just a matter of weeks or even days, considering the period of change relative to their current age. For older individuals, development generally refers to change over a period of months or years, typically years for adolescents and adults. Small groups may also develop over a period of months or years; for large social systems developmental change is generally observed over years or decades.

Second, developmental change is directed or regulated by internal organismic or systemic processes rather than being imposed by others or strongly shaped by environmental forces. Thus, development is not simply a matter of learning many things over a long period of time. Nativists see development as a process directed by the genes. Rational constructivists see development as the outcome of the rational and constructive processes of a self-regulating organism. The rational constructivist view also enables us to see developmental change in enduring groups and social systems.

Third, developmental change involves a succession of qualitatively distinct structures or modes of functioning. Growing larger is not, in itself, a developmental change. Among individuals, for example, development can be seen in the successive stages of metalogical understanding discussed earlier in the chapter or in the transition from objectivist to subjectivist to rationalist epistemologies noted above and discussed in Chapter 4. Among groups, similarly, development involves a transition to something new and different, not just more of the same.

Finally, to deem a change developmental we must show that it involves progress toward something better. A key purpose of the concept of development is to distinguish progressive changes from changes that are arbitrary, neutral, regressive, pathological, or specific to particular environments or cultures. In its original biological meaning, development is progress toward maturity, a conception that also works well in children's psychological development, where we can specify sequences of rational competencies all normal children construct over the course of their first 12 or so years. As we have repeatedly seen, however, there is no state of maturity in the future of all adolescents. Nevertheless, we can speak meaningfully of the development of rational agency beyond childhood in at least some individuals provided we can specify what they are constructing and how it represents an advance over what came before. Similarly, in the case of groups or societies there is no universal state of maturity toward which they naturally tend. Nevertheless, it seems reasonable to suggest that transitions to higher levels of deliberation and democracy can be seen as progress in rational self-governance and moral respect for persons. To the extent that progressive transitions are also extended, self-regulated, and qualitative, they qualify as development.

Do we really need to restrict the use of the term "development" in these ways? I suggest it is useful to do so. Individuals, groups, and social systems routinely change in a variety of ways. If we referred to all such changes as development, the term would serve no purpose. By limiting development to changes that are extended, self-regulated, qualitative, and progressive, we identify an important subcategory of change that transforms the individual, group, or social system, and that we may, in some cases, choose to promote.

It is common, for example, to speak of "economic development" when measures of economic activity show gains. Development in the strict sense, however, means something more than growth. To speak meaningfully of economic development, there must be a self-regulated and qualitative transition in economic structures or modes of functioning that can reasonably be seen as progress.

In *Development as Freedom*, the Nobel prize-winning economist Amartya Sen (1999) argued that development is furthered by conditions of liberty and respect for human agency. Freedoms of speech, press, and assembly, along with other civil liberties and opportunities, promote the economic development of nations. Sen rejected the common assumption that freedom must be sacrificed to make development possible and is thus a luxury to be enjoyed only in economically advanced societies. He showed instead that freedom is crucial to economic progress. Freedom, however, is not just the means of development but equally its end. Development is not just a matter of increasing wealth. Wealth, argued Sen, is valuable for the freedoms it permits. We can choose whether or not to have or do whatever we can afford. Genuine development, then, enhances our capabilities and options. Development, in Sen's analysis, is progress toward freedom.

Although Sen (1999) was concerned with the economic development of nations, his analysis applies to individual development as well. Both individuals and nations are active agents in their own development, not resources to be developed by others. People cannot develop other people, nor can nations develop other nations. We can promote the development of others, but only by enhancing their agency, not by restricting it. Restrictions on agency are in fact counterproductive; they generate resistance because consciousness of agency and commitment to freedom are universal. Thus, Sen concluded, we must respect freedom in order to promote development, which, it turns out, is the promotion of freedom. For both individuals and nations, freedom is both the means and the end of development.

One reason to promote the development of individual rational agency is to enhance the ability of individuals to participate in deliberative and democratic groups and social systems. It is likely, however, that such participation is crucial to individual development. Participation in childhood groups both requires and supports moral reasoning, for example. Participation in social systems both requires and supports precedent-based reasoning. This may seem paradoxical but it is simply developmental. We develop within groups and societies, with complex reciprocal influences across individual, group, and societal levels, and with meaningful potential for developmental change at each of these levels.

Conclusion

The emergence of rationality is neither a maturational process directed by genes nor a process of learning from one's environment, though genes and environments are obviously important. Moreover, it cannot be explained as an interaction of these two factors, though hereditary and environmental factors are deeply interconnected. Rather, rationality is constructed over time by increasingly rational agents through rational and social processes of reflection and coordination. Subjectivity is inevitable, but reflection on subjectivity enables progress to metasubjective forms of objectivity and increasingly rational self-governance at individual, social, and societal levels. The rational agency of an individual or group, I conclude, is the outcome of a rational process of construction whereby rational agents, individually and collectively, enhance their rationality.

This picture of rational agents becoming increasingly rational sounds pretty good, but of course it's an idealization. In the real world, rational agency and rational developmental processes are much more elusive than we would like them to be, which means there is plenty of room for improvement. We now consider how we can promote rationality by promoting its development.

8

EDUCATION FOR RATIONALITY

Education serves many purposes but is widely seen as concerned in large part, if not most centrally, with the promotion of rationality (Moshman, 2009b). If rationality were simply a collection of learnable skills, the challenge of education for rationality would be to identify those skills and determine how best each of them can be taught. Extensive research on development and education has made it clear, however, that rationality cannot be reduced to a set of discrete skills and cannot be learned by a direct process of social transmission. On the contrary, rationality develops through constructive processes and is best fostered by education aimed at promoting development.

As we saw in Chapter 7, peer interaction encourages processes of reflection and coordination central to development and thus plays a central role in the development of rationality. In this chapter we extend this insight to consider the role of peer argumentation in education for rationality. The discussion then turns to the prevalence of indoctrination in educational curricula in fields including science and history and to indoctrinative modes of instruction that circumvent or undermine rational agency rather than promoting its development. As a general response, I suggest a reconceptualization of academic freedom as intellectual freedom in academic contexts, including freedoms of teaching, learning, and inquiry. Academic institutions that respect the academic freedom of all engaged in academic work are most likely to succeed in promoting the development of rational agency. The chapter concludes with an overview of the skills, knowledge, and values of an ideal rational agent.

Critical Thinking

Critical thinking has long been seen by philosophers, educators, and others as a crucial part of education and arguably its most central goal. Although critical thinking has many definitions, it is widely seen as involving a concern for reasons and thus as closely connected to rationality. To think critically is to seek, respect, provide, and evaluate reasons. Thus critical thinking is, essentially, reasoning.

Harvey Siegel (1988, 1997, 2018) specifically advocated what he called "the reasons conception" of critical thinking, "which holds that the critical thinker is one who is *appropriately moved by reasons*" (Siegel, 1988, p. 2, emphasis in original). He suggested that critical thinking is the "educational cognate" of rationality. That is, "critical thinking involves bringing to bear all matters relevant to the rationality of belief and action." Thus, "education aimed at the promulgation of critical thinking is nothing less than education aimed at the fostering of rationality and the development of rational persons" (Siegel, 1988, p. 32).

Critical thinkers are logical when they ought to be, but it should be clear that critical thinking is much more than making logical inferences. It should also be clear (especially from Chapter 2) that there is no need to teach logic, at least not at the level of basic inferences. The basic logical inferences required in the notorious selection task (see Chapters 2 and 5), for example, are all routine in early childhood. What develops later, and what we ought to promote, is metalogical understanding and control of inferences.

Richard Paul (1990) distinguished "weak" from "strong" conceptions of critical thinking and advocated the latter. Students who learn to think critically, he warned, generally apply their critical abilities mostly to ideas they disagree with, thus enabling them to maintain their own ideas. Such thinking is critical only in a weak sense of the word. Critical thinking in the strong sense includes recognition of one's own ideological assumptions and identity commitments and active efforts to subject one's own ideas and those of one's groups to rigorous critique. The concept of strong critical thinking thus recognizes that people naturally tend to protect their ideologies and identities and that education for critical thinking must enable and encourage students to understand and overcome those tendencies.

Siegel (1988) similarly questioned whether someone who is capable of critical thinking but rarely thinks critically, or does so only in self-serving ways, is really a critical thinker. Critical thinking, he argued, is not just the *ability* to assess reasons. Critical thinking is the actual assessment of reasons, which cannot be explained by ability alone. The ideal critical thinker has "certain attitudes, dispositions, habits of mind, and character traits" that together comprise "the critical spirit" (Siegel, 1988, p. 39). Critical thinkers are not just *able* to assess reasons properly; they are disposed to do so. To have a critical spirit is to have a certain kind of character, one that (a) "is inclined to seek, and to base judgment and action upon, reasons;" (b) "rejects partiality and arbitrariness;" (c) "is committed to the objective evaluation of relevant evidence;" and (d) "values such aspects of critical thinking as intellectual honesty, . . . objectivity, and impartiality" (Siegel, 1988, p. 39). It is not enough that one is *able* to seek reasons or judge impartially; the critical thinker is *committed* to doing so, regardless of self-interest. To have a critical spirit is to be "inclined to seek reasons and evidence; to demand justification; to query and investigate unsubstantiated claims" (Siegel, 1988, p. 39). Critical thinkers ideally engage their reason assessment skills in all appropriate contexts, even when their own actions and most deeply held convictions are challenged. The critical spirit is most fundamentally "a deep commitment to and respect for reasons" (Siegel, 1988, p. 39). To have a critical spirit is "to *value* good reasoning, and to be disposed to believe and act on its basis" (Siegel, 1988, p. 39, emphasis in original).

Consideration of the critical spirit suggests the importance of teaching in what Siegel (1988) called "the critical manner."

> The critical manner is that manner of teaching that models and reinforces the critical spirit. A teacher who utilizes the critical manner seeks to encourage in his or her students the skills, habits and dispositions necessary for the development of the critical spirit. This means, first, that the teacher always recognizes the right of the student to question and demand reasons; and consequently recognizes an obligation to provide reasons wherever demanded. The critical manner thus demands of a teacher a willingness to subject all beliefs and practices to scrutiny, and so to allow students the genuine opportunity to understand the role reasons play in the justification of thought and action. . . . [T]he teacher must submit her reasons to the independent evaluation of the student.
>
> *(Siegel, 1988, p. 45)*

Deanna Kuhn (2019) conceptualized critical thinking as, most fundamentally, a matter of argumentation. Critical thinking is not so much an individual property one has to some degree as something one does with others: "Rather than a fixed attribute of an individual, critical thinking is a dynamic activity that may show itself to a greater or lesser extent and in varying forms depending on the affordances of the context" (p. 161). That is, critical thinking is collaborative reasoning. In the course of thinking critically with others, Kuhn has found, individuals may develop in ways that enhance their ability to think critically on their own. This insight is central to her argumentation curriculum, discussed in the next section.

Consistent with all of these conceptions, critical thinking can be seen as central to rational agency. To take critical thinking as the primary goal of education is to conceive education as the promotion of rational agency. As we saw in the previous chapter, rational agency is the outcome of a developmental process. To promote rationality, then, we must promote the processes central to its development.

Education as the Promotion of Development

As we saw in Chapter 7, the development of rationality is a constructive process in which rational agents further their own development through reflection and coordination. To promote the development of rationality we must engage students in processes of reflection and coordination. This is not just important in elementary education, where development in rationality is relatively rapid and universal. It is no less important in secondary and higher education, where the aim is to have students go beyond the "mature" level of rational agency typically achieved around the age of 12 years. There is no universal state of maturity beyond that, but there is plenty of room for further development.

As we also saw in Chapter 7, peer interaction is a crucial developmental context in which reflection and coordination promote advances in rational agency. Such interaction is routine across childhood but opportunities for more advanced argumentation and development are less universal. Education for rationality must provide such opportunities.

Kuhn (2005) advocated "education for thinking," and proposed that inquiry and argument are central to such education. Inquiry refers especially to scientific inquiry, which is both empirical and theoretical (see Chapter 3). It is not enough that students learn established scientific facts. They should learn how scientific knowledge is generated, including processes of seeking and interpreting evidence, proposing and evaluating theories, and participating in a community of inquiry. The point is not that they will learn to rely only, or even mostly, on the results of their own original research. We all rely on scientists and other experts. But to understand science and expertise, and thereby make good decisions about what to believe, we must understand the nature of science and the basis for expert conclusions. Education for thinking promotes knowledge of inquiry by engaging students in inquiry.

Education for thinking also engages students in argumentation, which has been central to Kuhn's subsequent work (Kuhn, Feliciano, & Kostikina, 2019; Zillmer & Kuhn, 2018; see also Dacey, 2020; Mercier, Boudry, Paglieri, & Trouche, 2017). In *Argue with Me: Argument as a Path to Developing Students' Thinking and Writing*, Kuhn, Hemberger, and Khait (2016) wrote directly for teachers. In a further effort to make her work even more accessible, Kuhn (2018a) has also published a student manual written directly for middle school students. In *Building Our Best Future: Thinking Critically About Ourselves and Our World*, she provided a detailed set of steps for undertaking productive argumentation, and furthering associated reasoning and writing skills, in middle school and beyond.

Building Our Best Future presents 44 topics in four categories. The categories are "A Personal Future" (including topics such as course selection, nutrition, alcohol, and money management), "A Community Future" (e.g., school curriculum, age of majority, taxes and services, elder care), "A National Future" (e.g., voting rights, health insurance, abortion, capital punishment), and "A World Future" (e.g., immigration, foreign aid, the United Nations, weapons of mass destruction). Students may also choose topics of their own.

For each agreed topic, two positions are identified and each student chooses a position, leading to a division into two teams. The teams ultimately compete in a "showdown" of argumentation including a series of face-to-face individual encounters. In preparation for the much-anticipated showdown, students engage in a sequence of activities in both small and large groups. Guided by the manual, they generate reasons, evaluate them, identify questions, seek relevant evidence, consider opposition arguments, formulate counterarguments, and prepare "comebacks" (rebuttals) to opposition counterarguments. For topics in the manual, lists of questions are provided, with online access to answers that students can draw on to construct and enhance their arguments.

After the showdown, in a phase called "sharing your thinking," students write individual short essays defending their current position. Regardless of whether their position has changed, their depth of understanding facilitates their writing and is reflected in the quality of the final product. For a greater challenge, students with differing views may collaborate on an essay explaining the issue and presenting the arguments and evidence for both sides.

There is also a Teachers Edition of *Building Our Best Future* (Kuhn, 2018b), which includes most of what appeared in the student edition plus explanatory notes and instructional suggestions. A concluding chapter, unique to the Teachers Edition, briefly reviews the substantial published evidence for the effectiveness of the curriculum and provides guidance on assessing progress in the reasoning and writing of individual students.

This curriculum promotes good reasoning and writing by engaging students deeply in the practice of argumentation. Argumentation promotes reasoning by engaging students in reflection on and coordination of diverse claims and reasons. The rich structure of arguments in which they participate also serves to make their subsequent writing increasingly rational and convincing.

The argumentation curriculum also has the potential to revitalize democratic deliberation. It highlights a variety of social and political issues that students may recognize as sources of controversy and engages them in rational discourse about such matters. Thus even as students develop individually, the potential for democracy also develops.

For the curriculum to reach its full potential, however, it must go beyond debate. The prospect of a "showdown" between opposing teams is highly motivating but insufficient for deliberative democracy, which requires an orientation toward achieving a rational consensus to the extent that this is possible. Thus, the collaborative essay written by students with differing views seems to me of particular importance. In some cases, collaboration may result in agreement on at least some key points. Even where it doesn't, there is value in the process of reaching agreement on an essay that both writers see as reasonable in its framing of the issue, its presentation of differing viewpoints, and its coverage of relevant arguments and evidence. When an essay like this is successful, the writers don't just agree to disagree but construct a more advanced understanding of the nature of their disagreement.

Indoctrination in Curriculum and Instruction

For education to promote the development of rationality, it is not enough to add a bit of argumentation or other opportunities for development. Real schools everywhere, especially at the elementary and secondary levels, are to a large extent centers of indoctrination, which is arguably not education at all, and certainly not the kind that promotes rationality or development (Moshman, 2009a; Ross, 2015).

Two forms of indoctrination can be distinguished, one related to curriculum and the other to instruction. A curriculum may be regarded as indoctrinative if it has been devised at least in part on nonacademic grounds to serve nonacademic purposes, such as getting students to be more patriotic or to support governmental or other policies. Regardless of the curriculum, moreover, instruction may be indoctrinative if it is designed to coerce belief rather than appealing to students' rational agency. In circumventing or undermining the rational agency of students, indoctrination fails to respect both reasons and persons, and is thus objectionable on both educational and moral grounds (Callan & Arena, 2009; Siegel, 1988). Education for rationality is the educational ideal in that it both respects and promotes students' rational agency.

I provide in this section examples of indoctrination in both curriculum and instruction. I begin with science education and then turn to aspects of education that raise issues of identity.

Science Education

Science education may fail to promote rationality to the extent that the curriculum has been shaped by political and religious pressures. I provide here, as an example, a brief history of science education in U.S. elementary and secondary schools (Laats & Siegel, 2016; Moshman, 2009a). As I will note, however, even when the curriculum is scientifically justified, science education fails to promote rational agency if it is presented in a manner that indoctrinates students.

In the early 20th century, although there was a consensus among scientists that species evolve over long periods of time, the teaching of evolution was seen by most Americans as a threat to the Christian conception of divine creation of a finite number of fixed "kinds" of organism; many also perceived a threat to the Biblical chronology that set the age of the Earth at 6,000 to 10,000 years. The highly publicized 1925 trial of John Scopes for teaching evolution brought the matter to national consciousness. Scopes was convicted, and it remained illegal to teach evolution in many states for the next several decades. Even in states that did not ban the teaching of evolution, the topic was generally deemed too controversial for the curriculum.

In 1957, the Soviet Union launched Sputnik, the Earth's first artificial satellite, raising concerns in the United States about trailing in the race for space and, more generally, falling behind in science. A resurgence of interest in science education led to a series of new curricula. As a result, beginning in the early 1960s, biology education increasingly recognized the central role of evolution in explaining life. Creationists objected, but the U.S. Supreme Court ruled in 1968 that laws banning the teaching of evolution were an unconstitutional establishment of religion.

Opponents of evolution education responded by developing a new version of creationism that omitted all mention of God and supernatural causation. New laws mandated that if public schools included evolution in the science curriculum they must provide "balanced treatment" by devoting equal attention to the new "scientific creationism." Those laws were struck down by federal courts, however, and ultimately in 1987 by the U.S. Supreme Court, which concluded that "scientific creationism" had no scientific basis and that balanced treatment laws thus served no purpose other than to promote Christianity.

Foes and skeptics of evolution now developed a new theory known as "intelligent design," which postulated that some biological systems are so "irreducibly complex" that they could not have evolved from simpler systems by a process of natural selection. Thus, they could only be the product of an intelligent designer. Although the intelligent designer was not identified as God, a federal court ruled in 2005 that intelligent design was no more scientific than earlier versions of creationism, and it became clear that efforts to mandate its inclusion in the curriculum were constitutionally doomed.

But efforts to undermine evolution education continue and, since the turn of the century, have been expanded to include attacks on teaching about climate change. New "academic freedom" laws recognized the right of individual teachers to discuss the "strengths and weaknesses" of evolution and alternative views, and extended this to multiple aspects of science deemed problematic, including climate science. The problem here is not that such laws protect the academic freedom of teachers but that they single out science and limit academic freedom to particular topics and theories. Teachers should be free to present the strengths and weaknesses of all ideas in all areas of study, and students should be encouraged to think critically in all their classes. Academic freedom does not permit a teacher to ignore an approved curriculum or to indoctrinate a captive audience of students in his or her religious or political views. It does, however, leave teachers free to present relevant arguments and alternatives and to promote critical thinking. As I will discuss in detail later in the chapter, academic freedom is for everyone engaged in teaching and learning. That certainly includes teaching and learning about the origin, history, current state, and potential futures of the Earth and its inhabitants. But it must include the rest of science as well, and the rest of education too.

It might be argued that science classes should simply require students to believe in evolution because this is simply a matter of believing the truth. Evolution is a well-established scientific theory with strong empirical support; the same cannot be said for any creationist alternative. Depending on exactly how we define science and what version of creationism we consider, creationist theories are either bad science (because they have been disconfirmed) or not science at all (because they make no testable predictions).

But science education is not a matter of instilling true or justified beliefs. Evolution education ought to be aimed at understanding evolution, including the evidence that supports it. This may be expected in most cases to lead to belief in evolution, because the evidence is so strong, but it is ultimately for students to determine what they believe. Although respect for reasons requires teachers to present a scientifically justifiable curriculum, respect for persons equally requires teachers to recognize the right of students to determine their own beliefs. Biology should be taught in a manner that respects all students, and their parents, regardless of their beliefs. Students should learn what scientists believe, and why, but the school cannot require them to change their own beliefs. Helping students understand evolutionary explanations, and the associated evidence, is fully consistent with respect for their ultimate right to believe as they will.

Education for rationality cannot require belief in evolution, climate change, or anything else. Coercing a student to believe something is indoctrination, even if the belief is true. We can require students to demonstrate understanding and, in some cases, can try to convince them to hold particular beliefs, but in the end it is for them to determine what to believe. Respect for reasons and persons requires an academically defensible curriculum but forbids us to undermine rational agency by coercing belief.

Education and Identity

These considerations of curriculum and instruction are relevant far beyond science education. In many domains, issues of indoctrination are deeply intertwined with issues of identity.

The teaching of history provides many such examples. In schools around the world, history is taught in large part with the purpose of creating patriotic citizens, which often means manipulating and framing what is taught so as to enhance nationalist identities and support for the current government and the ideologies of those in power (Moshman, 2009a, 2020). Most nations, for example, were founded in large part through processes of ethnic cleansing, including the elimination of indigenous groups with national identities of their own, but history education generally downplays, omits, or denies such uncomfortable aspects of nationhood (Moshman, 2007b, 2011b).

Many other areas of the curriculum are similarly compromised by ideological pressures and efforts to mold student identities. To the extent that the curriculum is not the outcome of academic decisions by teachers and other experts qualified and motivated to make such decisions, teaching and learning are distorted in ways that compromise student understanding and thus their capacity for rational decision-making. Even in the case of a problematic curriculum, there is some potential for rational agency and development if teachers and students are free to challenge the curriculum. All too often, however, both teachers and students understand the dangers of challenging curricular expectations on matters of ideology and identity.

Education may also be hindered by students harassing each other, often on the basis of ethnic, racial, religious, or political differences central to their identities. Such harassment undermines the mutual respect required for democratic deliberation, including argumentation among classmates. But school efforts to crack down on whatever they deem to be hate speech raise problems of their own, undermining the rights of belief and expression that are critical to argumentation (Moshman, 2009a, 2020).

Issues of intellectual freedom in education are not limited to elementary and secondary schools. Governmental, political, and religious pressures have compromised higher education for centuries, and continue to do so. Many of the current controversies relate to matters of social identity. Racial and ethnic minorities, political conservatives, supporters of Palestinian rights, and many others have claimed that their freedom of expression is restricted by a variety of institutional regulations and social pressures. Such concerns are often well justified, both within the academic context and on the campus at large (Lukianoff, 2014; Whittington, 2018).

Transforming Schools

Greater emphasis on peer argumentation, as discussed earlier in the chapter, has great potential for making instruction less indoctrinative by enhancing the role of students in their own learning. But student argumentation takes place within a larger context, which may greatly compromise it in two ways. First, if argumentation takes place within an indoctrinative curriculum it may fail to enhance rational agency. Second, control of speech by school officials, including teachers, may also undermine argumentation, even when it is intended to promote argumentation by enforcing civility.

Education for rationality requires a context of intellectual freedom. But the classroom is obviously not a forum for free speech by anyone on any topic. We need to look more seriously and rigorously at the nature and role of intellectual freedom in education, which requires a reconceptualization of academic freedom.

Intellectual Freedom in Education

As we have seen, what passes for education is often in large part a matter of indoctrination, especially in elementary and secondary education. This is inconsistent with the ideal of education for rationality, which requires an academic context of intellectual freedom in which rational agents can learn and develop.

Extending previous discussions about the role of intellectual freedom in collaborative reasoning (Chapter 5), deliberative democracy (Chapter 6), and the development of rational agency (Chapter 7), I now consider the central role of intellectual freedom in any educational institution or program aimed at the promotion of rationality. What we need to counter indoctrination in curriculum and instruction, I suggest, is a coherent and well-justified conception of academic freedom as the intellectual freedom to do academic work, including freedoms of teaching, learning, and inquiry (Moshman, 2009a, 2017). To the extent that an educational institution or program embraces academic freedom in this sense, it engages the rational agency of those involved and has the potential to promote better understanding and the further development of rational agency.

Academic Freedom as the Freedom to Do Academic Work

Academic freedom, I suggest, is best defined as the freedom to do academic work (Moshman, 2017). Academic work includes teaching, learning, and inquiry, all of which require intellectual freedom. Thus, academic freedom may be defined as intellectual freedom in academic contexts, including freedoms of teaching, learning, and inquiry (Moshman, 2009a).

Academic freedom, thus defined, is central to at least six distinct but overlapping traditions and literatures (Moshman, 2017). First, and most obvious, is the centuries-long tradition of academic freedom for college professors, which originated in European higher education and is represented in the United States in the policies of the American Association of University Professors (AAUP). In addition to freedoms of teaching and research, the literature in this tradition also addresses academic governance as the collective exercise of academic freedom (Finken & Post, 2009).

A second tradition addresses the intellectual freedom of college students, often as part of a larger concern with their individual rights and civil liberties. This literature usually encompasses students' intellectual freedom both within academic contexts (where I would call it academic freedom) and in their personal lives and political activities on campus and beyond (Lukianoff, 2014; Whittington, 2018).

A third tradition addresses intellectual freedom in elementary and/or secondary education. Restrictions on intellectual freedom at these levels are usually the result of community pressure, administrative action, and/or mandates from governing boards or legislatures, all of which typically infringe on the academic freedom of both teachers and students (Lent & Pipkin, 2013).

Fourth, legal and constitutional provisions may protect some aspects of academic freedom. In the United States, for example, First Amendment case law since the 1920s has provided some protection for intellectual freedom in public education, reaching a high point in the 1960s and 1970s and then declining as a result of decisions since the 1980s. Students and teachers have First Amendment rights as private individuals in their personal and political lives but generally cannot count on the First Amendment to protect their academic freedom (Driver, 2018; Moshman, 2009a; Ross, 2015).

Fifth, a great deal of academic work takes place in libraries or through access to their collections. This includes, but is not limited to, academic libraries. Librarians have been strong defenders of free access to information and ideas and have developed detailed policies to protect the intellectual freedom of their patrons and the integrity of their collections and operations (ALA Office for Intellectual Freedom, 2015).

Finally, many professional and disciplinary organizations have policies that explain and defend what they commonly call "intellectual freedom" in a variety of academic contexts. Topics addressed in these policies and related literatures include evolution, sexuality, morality, religion, and national histories (Moshman, 2009a).

The six traditions are largely isolated from each other, in part because they differ in focus and in part because they use different terminology. But they overlap in sharing a principled concern with the intellectual freedom of those who engage in academic work. Calling this *academic freedom* highlights that overlap and helps clarify its nature. Academic freedom is the intellectual freedom to teach, learn, or inquire in institutions devised for these purposes.

Academic Roles and Contexts

Education for rationality requires respect for the rational agency, and thus the academic freedom, of students. Such education is inconsistent with indoctrination, which aims to coerce rather than convince. Accordingly, teachers are responsible for identifying or preparing an academically justifiable curriculum and teaching it in academically justifiable ways that respect students' rational agency, and thus their academic freedom. The academic freedom of teachers with respect to curriculum and instruction is both justified and limited by their academic responsibility to respect and promote the rationality of their students, and thus their academic freedom. Academic freedom, then, protects the academic relation of teacher and student that distinguishes education from indoctrination. In addition to protecting the rights of individual teachers and students, academic freedom protects the process of education by orienting it toward rationality.

Academic work also includes inquiry, broadly defined to encompass everything from formal research intended for publication to informal processes of seeking, interpreting, and discussing information and ideas in order to reach justifiable conclusions. Freedom of inquiry is crucial not only to the pursuit and publication of formal research but also, as we have seen, to forms of student learning that engage students' rational agency and promote its further development.

It should be clear from this discussion that academic freedom is not just free speech for all. Neither classrooms nor scholarly journals are simply forums for freedom of expression. This is not to say that intellectual freedom is less important in academic contexts than in contexts of democratic deliberation. On the contrary, intellectual freedom is at least as crucial in academic contexts as in any other. But academic work requires a subtler conception of intellectual freedom that recognizes the aims of teaching, learning, and inquiry, and the crucial role of expertise (Post, 2012).

A classroom differs from a forum for free expression in at least three crucial ways. First, there is the identification of a teacher, who is deemed more expert than the students and has the responsibility and authority to organize the use of class time to achieve the academic goals of the course. Even when teachers allot time for student discussion, they frame and direct that discussion. Second, class sessions are generally devoted to specific topics within the broader topic of the course. Neither teachers nor students are free to talk about whatever they want. Finally, because academic work is concerned with knowledge, truth, and the promotion of rationality, it demands a focus on understanding and justification. Both students and teachers are expected to explain and justify their ideas and both may be evaluated on the quality of their explanations and justifications.

It is clear, then, that teachers may restrict student speech on the basis of its content in order to keep the class focused on the topic at hand. Moreover, they not only may but must discriminate on the basis of content in evaluating the quality of student work, assigning higher grades to students who show better understanding of important concepts and provide stronger justification of their ideas. Concern for intellectual freedom does not prevent teachers from giving students failing grades on the basis of what they say or write. In this respect, the classroom is neither a forum for free expression nor a deliberative democracy.

There is no academic reason, however, for discrimination on the basis of viewpoint. As discussed earlier in the chapter with respect to evolution education, students should be free to believe what they choose but may be evaluated on the basis of their understanding and their ability to justify their views. Intellectual freedom in academic contexts, then, is fully consistent with discrimination on the basis of the content of expression but not with discrimination on the basis of viewpoint. Viewpoint neutrality is crucial to intellectual freedom generally (Moshman, 2020) and to associated legal standards such as the First Amendment (Strossen, 2018). A standard of viewpoint neutrality shows respect for persons and reasons and furthers the promotion of rationality agency.

The standard of viewpoint neutrality applies equally with respect to research and publication. Respect for intellectual freedom is crucial to the academic integrity of a scholarly journal and of the field it represents, but no academic publication is a forum for free speech. Journals are limited to particular areas of study and only publish work that meets academic standards as determined by expert peer reviewers. Decisions about what to publish are not content neutral; they are based on the content of the submitted manuscript. Nevertheless, the process may be deemed a system of selection, rather than a regime of censorship, provided the selection process is viewpoint neutral. Ideally, manuscripts are rejected if they fail to justify their conclusions, regardless of viewpoint, and accepted for publication if they are found to meet academic standards, regardless of viewpoint. Authors may be required to justify conclusions reached in the manuscript and remove conclusions they cannot justify, but they should not be expected to remove viewpoints simply because reviewers deem those viewpoints false or offensive. Content discrimination is inherent in the process, but viewpoint discrimination would undermine the academic integrity of the journal.

Academic Freedom as Individual, Collective, and Institutional

Academic freedom is the freedom to do academic work, which is done by individuals, groups, and institutions. Thus, academic freedom is exercised individually, collectively, and institutionally. Education for rationality requires that students have the intellectual freedom to engage actively in learning through inquiry and argumentation. This requires that teachers have the academic freedom to teach an academically defensible curriculum in a non-indoctrinative manner. The academic freedom of teachers includes both the authority of individual teachers with respect to their own classes and the authority of the collective faculty to assure a coherent and defensible curriculum across a department or larger academic unit. The academic work of teachers and students, moreover, takes place within institutions which themselves require the academic freedom to conduct themselves in accord with academic norms of intellectual freedom.

When a college or school system resists political or religious pressures on the curriculum, for example, it is defending its academic freedom as an academic institution. But this doesn't mean administrators or governing boards control the curriculum. The academic institution must itself respect the academic freedom of its faculty and students, the collective faculty must respect the academic freedom of individual teachers and students, and individual teachers must respect the academic freedom of their students. Academic freedom is not a special power or privilege of some elite individual, group, or institution. It is a system of intellectual freedom that respects the rational agency of all involved in the academic enterprise and the goals of promoting the progress of knowledge and the rationality of students.

Academic freedom is thus central to the academic integrity of an academic institution. Intellectual freedom is what distinguishes education and research from indoctrination and propaganda. Without academic freedom, an academic institution is not really academic after all, and thus not what it claims to be.

Argumentation and Intellectual Freedom

In presenting her argumentation curriculum to teachers, Kuhn (2018b) noted that adults may be concerned about having young adolescents address controversial social and political issues in school. But the students, Kuhn observed, "are entirely comfortable and eager to talk about issues that they believe really matter" (p. 207). All that is needed, she has found, is an occasional reminder to criticize ideas, not people.

Higher education is sometimes singled out as special with respect to the need for intellectual freedom. There is no good reason, however, to distinguish secondary from higher education in this regard, and intellectual freedom is crucial to the construction of rational agency even in elementary schools (Chapter 7).

Even if students are comfortable and capable, however, their parents may fear the process of argumentation will somehow undermine their children's identities. A clear account of academic freedom that includes the right of students not to be indoctrinated may help convince them that they need not be threatened by a curriculum that gets their children thinking about matters they deem not debatable for reasons of ideology and identity.

The Rational Ideal

If the aim of education is to promote rationality, what outcomes would indicate we are succeeding? What would graduates ideally be like? I suggest here some aspects or components of what might be called the rational ideal. The rational ideal is not a state of maturity that everyone, or indeed anyone, fully achieves. It is an ideal intended to help orient our educational efforts. Its components include skills, knowledge, and values—some individual, some interpersonal, and some civic.

As discussed throughout this chapter, we cannot require students to adopt particular beliefs and values. Academically, this would stifle, rather than promote, rational agency. Morally, it would fail to respect students as persons (Siegel, 1988; Laats & Siegel, 2016). Requiring students to believe what we deem true and to value what we deem good is inconsistent with education for rationality, which requires respect for the rational agency of students.

Nevertheless, it is proper and important to have educational and developmental goals and to find productive and moral ways of maximizing progress toward them. With that in mind, drawing on discussion throughout the book, I sketch here some components of a rational ideal.

Skills

For a start, the ideal rational agent is good at reasoning, including logical, scientific, principled, and precedent-based reasoning. But we cannot promote rational agency by teaching children to make correct inferences. Young children already make correct inferences about a variety of logical, causal, moral, and social matters (Chapters 2–3). Progress toward the rational ideal requires the construction of self-regulatory abilities and epistemic cognition (Chapter 4).

Rational agents ideally participate rationally in groups (Chapter 5). But teachers cannot simply tell students what to do in groups. We enhance our ability to contribute to group rationality by engaging in actual argumentation with real peers about topics that matter to us in a context of intellectual freedom. Such experiences facilitate construction of the knowledge and values that support rational group functioning.

The rational ideal also includes rational agents reasoning collaboratively in contexts of deliberative democracy (Chapter 6). This includes practical skills, such as knowing where, when, and how to vote (Hart & Youniss, 2018). But the ideal member of an ideal society is a rational voter who also contributes to society in ways that go beyond voting. This requires developmental progress in civic knowledge and values.

Knowledge

The ideal rational agent understands both the inherent subjectivity of knowledge and the possibility of rational judgment despite this (Chapter 4). But we cannot promote rational agency by telling people what to believe about knowledge. Knowledge about knowledge is constructed in the course of inquiry and argumentation through processes of reflection and coordination (Chapter 7).

It would be impossible and counterproductive for anyone to rely entirely on the deliberate and reflective processes associated in dual process theories with System 2 (Chapter 1). Psychological functioning in daily life requires efficient heuristics and adaptive biases. Nevertheless, the ideal rational agent understands enough about dual processing to identify and address implicit biases, including social biases such as racism or sexism. In particular, the ideal rational agent recognizes and works to overcome the universal bias toward verification of one's beliefs and hypotheses (Chapters 5 and 6).

Rational agency ideally includes knowledge about the nature of identity and the role of identity commitments. We should not expect others to abandon their deeply-held views upon encountering ours, even if we have good reasons for our views. Ideal rational agents, however, may convince each other to modify their divergent views in ways that come closer to a justified consensus on at least some issues or considerations (Chapter 5). Regardless of their own ideologies and identities, ideal rational agents understand the dangers of dichotomization, dehumanization, and denial (Chapter 6).

Rational agents ideally show advanced understanding concerning the epistemologies of logic, science, morality, and social systems (Chapter 4). They coordinate these rigorously and effectively in reasoning about complex matters. They understand the nature and importance of expertise and its relation to democratic deliberation (Chapter 6).

Rational agents ideally understand the value of argumentation in seeking the truth. Ideal rational agents seek opportunities for collaborative reasoning (Chapter 5).

Finally, the ideal rational agent understands that the complexity of social problems makes strong disagreement virtually inevitable and resists the natural assumption that anyone with sharply differing views must be either ignorant or evil. Such understanding is critical to deliberative democracy (Chapter 6).

Values

The rational ideal is to value reasons and persons. We value reasons because respect for reasons is what makes us rational agents, which is how we choose to see ourselves. We value persons, at least in part, because it is persons that have reasons. In valuing reasons we value inquiry, argument, and expertise. In valuing persons, we value liberty, justice, and mutual respect. In valuing reasons and persons together, we highlight our rational agency.

The rational ideal is also to value truth (Moshman, 2015). Rationality can be merely instrumental, aimed at achieving whatever goals one might have. The rational ideal, however, is epistemic, valuing the truth for its own sake, expecting reasons for belief, and willing to question identity-defining beliefs for the sake of getting to the truth. As we saw earlier, theorists of critical thinking see active truth-seeking as fundamental to critical thinking in its "strong sense" (Paul, 1990) and to what Siegel (1988) calls the "critical spirit."

To be rational is also, ideally, to value rational agency. This includes valuing one's own rational agency. The rational ideal is a rationalist identity—a theory of oneself that highlights and takes pride in one's rational agency, construing this as central to one's personhood. The rational ideal also includes valuing the rational agency of others—seeing them as persons with whom one can engage in argumentation, sometimes as part of a larger deliberative democracy.

No one comes close to rational perfection, but we are all rational agents capable of making progress in rational agency, individually and collectively. We should value that too.

Conclusion

Education should aim to promote rational agency, keeping in mind an ideal rational agent not as a goal we expect to attain but as an ideal for which we strive. In the final chapter I aim to examine this ideal further, beginning by looking directly at its antithesis.

9

REASONS AND PERSONS

We live in a world of persons—of agents who have reasons for what they believe and do. Of course we also live in a physical and causal universe of objects, forces, and realities beyond our control. But we routinely see ourselves and each other as rational agents acting on the basis of reasons of our own, not simply caused to behave by physical, biological, psychological, or social forces. This world of reasons and persons would not exist without us, but it is nonetheless real to the extent that we make it real, and presumably consistent with the complex causal universe from which it emerges (Witherington, 2011).

The world of reasons and persons is the world of rationality, autonomy, personal identity, and moral responsibility (Korsgaard, 2009; Parfit, 1984). This is the world in which we have the opportunity to construct and promote our individual and collective rationality, rather than just believing whatever we happen to believe and doing whatever comes naturally (see Chapters 7 and 8). And this is the world in which we have the opportunity to create and maintain deliberation and democracy (see Chapters 5 and 6), rather than just be buffeted by social forces within our various groups and social systems.

The opposite of a world of reasons and persons is the world of the Borg. The Borg is a collective entity in the *Star Trek* universe that suppresses the individual personhood of those who compose it and those it assimilates. The prospect of the Borg is frightful, and not just in science fiction. We may ourselves be, or become, the Borg. In the first two sections of this chapter we confront the Borg and consider whether, as they never stop reminding us, resistance is futile. The remaining two sections of the chapter then consider, through a combination of history and science fiction, fundamental questions of who counts as a person and what counts as a reason.

Becoming the Borg

The Borg is a collective entity composed of biomechanical life forms with limited individual agency who arrive in huge cubic starships from a remote quadrant of the galaxy. The product of thousands of centuries of development, their powers are formidable. First seen in a 1989 episode of the television series *Star Trek: The Next Generation*, which takes place in 2365, the Borg played a major role in later episodes of that show and also in the subsequent series *Star Trek: Voyager*, the movie *Star Trek: First Contact*, and the 2020 series *Star Trek: Picard*.

We Borg

The Borg is a fearsome threat because it assimilates all societies and civilizations it encounters, incorporating diverse humanoid species and their knowledge and technologies in its ongoing program of self-improvement. "We are the Borg," they inform those they encounter. "You will be assimilated. Resistance is futile." This seems intended less as an effort to threaten or demoralize than as a simple statement of fact, which makes it all the more threatening and demoralizing.

Individual Borg drones are humanoid in appearance but with a variety of mechanical implants and attachments, typically including a mechanical eye and a mechanical arm. The transformation of individual humans and members of other sentient species into drones involves the injection of nanoprobes, microscopic robotic devices that take control at a cellular level and subsequently play a role in biological and mechanical maintenance and repair.

The standard Borg ship is a giant cube, highly decentralized, with no command center and extreme redundancy of functions. Like the Borg collective, it can remain functional even if much of it is destroyed. There are estimated to be millions of such ships, mostly in the distant Delta Quadrant, where the Borg originated and remain based as of the late 24th century. Borg ships can reach warp speeds exceeding those of Galaxy-class Federation starships, such the Enterprise, and have the power to destroy them. The Borg also maintain a network of transwarp corridors and hubs through which Borg ships achieve transwarp velocities that enable them to reach other regions of the galaxy, including Federation space (which includes Earth). Wherever they go, they assimilate entire species and civilizations.

Individual drones have no names. They are typically organized in small groups serving particular functions, with group members going by designations such as Third of Five or Seven of Nine. There is no group leader, nor does the group report to anyone in particular. Beyond the group level, the Borg are linked in a hive mind such that all individuals are in constant contact with all others, never alone with their own thoughts. They speak and act only on behalf of the collective. They have no beliefs or reasons of their own. When they announce that we will be assimilated, it's nothing personal. The progress of the Borg collective is all that matters for them and, they assume, for us.

Resistance is Futile

There is another sense to "We Borg." We ourselves may be the Borg. In the real world, I suggest, the threat is not that the Borg will arrive from a distant region of space and assimilate us, but that we ourselves are already the Borg, to a considerable extent, and naturally tend to become more so.

Have we already been assimilated? Is resistance indeed futile? As we will now see, a major theorist of dual processing has proposed that creating and maintaining a world of persons with reasons of their own requires active reflection on rationality.

"The Robot's Rebellion"

In *The Robot's Rebellion*, Keith Stanovich (2004) applied dual process theory to the question of respecting and maintaining our individuality in the face of something much like the Borg and its nanoprobes. Sticking to science, rather than science fiction, he addressed the fearsome threat of what he called "replicators," of which there are two types.

Genes and Memes

The first set of replicators are our genes. Their goal is to replicate themselves. They value us only to the extent that we serve that goal. They don't care about us as persons.

The second set of replicators are memes, units of cultural information. They too have no goal other than to replicate themselves. Such replication may have little relation to epistemic values of truth or justifiability. They just want to go viral. They don't care about reasons.

In considering the goals and values of our genes and memes, I hasten to add, I am speaking loosely and metaphorically, as if they had some degree of rational agency. Of course they don't. When I say that our genes and memes don't care about persons or reasons, I don't mean to suggest they care more about something else. What Stanovich (2004) wants us to keep in mind is that they don't care about anything. The robot's rebellion begins with understanding that our genes and memes are not rational agents and do not care about us as rational agents. To the extent that they direct our behavior, we are robots.

Stanovich's (2004) analysis seems to me somewhat reductionist (see Chapter 7) in its conception of the direct causal role of discrete genes and memes in determining behavior. His conception of our predicament, however, seems to me generally sound. We should not be robots in service to mindless genes and memes. We should not be part of the Borg. But we are, unless we rebel.

Metarationality

Is resistance futile? Stanovich (2004) does not think so. The possibility of rebellion lies in dual process theory. We may be robots, by which he means "vehicles designed for replicator propagation." But "we are the only robots who have discovered that we have interests that are separate from the interests of the replicators" (Stanovich, 2004, p. xii). The rebellion has two steps, corresponding to the two replicators.

The first step begins with the recognition that our interests as persons are not necessarily those of our genes. Our genes direct automatic processes that serve to replicate themselves. These processes compose System 1 of a generic dual process model, which can be seen as the genes keeping us on a short leash through automatic processes and intuitions. But System 2 allows us to conceptualize our own interests and to override our automatic impulses by thinking about how best to serve those interests.

The second step in the rebellion is to recognize that our thinking is infested with memes, the cultural baggage acquired from our societies precisely because of its ability to replicate itself, a process that does not depend on truth or justifiability. It is not enough to think instrumentally about how best to achieve what we take to be our goals given our current beliefs and values. We must engage in reasoning, taking truth as an ideal, requiring reasons from ourselves and others. That is, we must reflect critically on our beliefs and values, coordinating them in such a way as to achieve a broader and more stable equilibrium, a deeper level of justification. Humans, Stanovich (2004) insists, can and must "gain control of their lives in a way unique among lifeforms on Earth—by rational self-determination" (p. xiv).

This requires "meta-rationality" (Stanovich, 2004, p. 265). Rationality must critique and control itself. We must go beyond the instrumental rationality of serving what we take narrowly and without question to be our values, desires, and purposes. We need critical thinking in its strongest forms to achieve more advanced levels of equilibrium. In the words of economist and philosopher Amartya Sen (1999),

> It is the power of reason that allows us to consider our obligations and ideals as well as our interests and advantages. To deny this freedom of thought would amount to a severe constraint on the reach of our rationality.
>
> *(p. 272)*

We can't transcend our minds, one might think. But development, as we saw in Chapter 7, is an ongoing process of transcending our current mind through processes of reflection and coordination. Development beyond childhood is not automatic or inevitable, but progress in rational agency remains possible and, as argued in Chapter 8, should be the primary goal of education. The rebellion, it turns out, begins in early childhood and makes remarkable progress by the age of 12 or 13 years. The challenge is to keep it going.

"I, Borg"

In "I, Borg," a 1992 episode of *Star Trek: The Next Generation*, the Federation starship Enterprise, under the command of Captain Jean Luc Picard, responds to what seems to be a distress call from a nearby moon as they chart an unexplored star system. Commander William Riker, the first officer, beams down with security chief Worf and chief medical officer Beverly Crusher. They find that a small Borg starship has crashed, leaving four drones dead and the fifth unconscious and seriously injured.

Dr. Crusher insists on treating him, as she would anyone needing her medical assistance. Captain Picard is highly concerned because the Borg are known to retrieve lost drones, living or dead, but finally agrees to have the Borg drone beamed up to the Enterprise and isolated in a detention cell surrounded by a subspace damping field to prevent any communication between the drone and the collective. Dr. Crusher tends to him there, with help from chief engineer Geordi La Forge, who sets up the damping field and replaces the drone's damaged mechanical implants. Meanwhile, Picard, La Forge, and other crew members devise a plan to destroy the Borg collective from within by introducing into the drone an invasive program involving a topological anomaly that would spread through the collective after the drone is retrieved. Crusher is appalled by what she deems a plan for genocide, but the other senior staff believe the extraordinary threat posed by the Borg leaves no alternative.

The Borg drone finally regains consciousness and explores its cell, looking for an access terminal so it can interface with the collective. The search is unsuccessful, but Geordi La Forge later cautiously enters the cell to install a power conduit that will provide the energy the Borg uses for nourishment.

"We are Borg," the drone announces. "You will be assimilated. Resistance is futile."

When Geordi asks who "we" refers to, the drone simply repeats, "We are Borg." Geordi points out that the drone is alone and singular and asks if it has a name or means of identification. The drone responds, "Third of Five." Geordi remarks that the name does suit him.

In a later meeting with the Borg drone, Geordi introduces Dr. Crusher. When the drone asks what a doctor is, she replies that a doctor heals the sick and repairs the injured. The drone responds that the sick and injured are reabsorbed and others take their place. Dr. Crusher explains that she saved his life and, when he asks why, describes it as her duty.

The Borg drone asks Geordi his designation, leading Dr. Crusher to explain that they have names, not designations. The drone wonders about having a name and

Geordi asks if he wants one. They settle on "Hugh" and make introductions: "I'm Beverly." "I'm Geordi." "We are Hugh."

Shortly after, as Geordi examines Hugh's eyepiece, Hugh notes matter-of-factly that when they are assimilated they will have eyepieces too. Dr. Crusher responds that they don't want to be assimilated. Hugh remarks on how quiet it is, noting specifically the absence of other voices. He adds that on a Borg ship there are always thousands of voices because they all have each other's thoughts in their minds. Dr. Crusher suggests that Hugh is lonely.

Having second thoughts about the plan to use Hugh to destroy the Borg, Geordi goes to Ten Forward, the Enterprise bar, where he talks with the bartender Guinan, a recurring character played by Whoopi Goldberg. Guinan appears human but is actually an El-Aurian at least five centuries old. She is known for listening and is generally mild and nonjudgmental, but she has a history with the Borg, which virtually destroyed her people, leaving her among a remnant of survivors scattered around the galaxy. She had already cautioned Picard strongly that the Borg would come to find their lost drone and would assimilate or destroy the Enterprise. Now, hearing Geordi refer to the drone as Hugh, she is incredulous: "You *named* the Borg?"

Geordi insists she go talk to Hugh. When she responds that she has nothing to say, he suggests she listen. She resists, but later goes. Standing outside the detention cell and observing the drone through the force field, she remarks that he doesn't look so tough. "We are Borg," he says, adding, after some prodding from her about assimilation and resistance, that resistance is futile.

"Resistance is not futile," she replies, noting that her people resisted the Borg and some survived, albeit scattered and isolated. To her amazement, Hugh reflects on the possibility that resistance is not futile and then comments on her being lonely, adding, "We are also lonely."

Later, as the crew proceed with their plan, Geordi tells Hugh that they are studying him because the Federation is interested in learning about other species. Hugh responds, "We assimilate species. Then we know everything about them." Geordi explains that he and others do not wish to be assimilated because they value their individuality and sense of self. In response to Hugh's questions he acknowledges that individuation can be lonely and explains friendship. Hugh concludes that what he is describing is "like Geordi and Hugh."

In a subsequent discussion of the plan to destroy the Borg, Geordi tells Captain Picard of his reservations. Picard likens the drone to a laboratory animal and strongly suggests that Geordi "unattach." But later, Guinan shows up to urge Picard to meet with Hugh, arguing that he should at least look him in the eye before using "this person" to destroy his race. Picard interrupts: "It's not a person, dammit, it's a Borg."

Eventually, however, he does meet with Hugh. Drawing on his personal experience with the Borg, he successfully poses as a fellow member of the collective and states that the Enterprise and its culture will be assimilated. To Hugh's objection that they do not wish it, he responds that their wishes are irrelevant. To Hugh's observation that they will resist, Picard responds that resistance is futile. When Hugh replies that resistance is not futile and that some have escaped, Picard insists they will be found and assimilated, and when Hugh asks about Geordi, describing him as his friend, Picard responds that Geordi too will be assimilated and that Hugh must cooperate in the assimilation. "I will not," he says, and when Picard reminds him that he is Borg he replies, "No, I am Hugh."

Picard is taken aback by Hugh's rejection of Borg aims and astonished by his use of the first person. Having heard what he didn't want to hear, he concludes that the Enterprise cannot proceed with the plan to use Hugh as an instrument to destroy the Borg.

The senior staff meet to consider alternative options, which include erasing Hugh's memory of everything that happened on the Enterprise and then beaming him down to the moon to be found by the Borg. They decide instead to beam him down with his memory intact in the hope that his reconnection to the Borg will result in his new knowledge of self and sense of individuality spreading rapidly through the collective. But Dr. Crusher points out that he may not want to go. They agree that the choice is his.

Picard and Geordi explain to Hugh that it is up to him to choose whether to beam down and be retrieved by a Borg ship, which is approaching, or seek asylum and stay on the Enterprise. "Choose what I want," says Hugh in wonderment, trying to grasp the concept. He wants to stay with Geordi, whom he regards as his friend. But he knows the Borg will come for him, endangering Geordi and others. In what Stanovich (2004) would call meta-rationality, he recognizes his good reasons for wanting to stay but overrides them on the basis of further reflection, choosing to beam down despite what he wants. On the transporter pad about to beam down, he tells Captain Picard, "I do not want to forget that I am Hugh." At a loss for any response, Picard simply says "energize," instructing the transporter chief to beam Hugh down.

Subsequent episodes of *Next Generation* showed that Hugh's link to other Borg in his ship resulted in a spread of individuality that, at least initially, radically disrupted their collective functioning, with dire consequences for former drones unable to function as persons, many of whom fell under the spell of an unscrupulous leader. The long-term consequences of Borg individuality played a central role in the 2020 series *Picard*, which takes place decades later.

Is there hope for the Borg, or for us? To avoid becoming the Borg, or at least to be less like them, we must respect reasons and persons. But to do that we must address difficult issues of who counts as a person and what counts as a reason.

Who Counts as a Person?

Ancient Athens is properly lauded for its direct democracy and equal respect for all who participated, including equal opportunity to speak (Saxonhouse,

2006). It was simply a matter of common sense, however, that slaves and women did not count as persons entitled to equal respect or freedom of speech. Looking back now, almost everyone reading this book will probably consider it obvious that no one should be a slave and that women should count fully as persons. But the question of who counts as a person and in what sense remains fundamental to any social system. It is inconsistent with democracy for some persons to count more or less than others. All those who count as persons, at least in some full sense of personhood, must count equally. But who counts as a person?

"Standing Bear Becomes a Person"

I first learned of Standing Bear around 1980 when I read the chapter "Standing Bear Becomes a Person" in Dee Brown's (1970) classic *Bury My Heart at Wounded Knee: An Indian History of the American West* (see Starita, 2008, for a more comprehensive account). Wounded Knee was the South Dakota site of an 1890 massacre in which U.S. troops shot helpless members of a Minneconjou Lakota community of several hundred, killing most of them. It was far from the only such massacre. But in the expansion and consolidation of the United States, mass killing was not the only, or even the primary, means of genocide:

> From the late nineteenth century to the mid-twentieth century, the governments of the United States and Canada ran boarding schools for indigenous children from dozens of tribes (Adams, 1995; Churchill, 2004). The intent was to eliminate indigenous cultures by severing the link between generations and assimilating the children to American society. No one would be killed, in theory, but the indigenous cultures would disappear with the passing of the present generation.
>
> The students, accordingly, were isolated from their families and communities. They received "white man's" names to replace those by which they had been known. They were issued clothing appropriate for their gender in "civilized" society. Boys, often to their great dismay, had their long hair cut. They were required to learn English and forbidden to speak their native languages. Christian beliefs and middle-class values dominated the curriculum. History was taught as the progress of civilization in the Americas since 1492. Girls were trained in domestic skills and boys in agricultural and industrial skills so they could function in society.
>
> The motto was "Kill the Indian, save the man." Indian schools proudly illustrated their success with before-and-after photographs that showed young savages transformed into civilized Americans. The children were "saved." What was "killed" was the social identity that would otherwise have linked them to their childhoods and ancestral cultures.
>
> *(Moshman, 2011b, p. 925)*

In the era of genocidal massacres such as Wounded Knee, the boarding schools were supported by liberals as the more humane approach to what was seen as an inexorable historical process. The "vanishing" of the "Indian" was deemed inherent to the progress of civilization, a matter of "manifest destiny." The natives and their cultures would be assimilated. Resistance was futile.

But resistance was not always futile. The Ponca are a small tribe with a long history on land by the Niobrara River in what is now northeast Nebraska, near the South Dakota border. Their number dropped as low as 200 after a smallpox epidemic wiped most of them out in the winter of 1800–1801. Over the following decades they suffered many hardships, including repeated attacks by other tribes, until eventually they were informed that their land had been given away by the U.S. government in a treaty with a more troublesome tribe and were forced in 1877 to move to "Indian Country," in what is now Oklahoma, despite the strong objections of the Ponca chiefs, including Standing Bear. Many died along the way, especially children, as they walked 600 miles south over the course of two months, often in harsh weather, on what became known as the Ponca trail of tears. (The term "trail of tears" originated in connection with earlier removals of the Cherokee and other nations from the Southeastern U.S. to lands beyond the Mississippi.)

Within 18 months, a quarter of the tribe had perished, mostly of disease in what the Ponca called "the Warm Country." Acceding to his teenage son's dying wish, Standing Bear promised to bury his bones back by the Niobrara. The other chiefs thought the trip back beyond the capability of the surviving Ponca, but Standing Bear set off with 30 men, women, and children and returned to Nebraska, in another harrowing trip. There, he and his people were apprehended by the U.S. military under the command of General George Crook, who had orders to return them to Indian Country.

General Crook, based at Fort Omaha, was responsible for the Department of the Platte, a region stretching from Nebraska west to Montana, north to Canada, and south to Texas. He was the veteran of more than two decades of military campaigns against western tribes, and had long seen the natives and their ways as a primitive roadblock to the progress of civilization.

> But in recent years, he had grown weary of the broken treaties, the unprovoked massacres of women and children, the corruption in Washington, the moral bankruptcy of the reservation agents. And after more and more contact . . ., [h]e began to see the Indian as a person whose beliefs and culture had sustained him for centuries, someone who could not be forced to adopt radically new values and traditions in a few short years.
>
> *(Starita, 2008, p. 118)*

Crook would follow his orders if he had to, but he did not wish to. He contacted Thomas Henry Tibbles, assistant editor of the *Omaha Daily Herald*, who interviewed Standing Bear and wrote extensively about the plight of the Ponca, leading to an upsurge in popular sympathy and national publicity. Tibbles also recognized the possibility of a lawsuit based on the 14th Amendment and convinced two of Omaha's top lawyers to take the case pro bono (without pay). One, John Lee Webster, was an expert on constitutional matters. The other, Andrew Jackson Poppleton, was general counsel of the Union Pacific Railroad and later the first president of the Nebraska Bar Association. Meanwhile, General Crook, still sitting on his orders to get the Ponca to Indian Country, could only delay so long. Apparently at his suggestion, Standing Bear's attorneys sought a writ of habeas corpus from Judge Elmer Dundy requiring General Crook to bring Standing Bear to court and respond to Standing Bear's charge that he was unlawfully detained.

Dundy issued the writ and the trial took place in May 1879. After the lawyers for Standing Bear and for the government had completed their arguments, Judge Dundy announced that Standing Bear had requested permission to make a closing statement and, though this was unprecedented, he had granted the request. Standing Bear faced the audience, holding out his arm, and then turned to the judge (assisted by a translator):

> That hand is not the color of yours, but if I pierce it, I shall feel pain. If you pierce your hand, you also feel pain. The blood that will flow from mine will be of the same color as yours. I am a man. The same God made us both.
>
> *(Starita, 2008, p. 151)*

Turning back to the audience, Standing Bear went on to tell a story of standing with his wife and little girl on the bank of a wide and impassable river, its waters rising rapidly, with cliffs all around, and finally, scanning the cliffs in desperation, spotting a steep, rocky path to safety. But as they climb the path, waters rushing in behind them,

> a man bars the passage. . . . If he says that I cannot pass, I cannot. The long struggle will have been in vain. My wife and child and I must return and sink beneath the flood. We are weak and faint and sick. I cannot fight.

Turning again to face the judge, he added, "You are that man" (Starita, 2008, p. 151).

There was silence in the court. The judge struggled to maintain his composure. Some women in the back could be heard weeping. General Crook leaned forward on the table, his head in his hands. Then he stood up, walked across the courtroom, and shook Standing Bear's hand.

Ten days later, Judge Dundy released his detailed ruling. He noted that if sympathy were decisive he would have ruled for Standing Bear immediately after the closing arguments. But the case must be decided on the basis of law, and given the state of the law, the ruling did not challenge governmental authority over tribes. It implicitly accepted without question that, for Indians, the only alternatives to mass killing were (1) ethnic cleansing by the removal of tribes to reservations or Indian Country or (2) the assimilation of individuals into American life. Drawing on arguments from Standing Bear's attorneys, he carefully responded point by point to the government's legal arguments. There were two key aspects to the ruling.

First, Dundy rejected the government's argument that the writ of habeas corpus was illegitimate because Standing Bear was not a citizen. Careful examination of the law made it clear that any person, regardless of citizenship, could file for a writ of habeas corpus. Was Standing Bear a person? Dundy quoted from Webster's dictionary a definition of a person as, "a living soul; a self conscious being; a moral agent; especially a living human being; a man, woman, or child; an individual of the human race" (Starita, 2008, p. 155). He found this definition satisfactory for legal purposes and concluded that an Indian is a person and that the writ was thus proper.

Second, without questioning governmental authority over native tribes, Dundy argued that the law supported Standing Bear's case that natives can expatriate from their tribes and the facts of the case showed that he had done so and had a history of farming, educating his children, and living a praiseworthy American life. Thus, he was protected by the Fourteenth Amendment to the U.S. Constitution, adopted in 1868, three years after the Civil War, the first section of which reads:

> All persons born or naturalized in the United States, and subject to the jurisdiction thereof, are citizens of the United States and of the state wherein they reside. No state shall make or enforce any law which shall abridge the privileges or immunities of citizens of the United States; nor shall any state deprive any person of life, liberty, or property, without due process of law; nor deny to any person within its jurisdiction the equal protection of the laws.

The interpretation of the 14th Amendment was and remains a matter of considerable uncertainty and dispute, but Judge Dunby concluded that there was no valid legal basis for Standing Bear's imprisonment and ordered his release. He and other Ponca eventually returned to their homelands, though not without further difficulties. After much deliberation, the government decided not to pursue an appeal, worried that the U.S. Supreme Court might uphold the decision and set a national precedent that would undermine its Indian policy. Psychologically, Standing Bear had already been a rational agent, and thus a person. Now he was a person in the eyes of the law, with a right to choose for himself.

"The Measure of a Man"

Nearly five centuries later, in 2365, the starship Enterprise arrives at Starbase 173, a new outpost of the United Federation of Planets (in "The Measure of a Man," a

1989 episode of *Star Trek: The Next Generation*). Commander Bruce Maddox, an expert on robotics, comes aboard and takes immediate notice of Lt. Commander Data, an android who serves as a senior officer, who likewise takes notice of Maddox. Maddox explains to Captain Picard that he evaluated Data's application to Starfleet Academy, and Data adds that Maddox cast the sole vote against his admission on grounds that he was not a "sentient being."

Maddox explains that he has made it his life's work to understand Data, who was created by an eccentric genius in work that has never been replicated, and is close to a breakthrough that will enable the production of multiple androids like Data. The next step in his research requires him to "disassemble" Data, which will include downloading the memories from his positronic brain to the Starbase 173 computer. Mr. Data, who has devoted substantial effort to studying himself, is initially intrigued. After questioning Maddox about technical specifics, however, he concludes that Maddox lacks the knowledge to carry out the procedures safely and successfully. Picard tells Maddox he cannot permit the research.

Maddox responds with a step that he says he had hoped would not be necessary. He produces Starfleet orders transferring Data from the Enterprise to Starbase 173, where he would be under Maddox's command. Data later informs Picard that he will not submit to the procedure. Looking for legal options, Picard consults Captain Philippa Louvois, who has been appointed to set up and head the new Judge Advocate General's office for the sector. She says Mr. Data can refuse to undergo the procedure, but the transfer cannot be stopped. Picard worries that once Maddox is in charge of Data he will do whatever he wants. Is there no other option? There is always an option, responds Louvois. Data can resign.

Data promptly resigns from Starfleet. He describes himself to Maddox as "the culmination of one man's dream," an addition to "the substance of the universe." "If by your experiments I am destroyed," he explains, "something unique, something wonderful will be lost. I cannot permit that."

At a subsequent meeting with Louvois and Picard, Maddox dismisses Picard's concern about Mr. Data's rights as a sentimental reaction to Data's human appearance. "If it were a box on wheels," he insists, he would not be facing this opposition, asking them to imagine a future in which every ship in Starfleet has a Data on board. He argues that Data cannot resign because he is not a person. He is the property of Starfleet. He cannot refuse the procedure any more than the ship's computer can refuse a refit.

After looking into the matter, Captain Louvois rules that the law supports Maddox's position. Pressed by Picard, she tells him that if he challenges the decision she must arrange a hearing but reminds him that she does not yet have sufficient legal staff to conduct the hearing. When Picard insists there must be regulations to cover the situation, she replies that there are. Mr. Data may appeal, she will serve as judge, Picard will represent him, and Commander Riker, the next-ranking officer, will make the case against him. Riker protests that he cannot do so because Data is his comrade and he regards him as a friend, but the judge threatens that she will dismiss the appeal if he declines the role or does not take it seriously.

Riker prepares for the hearing by studying Data's technical schematics. As the hearing begins, he calls Data to the stand and demonstrates that Data is a machine, questioning him about his storage and processing capacity, illustrating his great strength. He removes Data's hand and shows it to the judge. Finally, based on his technical research, he does something few knew was even possible. Reaching behind Mr. Data, he turns him off.

The demonstration is stunning, and Picard requests a recess. He goes to Ten Forward, where Guinan tends bar, to express his dismay about the case. Guinan notes that if Maddox somehow succeeds in creating a multitude of Datas they would all be very valuable, adding, "and now he's been ruled the property of Starfleet. That should increase his value." How so, asks Picard. Guinan responds that there have been disposable people in the history of many worlds who do the dirty work that no one else wants to do because it is too difficult or too hazardous. No one need think about the welfare of such people or worry about how they feel. The replication of Data, now that he is Starfleet property, would create whole generations of disposable people. "You're talking about slavery," says Picard, to which Guinan responds in her usual mild manner that this characterization seems a bit harsh.

But Captain Picard does not think this is too harsh, and when the trial resumes he acknowledges immediately that Data is a machine, as are we all, though of different types, and calls him to the witness stand. He asks Data about several items he packed after resigning. Why did he pack a display of his medals? What purpose do they serve? Data responds that he just wanted them, wondering, "Is that vanity?" Asked about a book Picard gave him, he says he values it as a reminder of friendship and service. Finally, there is a holocube of Tasha Yar, an Enterprise security chief who died dramatically in a previous episode. At first Data declines to discuss it, explaining only "I gave my word." Picard convinces him Tasha would have wanted him to speak under these circumstances. Data finally says she was "special" to him, adding, "we were intimate."

Picard now calls Commander Maddox to the stand and questions him about the criteria that must be met to qualify as a "sentient being" and thus a person with rights. Maddox refers to intelligence, self-awareness, and consciousness. Picard challenges Maddox to prove to the court that he, Picard, is sentient. Maddox scoffs. Picard asks whether Data is intelligent. Maddox acknowledges that Data is intelligent in that "it" is capable of learning, understanding, and coping with new situations. And self-awareness?

Picard asks Data what he is doing. "I am taking part in a legal hearing to determine my rights and my status," replies Data. "Am I a person or property?" And what is at stake? "My right to choose, perhaps my very life." Data is clearly intelligent and self-aware, concludes Picard, meeting two of Maddox's three criteria. And consciousness? How does anyone know Data lacks whatever that is?

But Maddox insists his research on Data is crucial so that he can "learn from it and construct more." How many more? "As many as are needed," responds Maddox, suggesting the number could be in the hundreds, even in the thousands. A single Data is a curiosity, says Picard, maybe even a wonder, "but thousands of Datas, isn't that becoming a race? And won't we be judged by how we treat that race?" Reminding the court that Starfleet was founded to seek out new life, he concludes: "Well there it sits, waiting."

"It sits there looking at me," says the judge after a moment of uncertainty, "and I don't know what it is." She complains that she is not competent to address matters of metaphysics or questions best left to saints and philosophers, but accepts that she must make a ruling. Data is a machine, she grants, but he is not the property of Starfleet. The basic issue, which she suggests everyone has been dancing around, is whether Data has a soul, adding that she doesn't know whether he does or whether she herself has one. "But I have got to give him the freedom to explore that question himself. It is the ruling of this court that Lieutenant Commander Data has the freedom to choose."

Mr. Data promptly chooses not to undergo Maddox's procedure but urges him to continue his research, which he still finds intriguing. "He is remarkable," says Maddox after Data leaves. "You didn't call him 'it,'" observes the judge.

Riker stays away from the later celebration as Mr. Data resumes his position as an officer on the Enterprise. Data seeks him out and Riker explains he wouldn't feel welcome because he argued so strongly against Data. But Data already knows Riker did that so the appeal would not be summarily dismissed. "That action injured you and saved me," he says. "I will not forget it." Commander Riker calls him a wise man. "Not yet, sir" replies Mr. Data, "but with your help, I am learning."

What Counts as a Reason?

Respect for reasons is crucial to argumentation and lies at the heart of rational belief and action, and thus of personhood. But does respect for persons and reasons mean we must accept all beliefs and actions as equally justified and all reasons as equally strong? Is knowledge simply a matter of perspective? Is truth ultimately relative to our various cultural, political, and religious worldviews? Are there many truths, or none at all? Are we now, as many have suggested, in a "post-truth" universe of "alternative facts"? Such questions were central to the discussion of epistemic cognition and development in Chapter 4, in which I argued on the basis of extensive evidence that radical subjectivism is not the last word, developmentally or epistemologically (see also Moshman, 2015). For another approach to these questions, I go back to a 1968 episode of the original *Star Trek*.

In "For the World is Hollow and I Have Touched the Sky," the starship Enterprise encounters an isolated asteroid 200 miles in diameter. Analysis shows that it is moving on an independent course, at sub-light speed, correcting for gravitational forces. It is composed, moreover, of a hollow outer shell and breathable air within. Further analysis of the asteroid's trajectory shows more: It is on course to collide in 396 days with a planet inhabited by over 3 billion people.

Captain Kirk, Mr. Spock, and Dr. McCoy beam inside to investigate. The asteroid turns out to be a multigenerational ship that has been en route for at least 10,000 years. Its current inhabitants, however, many generations removed from those who initially populated the huge ship, believe themselves to be on a planet called Yonada. The three officers meet "the High Priestess of the People." This being classic *Star Trek*, she is young, beautiful, scantily clad, and, it soon turns out, ready for love. She introduces them to "the Oracle of the People," the source of all knowledge about the will of "the creators."

Later, Spock reminds Kirk of the prime directive, which forbids interference with other cultures. Kirk concludes, however, that the prime directive is overridden in this case by the clear and present danger of planetary collision.

Suddenly, an old man, who has apparently sought them out, observes that they are not of Yonada. "No, we're from outside your world," replies Kirk. The old man asks where that is. "Up there," replies Kirk, "outside, up there, everywhere." The man nods, knowingly. Many years ago, he tells them, he climbed the mountains, which is strictly forbidden. "Things are not as they teach us," he laments, "for the world is hollow and I have touched the sky." Then he drops dead before them. The Oracle has formidable powers.

Meanwhile, the High Priestess has been falling in love with McCoy, much to his (and perhaps Kirk's) surprise. But she remains serious about her responsibilities to her people, which include enforcing the truth of the creators as revealed by the Oracle. Sacrilege is punishable by death. "I hope you men of space, of other worlds, hold truth as dear as we do," she says to McCoy. "We do," he replies.

While McCoy dallies with the High Priestess, Kirk and Spock try to determine how to adjust the course of the asteroid ship but are repulsed by the Oracle and barely escape with their lives. In the end, armed with nothing but the truth, Kirk confronts the High Priestess. "Now listen to me," he demands repeatedly, insisting she hear what she vehemently rejects as "your truth of your world." What she and her people have believed, he maintains, is false. Yonada is a giant spaceship that has gone perilously off course. The High Priestess listens but seemingly still rejects it all. "Why should the truth be kept from us? Why should the creators keep us in darkness?"

The episode reaches its epistemic climax as she abruptly runs off to consult the Oracle, which immediately accuses her of having listened to the words of the nonbelievers. "They said they spoke the truth," says the High Priestess, but the Oracle dismisses whatever they said as "their truth." In response to her suggestion that truth is "truth for all," the Oracle maintains there can be no other truth for her than "the truth of Yonada," which is her truth. But this no longer satisfies her. "I must know the truth of the world," she insists.

In the end, Spock and Kirk correct the flaw in the ship's control system and get it back on course for the planet it was meant to reach. McCoy asks the High Priestess to return to the Enterprise with him. But despite her love for him and her new knowledge of the world, she remains with her people, explaining that she understands the great purpose of the creators and will honor it.

This episode strongly rejects epistemological relativism. We all have our own ideas, but we don't have our own truths. The prime directive requires respect for other cultures but it does not render all their beliefs correct. Group beliefs can be wrong, and ignorance can be deadly. We should all seek "the truth of the world."

I'm pretty sure the eight billion people of Earth are not living inside an asteroid, but we may well be on course toward disaster. We can't count on Captain Kirk and Mr. Spock to come back in time and beam down to set us right. Our only hope is to enhance our own rational functioning, individually and collectively.

Conclusion

We live in a world of reasons and persons, but only if we choose to do so. We are also the Borg, except to the extent that we choose to be something more. We are vehicles for genes and memes, except to the extent that we choose to value ourselves as individual persons. We become and remain rational agents to the extent that we exercise and reflect on our rational agency, individually and collectively.

We will not achieve a utopia of justification, truth, justice, and democracy, but we have the psychological competence to make real progress toward such ideals and to maintain them at a high level. But this requires that we work together, which requires mutual respect. Without respect for persons, respect for reasons cannot be fully realized.

But we cannot just get together in groups and work things out. We must devise and respect institutions that make collaborative reasoning possible and that direct our argumentation toward truth and rational decision making. The ideal social institution, the sort of group or society within which rational and epistemic ideals are best realized, is deliberative democracy. The corresponding educational ideal is the promotion of rational agency, which requires a focus on the developmental construction of knowledge and reasoning under conditions of intellectual freedom.

The Borg have already arrived, but resistance is not futile.

GLOSSARY

Academic freedom	The intellectual freedom to do academic work, including teaching, learning, and inquiry.
Agent	An actor or subject; one who acts or knows.
Agent, rational	One who believes or acts on the basis of reasons, preferably good reasons.
Argument	A justification, especially a complex one.
Argumentation	A social process of rational debate or collaborative reasoning.
Belief	Roughly, acceptance of a proposition as true.
Cognition	Knowledge and associated inferential processes, including perception, representation, conceptualization, interpretation, memory, thinking, and reasoning.
Constructivism	A theoretical perspective emphasizing the active role of the organism in the construction of knowledge.
Coordination	A process of developmental change involving structural integration and reorganization.
Deductive reasoning	Logical reasoning in the strict sense of reaching only logically necessary conclusions.
Dehumanization	A process in which those categorized as other come to be seen as less than persons.
Democracy, deliberative	A form of liberal democracy that takes as its ideal the achievement of consensus through rational processes of argumentation.

Democracy, liberal	A social system based on equal respect for all persons.
Denial	Rejection of the truth, especially to maintain one's moral identity.
Development	A type or pattern of change that is extended, self-regulated, qualitative, and progressive.
Dichotomization	A process by which the multidimensional complexity of social identity is reduced to two categories.
Domain, cognitive	A broad field or topic of knowledge that may or may not correspond to an academic discipline.
Domain, epistemic	A cognitive domain with a distinct epistemology, including a distinct conception of justification and/or truth and a correspondingly distinct form of prototypical reasoning.
Dual process theory	A theory of thinking or reasoning that distinguishes (a) automatic and/or intuitive processes from (b) deliberate and/or reflective processes.
Empiricism	A conception of development that highlights learning from the environment.
Epistemic cognition	Knowledge about matters of epistemology—that is, knowledge about the justification and truth of beliefs.
Epistemic development	The development of epistemic cognition.
Epistemic domain	A cognitive domain with a distinct epistemology, including a distinct conception of justification and/or truth and a correspondingly distinct form of prototypical reasoning.
Epistemology	The study of knowledge, especially with regard to normative matters of justification and truth.
Hypothetico-deductive reasoning	Deductive reasoning from premises deemed to be hypothetical or false.
Identity	An explicit theory of oneself as a person.
Identity, moral	An explicit theory of oneself as a moral person.
Identity, rational	An explicit and justifiable theory of oneself as a person.
Identity, rationalist	An explicit theory of oneself that highlights and values one's rationality.
Inference	Going beyond the data.
Intellectual freedom	Freedoms of belief, expression, discussion, inquiry, and access to information and ideas.

Justification	A reason for belief or action, especially as offered in a context of argumentation.
Knowledge	Roughly, justified true belief.
Logic	Strict norms of good reasoning, especially rules of deductive necessity.
Logical necessity	Truth based on logical proof rather than empirical evidence.
Logical reasoning	Reasoning in accord with norms of logic.
Metacognition	Cognition about cognition, including (a) conceptual knowledge about knowledge and inference and (b) procedural knowledge implicit in cognitive self-regulation.
Metalogical understanding	Explicit or theoretical knowledge about logic.
Metasubjective objectivity	Progress in objectivity through (subjective) reflection on and reconstruction of one's subjectivity.
Metasubjectivity	Knowledge about or reflection on subjectivity.
Moral epistemology	A theory concerning the justification and truth of moral beliefs and the corresponding rationality of moral action.
Moral identity	An explicit theory of oneself as a moral person.
Morality	Respect or concern for the rights or welfare of others.
Nativism	A conception of development that highlights the direct causal role of genes.
Norm	A rule, principle, or ideal against which action, inference, belief, or reality can be evaluated.
Normative	Referring to norms, and thus to what ought to be.
Objectivism	An epistemology that holds there to be ultimate truths that are directly observable, provable, or known to infallible authorities.
Objectivity	Truth in relation to reality regardless of subjective perspective.
Peer interaction	Reciprocal social interaction of rational agents who are, and perceive themselves to be, equal in authority, status, and power.
Person	At minimum, a rational agent.
Perspective	A (subjective) orientation or point of view.
Perspective taking	Seeing from perspectives other than one's own.
Precedent	A judgment that is (to some degree) binding on future judgments in analogous cases.

Precedent-based reasoning	Reasoning on the basis of precedents.
Principle	An abstract norm whose application to cases requires rational judgment rather than strict imposition of a concrete rule.
Principled reasoning	Reasoning on the basis of explicit principles, especially moral principles.
Progressive change	Change that can be normatively judged to make progress toward maturity, rationality, or some other justifiable end.
Qualitative change	Change in kind, not just amount.
Rational	Minimally, acting on the basis of reasons. More stringently, having good reasons for one's beliefs and actions.
Rational agency	The competence to believe or act on the basis of reasons.
Rational agent	One who believes or acts on the basis of reasons, preferably good reasons.
Rational constructivism	A form of constructivism in which organisms are seen as rational agents making developmental progress.
Rational identity	An explicit and justifiable theory of oneself as a person.
Rationalism	A postsubjectivist epistemology in which reasons short of proof provide bases for beliefs and actions.
Rationalist identity	An explicit theory of oneself that highlights and values one's rationality.
Rationality	The quality of having reasons, especially good reasons.
Reason	A rational basis, and potential justification, for belief or action.
Reasoning	Epistemologically self-regulated thinking—that is, forms of thinking, such as argumentation, that are aimed at reaching justifiable and/or true conclusions.
Reasoning, deductive	Logical reasoning in the strict sense of reaching only logically necessary conclusions.
Reasoning, hypothetico-deductive	Deductive reasoning from premises deemed to be hypothetical or false.
Reasoning, logical	Reasoning in accord with norms of logic.
Reasoning, precedent-based	Reasoning on the basis of precedents.

Reasoning, principled	Reasoning on the basis of explicit principles, especially moral principles.
Reasoning, scientific	Reasoning aimed at empirical justification and truth.
Reflection	A metacognitive process of consciousness and developmental change.
Science	Empirical study and theoretical explanation of the world.
Scientific reasoning	Reasoning aimed at empirical justification and truth.
Self-regulated change	Change that is directed or regulated from within.
Social convention	A norm of behavior binding only within a particular social system.
Subjectivism	An epistemology in which knowledge is seen as constructed from, and thus determined by, one's point of view.
Subjectivity	Perspective or point of view, involving the contribution of mind to knowledge.
Theory	A structure of knowledge that organizes and explains some domain or set of facts.
Thinking	The deliberate application and coordination of one's inferences to serve one's purposes, including problem solving, decision making, judgment, planning, and various forms of reasoning.
Third-party perspective taking	Seeing one's reciprocal relation to another person from the (meta)perspective of a real or hypothetical third party.
Truth	Objectivity, as a matter of concrete fact or epistemic ideal.
Understanding	Theoretical knowledge.
Verification bias	A natural tendency to seek and attend to evidence supporting one's beliefs and hypotheses.

REFERENCES

Adams, D. W. (1995). *Education for extinction: American Indians and the boarding school experience, 1875–1928*. Lawrence: University of Kansas Press.

Aikin, S. F., & Talisse, R. B. (2019). *Why we argue (and how we should): A guide to political disagreement in an age of unreason* (2nd ed.). New York: Routledge.

ALA Office for Intellectual Freedom. (2015). *Intellectual freedom manual* (9th ed.). Chicago: American Library Association.

Allen, J. W. P., & Bickhard, M. H. (2018). Stage fright: Internal reflection as a domain general enabling constraint on the emergence of explicit thought. *Cognitive Development, 45*, 77–91.

Amar, A. R. (2012). *America's unwritten constitution: The precedents and principles we live by*. New York: Basic Books.

Amsel, E., Klaczynski, P. A., Johnston, A., Bench, S., Close, J., Sadler, E., & Walker, R. (2008). A dual-process account of the development of scientific reasoning: The nature and development of metacognitive intercession skills. *Cognitive Development, 23*, 452–471.

Appiah, K. A. (2005). *The ethics of identity*. Princeton, NJ: Princeton University Press.

Appiah, K. A. (2017). *As if: Idealization and ideals*. Cambridge, MA: Harvard University Press.

Appiah, K. A. (2018). *The lies that bind: Rethinking identity*. New York: Norton.

Ash, T. G. (2016). *Free speech: Ten principles for a connected world*. New Haven, CT: Yale University Press.

Augustinova, M. (2008). Falsification cueing in collective reasoning: Example of the Wason selection task. *European Journal of Social Psychology, 38*, 770–785.

Bächtiger, A., Dryzek, J. S., Mansbridge, J., & Warren, M. E. (2018a). Deliberative democracy: An introduction. In A. Bächtiger, J. S. Dryzek, J. Mansbridge, & M. E. Warren (Eds.). *The Oxford handbook of deliberative democracy* (pp. 1–31). New York: Oxford University Press.

Bächtiger, A., Dryzek, J. S., Mansbridge, J., & Warren, M. E. (Eds.). (2018b). *The Oxford handbook of deliberative democracy*. New York: Oxford University Press.

Bächtiger, A., & Wegmann, A. (2014). "Scaling up" deliberation. In S. Elstub & P. McLaverty (Eds.), *Deliberative democracy: Issues and cases* (pp. 118–135). Edinburgh: Edinburgh University Press.

Baillon, A., Bleichrodt, H., Liu, N., & Wakker, P. P. (2016). Group decision rules and group rationality under risk. *Journal of Risk and Uncertainty, 52*, 99–116.
Baldwin, J. M. (1895). *Mental development in the child and the race*. New York: Macmillan.
Bardon, A. (2020). *The truth about denial: Bias and self-deception in science, politics, and religion*. New York: Oxford University Press.
Barrouillet, P., & Gaillard, V. (Eds.). (2011). *Cognitive development and working memory: A dialogue between neo-Piagetian theories and cognitive approaches*. New York: Psychology Press.
Barrouillet, P., & Gauffroy, C. (2013). Dual processes and mental models in the development of conditional reasoning. In P. Barrouillet & C. Gauffroy (Eds.), *The development of thinking and reasoning* (pp. 95–121). New York: Psychology Press.
Bearison, D. J., & Dorval, B. (2002). *Collaborative cognition: Children negotiating ways of knowing*. Westport, CT: Ablex.
Bloom, P. (2013). *Just Babies: The origins of good and evil*. New York: Crown.
Bloom, P. (2016). *Against empathy: The case for rational compassion*. New York: HarperCollins.
Boyes, M. C., & Chandler, M. (1992). Cognitive development, epistemic doubt, and identity formation in adolescence. *Journal of Youth and Adolescence, 21*, 737–763.
Braine, M. D. S., & O'Brien, D. P. (Eds.). (1998). *Mental logic*. Mahwah, NJ: Erlbaum.
Brown, A. L. (1978). Knowing when, where, and how to remember: A problem in metacognition. In R. Glaser (Ed.), *Advances in instructional psychology*. New York: Halsted Press.
Brown, D. (1970). *Bury my heart at Wounded Knee: An Indian history of the American West*. New York: Bantam.
Brown, M. B. (2014). Expertise and deliberative democracy. In S. Elstub & P. McLaverty (Eds.), *Deliberative democracy: Issues and cases* (pp. 50–68). Edinburgh: Edinburgh University Press.
Bryant, P. E., & Trabasso, T. R. (1971). Transitive inferences and memory in young children. *Nature, 232*, 456–458.
Callan, E., & Arena, D. (2009). Indoctrination. In H. Siegel (Ed.), *Oxford handbook of philosophy of education* (pp. 104–121). Oxford, UK: Oxford University Press.
Campbell, R. L., & Bickhard, M. H. (1986). *Knowing levels and developmental stages*. Basel, Switzerland: Karger.
Carey, S., & Smith, C. (1993). On understanding the nature of scientific knowledge. *Educational Psychologist, 28*, 235–251.
Carpendale, J. I. M., & Chandler, M. J. (1996). On the distinction between false belief understanding and subscribing to an interpretive theory of mind. *Child Development, 67*, 1686–1706.
Cauley, K. M. (1992). Children's construction of the logic of arithmetic. *Journal of Applied Developmental Psychology, 13*, 65–74.
Cesana-Arlotti, N., Martín, A., Téglás, E., Vorobyova, L., Cetnarski, R., & Bonatti, L. L. (2018). Precursors of logical reasoning in preverbal human infants. *Science, 359*, 1263–1266.
Chandler, M. J. (1975). Relativism and the problem of epistemological loneliness. *Human Development, 18*, 171–180.
Chandler, M. J. (1987). The Othello effect: Essay on the emergence and eclipse of skeptical doubt. *Human Development, 30*, 137–159.
Chandler, M. J., Boyes, M., & Ball, L. (1990). Relativism and stations of epistemic doubt. *Journal of Experimental Child Psychology, 50*, 370–395.
Chandler, M. J., Hallett, D., & Sokol, B. W. (2002). Competing claims about competing knowledge claims. In B. K. Hofer & P. R. Pintrich (Eds.), *Personal epistemology: The psychology of beliefs about knowledge and knowing* (pp. 145–168). Mahwah, NJ: Erlbaum.

Chapman, L. J., & Chapman, J. P. (1959). Atmosphere effect re-examined. *Journal of Experimental Psychology, 58*, 220–226.

Churchill, W. (2004). *Kill the Indian, save the man: The genocidal impact of American Indian residential schools*. San Francisco: City Lights Books.

Cinalli, M., & O'Flynn, I. (2014). Pluralism and deliberative democracy. In S. Elstub & P. McLaverty (Eds.), *Deliberative democracy: Issues and cases* (pp. 82–97). Edinburgh: Edinburgh University Press.

Curşeu, P. L., Jansen, R. J. G., & Chappin, M. M. H. (2013). Decision rules and group rationality: Cognitive gain or standstill? *PLOS One*, *8*(2), e56454. doi: 10.1371/journal.pone.0056454

Curşeu, P. L., Mesiec, N., Pluut, H., & Lucas, G. J. M. (2015). Cognitive synergy in groups and group-to-individual transfer of decision-making competencies. *Frontiers in Psychology*, *6*, 1375. doi: 10.3389/fpsyg.2015.01375

Dacey, A. (2020). Come now, let us reason together: Cognitive bias, individualism, and interactionism in critical thinking education. *Informal Logic*, *40*, 47–76.

De Brasi, L. (2018). Citizenry incompetence and the epistemic structure of society. *Unisinos Journal of Philosophy, 19*, 201–212.

De Neys, W. (2012). Bias and conflict: A case for logical intuitions. *Perspectives on Psychological Science,* 7, 28–38.

De Neys, W. (2018). Bias, conflict, and fast logic: Towards a hybrid dual process future? In W. De Neys (Ed.), *Dual process theory 2.0* (pp. 47–65). New York: Routledge.

Demetriou, A., Makris, N., Kazi, S., Spanoudis, G., & Shayer, M. (2018). The developmental trinity of mind: Cognizance, executive control, and reasoning. *WIREs Cognitive Science*, doi: 10.1002/wcs.1461

Demetriou, A., & Spanoudis, G. (2018). *Growing minds: A developmental theory of intelligence, brain, and education*. New York: Routledge.

Dewey, J. (1997). *How we think*. Mineola, NY: Dover. (Original work published 1910)

Doise, W., & Mugny, G. (1984). *The social development of the intellect*. Oxford: Pergamon.

Domberg, A., Köymen, B., & Tomasello, M. (2018). Children's reasoning with peers in cooperative and competitive contexts. *British Journal of Developmental Psychology, 36*, 64–77.

Driver, J. (2018). *The schoolhouse gate: Public education, the Supreme Court, and the battle for the American mind*. New York: Pantheon.

Dworkin, R. (1985). *A matter of principle*. Cambridge, MA: Harvard University Press.

Dworkin, R. (1996). *Freedom's law: The moral reading of the American Constitution*. Cambridge, MA: Harvard University Press.

Dworkin, R. (2011). *Justice for hedgehogs*. Cambridge, MA: Harvard University Press.

Elstub, S., & McLaverty, P. (Eds.). (2014). *Deliberative democracy: Issues and cases*. Edinburgh: Edinburgh University Press.

Erikson, E. H. (1968). *Identity: Youth and crisis*. New York: Norton.

Estlund, D., & Landemore, H. (2018). The epistemic value of democratic deliberation. In A. Bächtiger, J. S. Dryzek, J. Mansbridge, & M. E. Warren (Eds.), *The Oxford handbook of deliberative democracy* (pp. 113–131). New York: Oxford University Press.

Evans, J. St. B. T. (2007). *Hypothetical thinking: Dual processes in reasoning and judgement*. New York: Psychology Press.

Evans, J. St. B. T. (2017). *Thinking and reasoning: A very short introduction*. Oxford: Oxford University Press.

Evans, J. St. B. T., & Stanovich, K. E. (2013). Dual-process theories of higher cognition: Advancing the debate. *Perspectives on Psychological Science, 8*, 223–241.

Fallon, R. H., Jr. (1987). A constructivist coherence theory of constitutional interpretation. *Harvard Law Review, 100*, 1189–1286.

Fallon, R. H., Jr. (2018). *Law and legitimacy in the Supreme Court*. Cambridge, MA: Harvard University Press.

Feiman, R., Hartshorne, J. K., & Barner, D. (2019). Contrast and entailment: Abstract logical relations constrain how 2- and 3-year-old children interpret unknown numbers. *Cognition, 183*, 192–207.

Finken, M. W., & Post, R. C. (2009). *For the common good: Principles of American academic freedom*. New Haven, CT: Yale University Press.

Flavell, J. H. (1979). Metacognition and cognitive monitoring: A new area of cognitive-developmental inquiry. *American Psychologist, 34*, 906–911.

Gelman, R., & Gallistel, C. R. (1978). *The child's understanding of number*. Cambridge, MA: Harvard University Press.

Gibbs, J. C. (2019). *Moral development and reality: Beyond the theories of Kohlberg, Hoffman, & Haidt* (4th ed.). Oxford: Oxford University Press.

Gopnik, A. (2009). *The philosophical baby: What children's minds tell us about truth, love, and the meaning of life*. New York: Farrar, Straus, and Giroux.

Gopnik, A. (2012). Scientific thinking in young children: Theoretical advances, empirical research, and policy implications. *Science, 337* (6102), 1623–1627.

Goswami, U. (1992). *Analogical reasoning in children*. New York: Psychology Press.

Graesser, A. C., Singer, M., & Trabasso, T. (1994). Constructing inferences during narrative text comprehension. *Psychological Review, 101*, 371–395.

Greene, J. A., Sandoval, W. A., & Bråten, I. (Eds.) (2016). *Handbook of epistemic cognition*. New York: Routledge.

Gutmann, A., & Thompson, D. (2004). *Why deliberative democracy?* Princeton, NJ: Princeton University Press.

Gutmann, A., & Thompson, D. (2018). Reflections on deliberative democracy: When theory meets practice. In A. Bächtiger, J. S. Dryzek, J. Mansbridge, & M. E. Warren (Eds.), *The Oxford handbook of deliberative democracy* (pp. 900–912). New York: Oxford University Press.

Habermas, J. (1990). *Moral consciousness and communicative action*. Cambridge, MA: MIT Press.

Habermas, J. (1996). *Between facts and norms: Contributions to a discourse theory of law and democracy*. Cambridge, MA: MIT Press.

Haidt, J. (2001). The emotional dog and its rational tail: A social intuitionist approach to moral judgment. *Psychological Review, 108*, 814–834.

Hans, V. P. (2007). Deliberation and dissent: *12 Angry Men* versus the empirical reality of juries. *Chicago-Kent Law Review, 82*, 579–589.

Hart, D., & Youniss, J. (2018). *Renewing democracy in young America*. Oxford: Oxford University Press.

Helwig, C. C. (1995). Adolescents' and young adults' conceptions of civil liberties: Freedom of speech and religion. *Child Development, 66*, 152–166.

Helwig, C. C., Ruck, M. D., & Peterson-Badali, M. (2014). Rights, civil liberties, and democracy. In M. Killen & J. G. Smetana (Eds.), *Handbook of moral development* (2nd ed.) (pp. 46–69). New York: Psychology Press.

Henle, M. (1962). On the relation between logic and thinking. *Psychological Review, 69*, 366–378.

Inhelder, B., & Piaget, J. (1958). *The growth of logical thinking from childhood to adolescence*. New York: Basic Books. (Original work published 1955)

Inhelder, B., & Piaget, J. (1964). *The early growth of logic in the child: Classification and seriation*. London: Routledge. (Original work published 1959)

Iordanou, K. (2016). From theory of mind to epistemic cognition. A lifespan perspective. *Frontline Learning Research, 4*, 106–119.

Johnson-Laird, P. N. (1983). *Mental models*. Cambridge, MA: Harvard University Press.

Johnson-Laird, P. N. (2006). *How we reason*. Oxford: Oxford University Press.

Johnson-Laird, P. N., & Byrne, R. M. J. (1991). *Deduction*. Hillsdale, NJ: Erlbaum.

Kahneman, D. (2011). *Thinking, fast and slow*. New York: Farrar, Straus, & Giroux.

Karmiloff-Smith, A. (1992). *Beyond modularity: A developmental perspective on cognitive science*. Cambridge, MA: MIT Press.

Karpowitz, C. E., & Mendelberg, T. (2018). The political psychology of deliberation. In A. Bächtiger, J. S. Dryzek, J. Mansbridge, & M. E. Warren, *The Oxford handbook of deliberative democracy* (pp. 535–555). New York: Oxford University Press.

Kazi, S., Kazali, E., Makris, N., Spanoudis, G., & Demetriou, A. (2019). Cognizance in cognitive development: A longitudinal study. *Cognitive Development, 52*.

Killen, M., & Rutland, A. (2011). *Children and social exclusion: Morality, prejudice, and group identity*. Malden, MA: Wiley-Blackwell.

King, P. M., & Kitchener, K. S. (1994). *Developing reflective judgment: Understanding and promoting intellectual growth and critical thinking in adolescents and adults*. San Francisco: Jossey-Bass.

Klaczynski, P. A. (2000). Motivated scientific reasoning biases, epistemological beliefs, and theory polarization: A two-process approach to adolescent cognition. *Child Development, 71*, 1347–1366.

Klaczynski, P. A. (2011). Age differences in understanding precedent-setting decisions and authorities' responses to violations of deontic rules. *Journal of Experimental Child Psychology, 109*, 1–24.

Klaczynski, P. A., & Felmban, W. S. (2019). When (and when not) to make exceptions: Links among age, precedent setting decisions, and argument evaluation. *Journal of Genetic Psychology, 180*, 170–184.

Klein, E. (2020). *Why we're polarized*. New York: Avid Reader Press.

Kohlberg, L. (1981). *The philosophy of moral development*. San Francisco: Harper & Row.

Kohlberg, L. (1984). *The psychology of moral development*. San Francisco: Harper & Row.

Korsgaard, C. M. (2009). *Self-constitution: Agency, identity, and integrity*. Oxford: Oxford University Press.

Koslowski, B. (1996). *Theory and evidence: The development of scientific reasoning*. Cambridge, MA: MIT Press.

Koslowski, B. (2013). Scientific reasoning: Explanation, confirmation bias, and scientific practice. In G. J. Feist & M. E. Gorman (Eds.), *Handbook of the psychology of science* (pp. 151–192). New York: Springer.

Koslowski, B., Marasia, J., Chelenza, M., & Dublin, R. (2008). Information becomes evidence when an explanation can incorporate it into a causal framework. *Cognitive Development, 23*, 472–487.

Kuhn, D. (1989). Children and adults as intuitive scientists. *Psychological Review, 96*, 674–689.

Kuhn, D. (1991). *The skills of argument*. Cambridge, UK: Cambridge University Press.

Kuhn, D. (2005). *Education for thinking.* Cambridge, MA: Harvard University Press.

Kuhn, D. (2018a). *Building our best future: Thinking critically about ourselves and our world* (student ed.). New York: Wessex.

Kuhn, D. (2018b). *Building our best future: Thinking critically about ourselves and our world* (teachers ed.). New York: Wessex.

Kuhn, D. (2019). Critical thinking as discourse. *Human Development, 62*, 146–164.

Kuhn, D., Amsel, E., & O'Loughlin, M. (1988). *The development of scientific thinking skills.* San Diego, CA: Academic Press.

Kuhn, D., Cheney, R., & Weinstock, M. (2000). The development of epistemological understanding. *Cognitive Development, 15*, 309–328.

Kuhn, D., Feliciano, N., & Kostikina, D. (2019). Engaging contemporary issues as practice for citizenship. *The Social Studies, 110*, 207–219.

Kuhn, D., Hemberger, L., & Khait, V. (2016). *Argue with me: Argument as a path to developing students' thinking and writing* (2nd ed.). New York: Routledge.

Kuhn, D. & Weinstock, M. (2002). What is epistemological thinking and why does it matter? In B. K. Hofer & P. R. Pintrich (Eds.), *Personal epistemology: The psychology of beliefs about knowledge and knowing* (pp. 121–144). Mahwah, NJ: Erlbaum.

Laats, A., & Siegel, H. (2016). *Teaching evolution in a creation nation.* Chicago: University of Chicago Press.

Laden, A. S. (2012). *Reasoning: A social picture.* Oxford: Oxford University Press.

Lalonde, C. E., & Chandler, M. J. (2002). Children's understanding of interpretation. *New Ideas in Psychology, 20*, 163–198.

Landemore, H. (2013). *Democratic reason: Politics, collective intelligence, and the rule of the many.* Princeton, NJ: Princeton University Press.

Landy, J. F., & Royzman, E. B. (2018). The moral myopia model: Why and how reasoning matters in moral judgment. In G. Pennycook (Ed.), *The new reflectionism in cognitive psychology: Why reason matters* (pp. 70–92). New York: Routledge.

Langer, J. (1980). *The origins of logic: From six to twelve months.* San Francisco: Academic Press.

Langer, J. (1986). *The origins of logic: One to two years.* Orlando, FL: Academic Press.

Laughlin, P. R. (2011). *Group problem solving.* Princeton, NJ: Princeton University Press.

Lent, R. C., & Pipkin, G. (2013). *Keep them reading: An anti-censorship handbook for educators.* New York: Teachers College Press.

Lerner, R. M., & Overton, W. F. (2017). Reduction to absurdity: Why epigenetics invalidates all models involving genetic reduction. *Human Development, 60*, 107–123.

Lickliter, R., & Witherington, D. C. (2017). Towards a truly developmental epigenesis. *Human Development, 60*, 124–138.

Lukianoff, G. (2014). *Unlearning liberty: Campus censorship and the end of American debate.* New York: Encounter.

Maalouf, A. (2001). *In the name of identity: Violence and the need to belong.* New York: Arcade.

Mansfield, A. F., & Clinchy, B. M. (2002). Toward the integration of objectivity and subjectivity: Epistemological development from 10 to 16. *New Ideas in Psychology, 20*, 225–262.

Markovits, H. (2013). The development of abstract conditional reasoning. In P. Barrouillet & C. Gauffroy (Eds.), *The development of thinking and reasoning* (pp. 71–91). New York: Psychology Press.

Markovits, H. (Ed.). (2014). *The developmental psychology of thinking and decision-making.* New York: Psychology Press.

Markovits, H. (2020). The development of logical reasoning. In G. W. Noblit (Ed.), *Oxford research encyclopedia of education*. Oxford: Oxford University Press. doi: 10.1093/acrefore/9780190264093.013.873

Markovits, H., Brunet, M.-L., Thompson, V., & Brisson, J. (2013). Direct evidence for a dual process model of deductive inference. *Journal of Experimental Psychology: Learning, Memory and Cognition, 39*, 1213–1222.

Markovits, H., Thompson, V., & Brisson, J. (2015). Metacognition and abstract reasoning. *Memory & Cognition, 43*, 681–693.

Maynard, J. L. (forthcoming). Ideologies, identities and speech in atrocity crimes. In B. Hola, H. N. Brehm, & M. Weerdesteijn (Eds.), *Oxford handbook of atrocity crime*. Oxford: Oxford University Press.

McCulloch, W. S. (1961). What is a number, that a man may know it, and a man, that he may know a number? *General Semantics Bulletin, 26–27*, 7–18. [Reprinted in W. S. McCulloch (Ed.). (1965). *Embodiments of mind* (pp. 1–18). Cambridge, MA: MIT Press.]

McCulloch, W. S., & Pitts, W. H. (1943). A logical calculus of the ideas immanent in nervous activity. *Bulletin of Mathematical Biophysics, 5*, 115–133. [Reprinted in W. S. McCulloch (Ed.). (1965). *Embodiments of mind* (pp. 19–39). Cambridge, MA: MIT Press.]

Mercier, H., Boudry, M. Paglieri, F., & Trouche, E. (2017). Natural-born arguers: Teaching how to make the best of our reasoning abilities. *Educational Psychologist, 52*, 1–16.

Mercier, H., & Sperber, D. (2017). *The enigma of reason*. Cambridge, MA: Harvard University Press.

Mercier, H., & Sperber, D. (2019). Replies to critics. *Teorema, 38*, 139–156.

Miller, S. A. (2012). *Theory of mind: Beyond the preschool years*. New York: Psychology Press.

Moshman, D. (1979). Development of formal hypothesis-testing ability. *Developmental Psychology, 15*, 104–112.

Moshman, D. (1982). Exogenous, endogenous, and dialectical constructivism. *Developmental Review, 2*, 371–384.

Moshman, D. (1990). The development of metalogical understanding. In W. F. Overton (Ed.), *Reasoning, necessity, and logic: Developmental perspectives* (pp. 205–225). Hillsdale, NJ: Erlbaum.

Moshman, D. (1995). The construction of moral rationality. *Human Development, 38*, 265–281.

Moshman, D. (2004a). False moral identity: Self-serving denial in the maintenance of moral self-conceptions. In D. K. Lapsley & D. Narvaez (Eds.), *Moral development, self, and identity* (pp. 83–109). Mahwah, NJ: Erlbaum.

Moshman, D. (2004b). From inference to reasoning: The construction of rationality. *Thinking & Reasoning, 10*, 221–239.

Moshman, D. (2007a). Social identity and its discontents. *Journal of Applied Developmental Psychology, 28*, 184–187.

Moshman, D. (2007b). Us and them: Identity and genocide. *Identity, 7*, 115–135.

Moshman, D. (2009a). *Liberty and learning: Academic freedom for teachers and students*. Portsmouth, NH: Heinemann.

Moshman, D. (2009b). The development of rationality. In H. Siegel (Ed.), *Oxford handbook of philosophy of education* (pp. 145–161). Oxford, UK: Oxford University Press.

Moshman, D. (2011a). *Adolescent rationality and development: Cognition, morality, and identity* (3rd ed.). New York: Psychology Press.

Moshman, D. (2011b). Identity, genocide, and group violence. In S. J. Schwartz, K. Luyckx, & V. L. Vignoles (Eds.), *Handbook of identity theory and research* (pp. 917–932). New York: Springer.

Moshman, D. (2013). Adolescent rationality. *Advances in Child Development and Behavior, 45*, 155–183.

Moshman, D. (2015). *Epistemic cognition and development: The psychology of justification and truth*. New York: Psychology Press.

Moshman, D. (2017). Academic freedom as the freedom to do academic work. *AAUP Journal of Academic Freedom, 8*. www.aaup.org/JAF8/academic-freedom-freedom-do-academic-work#.Wcqm7I6QzuR

Moshman, D. (2018). Reasoning, logic, and development: Essay review of *The enigma of reason* by Hugo Mercier and Dan Sperber. *Human Development, 61*, 60–64.

Moshman, D. (2020). "Hate speech," free speech, and group violence. In R. J. Sternberg (Ed.), *Perspectives on hate: How it originates, develops, manifests, and spreads* (pp. 203–224). Washington, DC: APA Books.

Moshman, D., & Franks, B. A. (1986). Development of the concept of inferential validity. *Child Development, 57*, 153–165.

Moshman, D., & Geil, M. (1998). Collaborative reasoning: Evidence for collective rationality. *Thinking & Reasoning, 4*, 231–248.

Nagel, T. (1986). *The view from nowhere*. New York: Oxford University Press.

Neimark, E. D. (1970). Model for a thinking machine: An information-processing framework for the study of cognitive development. *Merrill-Palmer Quarterly of Behavior and Development, 16*, 345–368.

Neimark, E. D. (1975). Intellectual development during adolescence. In F. D. Horowitz (Ed.), *Review of child development research* (Vol. 4, pp. 541–594). Chicago: University of Chicago Press.

Neimark, E. D. (1987). *Adventures in thinking*. San Diego: Harcourt Brace Jovanovich.

Neimark, E. D., & Santa, J. L. (1975). Thinking and concept attainment. *Annual Review of Psychology, 26*, 173–205.

Neimark, E. D., & Slotnick, N. S. (1970). Development of the understanding of logical connectives. *Journal of Educational Psychology, 61*, 451–460.

Nino, C. S., (1996). *The constitution of deliberative democracy*. New Haven, CT: Yale University Press.

Noveck, I. (2019). From Queensbury rules to argumentative theory: A review of Mercier & Sperber's *The enigma of reason*. *Teorema, 38*, 121–138.

Nucci, L. P. (2001). *Education in the moral domain*. Cambridge, UK: Cambridge University Press.

Nucci, L. P. (2014). The personal and the moral. In M. Killen & J. G. Smetana (Eds.), *Handbook of moral development* (2nd ed.) (pp. 538–558). New York: Psychology Press.

O'Madagain, C., & Tomasello, M. (2019). Joint attention to mental content and the social origin of reasoning. *Synthese*. doi: 10.1007/s11229-019-02327-1

Overton, W. F. (Ed.). (1990). *Reasoning, necessity, and logic: Developmental perspectives*. Hillsdale, NJ: Erlbaum.

Parfit, D. (1984). *Reasons and persons*. Oxford: Oxford University Press.

Parkinson, J. (2018). Deliberative systems. In A. Bächtiger, J. S. Dryzek, J. Mansbridge, & M. E. Warren (Eds.). *The Oxford handbook of deliberative democracy* (pp. 432–446). New York: Oxford University Press.

Paul, R. W. (1990). *Critical thinking: What every person needs to survive in a rapidly changing world*. Rohnert Park: CA: Center for Critical Thinking and Moral Critique, Sonoma State University.

Pennycook, G. (2018). A perspective on the theoretical foundation of dual process models. In W. De Neys (Ed.), *Dual process theory 2.0* (pp. 5–27). New York: Routledge.

Perry, W. G. (1999). *Forms of intellectual and ethical development in the college years: A scheme*. San Francisco: Jossey-Bass. (Original work published 1970)

Piaget, J. (1954). *The construction of reality in the child*. New York: Basic Books. (Original work published 1937)

Piaget, J. (1963). *The origins of intelligence in children*. New York: Norton. (Original work published 1936)

Piaget, J. (1965a). *The child's conception of number*. New York: Norton. (Original work published 1941)

Piaget, J. (1965b). *The moral judgment of the child*. New York: Free Press. (Original work published 1932)

Piaget, J. (1971). *Biology and knowledge: An essay on the relations between organic regulations and cognitive processes*. Chicago: University of Chicago Press. (Original work published 1967)

Piaget, J. (1972). *Judgment and reasoning in the child*. Totowa, NJ: Littlefield, Adams. (Original work published 1928)

Piaget, J. (1974). *Understanding causality*. New York: Norton. (Original work published 1971)

Piaget, J. (1985). *The equilibration of cognitive structures: The central problem of intellectual development*. Chicago: University of Chicago Press. (Original work published 1975)

Piaget, J. (1995). *Sociological studies*. New York: Routledge. (Original works published 1928–1977)

Piaget, J. (2001). *Studies in reflecting abstraction*. Hove, UK: Psychology Press. (Original work published 1977)

Piaget, J., & Inhelder, B. (1975). *The origin of the idea of chance in children*. New York: Norton. (Original work published 1951)

Pillow, B. H. (2012). *Children's discovery of the active mind: Phenomenological awareness, social experience, and knowledge about cognition*. New York: Springer.

Post, R. C. (2012). *Democracy, expertise, and academic freedom: A First Amendment jurisprudence for the modern state*. New Haven, CT: Yale University Press.

Premack, D., & Woodruff, G. (1978). Does the chimpanzee have a theory of mind? *Behavioral and Brain Sciences, 1*, 515–526.

Rawls, J. (1971). *A theory of justice*. Cambridge, MA: Harvard University Press.

Rawls, J. (2001). *Justice as fairness: A restatement*. Cambridge, MA: Harvard University Press.

Ricco, R. B. (2015). Development of reasoning. In R. M. Lerner (Ed.), *Handbook of child psychology and developmental science* (7th ed., Vol. 2) (pp. 519–570). Hoboken, NJ: Wiley.

Ricco, R. B., & Overton, W. F. (2011). Dual systems competence <—> procedural processing: A relational developmental systems approach to reasoning. *Developmental Review, 31*, 119–150.

Richard, M. (2019). Is reasoning a form of agency? In M. Balcerak Jackson & B. Balcerak Jackson (Eds.), *Reasoning: New essays on theoretical and practical thinking* (pp. 91–100). New York: Oxford University Press.

Rips, L. J. (1994). *The psychology of proof: Deductive reasoning in human thinking*. Cambridge, MA: MIT Press.

Rosenberg, A., & McIntyre, L. (2020). *Philosophy of science: A contemporary introduction* (4th ed.). New York: Routledge.

Rosenberg, S. W. (2014). Citizen competence and the psychology of deliberation. In S. Elstub & P. McLaverty (Eds.), *Deliberative democracy: Issues and cases* (pp. 98–117). Edinburgh: Edinburgh University Press.

Rosenfeld, S. (2019). *Democracy and truth: A short history*. Philadelphia: University of Pennsylvania Press.

Ross, C. J. (2015). *Lessons in censorship: How schools and courts subvert students' First Amendment rights*. Cambridge, MA: Harvard University Press.

Saxonhouse, A. W. (2006). *Free speech and democracy in ancient Athens*. New York: Cambridge University Press.

Scholnick, E. K., & Wing, C. S. (1991). Speaking deductively: Preschoolers' use of *If* in conversation and in conditional inference. *Developmental Psychology, 27*, 249–258.

Scholnick, E. K., & Wing, C. S. (1992). Speaking deductively: Using conversation to trace the origins of conditional thought in children. *Merrill-Palmer Quarterly, 38*, 1–20.

Scholnick, E. K., & Wing, C. S. (1995). Logic in conversation: Comparative studies of deduction in children and adults. *Cognitive Development, 10*, 319–345.

Schraw, G., & Moshman, D. (1995). Metacognitive theories. *Educational Psychology Review, 7*, 351–371.

Sells, S. B. (1936). The atmosphere effect: An experimental study of reasoning. *Archives of Psychology (Columbia University), 29*, 3–72.

Selman, R. L. (1980). *The growth of interpersonal understanding: Developmental and clinical analyses*. New York: Academic Press.

Sen, A. (1999). *Development as freedom*. New York: Knopf.

Siegel, H. (1988). *Educating reason: Rationality, critical thinking, and education*. New York: Routledge.

Siegel, H. (1997). *Rationality redeemed? Further dialogues on an educational ideal*. New York: Routledge.

Siegel, H. (2018). *Education's epistemology: Rationality, diversity, and critical thinking*. Oxford: Oxford University Press.

Siegel, S. (2019). Inference without reckoning. In M. Balcerak Jackson & B. Balcerak Jackson (Eds.), *Reasoning: New essays on theoretical and practical thinking* (pp. 15–31). New York: Oxford University Press.

Smetana, J. G. (2011). *Adolescents, families, and social development: How teens construct their worlds*. Malden, MA: Wiley-Blackwell.

Smetana, J. G., Jambon, M., & Ball, C. (2014). The social domain approach to children's moral and social judgments. In M. Killen & J. G. Smetana (Eds.), *Handbook of moral development* (2nd ed., Vol. 2) (pp. 23–45). New York: Psychology Press.

Smith, L. (1993). *Necessary knowledge: Piagetian perspectives on constructivism*. Hillsdale, NJ: Erlbaum.

Smith, L. (2002). *Reasoning by mathematical induction in children's arithmetic*. Oxford: Pergamon.

Sobel, D. M., & Kirkham, N. Z. (2007). Bayes nets and babies: Infants' developing statistical reasoning abilities and their representation of causal knowledge. *Developmental Science, 10*, 298–306.

Sodian, B. (2011). Theory of mind in infancy. *Child Development Perspectives, 5*, 39–43.

Sodian, B. (2018). The development of scientific thinking in preschool and elementary school age: A conceptual model. In F. Fischer, C. A. Chinn, K. Engelmann, & J. Osborne

(Eds.), *Scientific reasoning and argumentation: The roles of domain-specific and domain-general knowledge*. New York: Routledge.
Sodian, B., & Kristen, S. (2016). Theory of mind. In J. A. Greene, W. A. Sandoval, & I. Bråten (Eds.), *Handbook of epistemic cognition* (pp. 68–85). New York: Routledge.
Sodian, B., & Wimmer, H. (1987). Children's understanding of inference as a source of knowledge. *Child Development, 58*, 424–433.
Staffel, J. (2019). Attitudes in active reasoning. In M. Balcerak Jackson & B. Balcerak Jackson (Eds.), *Reasoning: New essays on theoretical and practical thinking* (pp. 44–67). New York: Oxford University Press.
Stanovich, K. E. (2004). *The robot's rebellion: Finding meaning in the age of Darwin*. Chicago: University of Chicago Press.
Stanovich, K. E. (2011). *Rationality and the reflective mind*. Oxford: Oxford University Press.
Starita, J. (2008). *"I am a man": Chief Standing Bear's journey for justice*. New York: St. Martin's Griffin.
Strossen, N. (2018). *Hate: Why we should resist it with free speech, not censorship*. Oxford: Oxford University Press.
Tarricone, P. (2011). *The taxonomy of metacognition*. New York: Psychology Press.
Taylor, A. (2019). *Democracy may not exist, but we'll miss it when it's gone*. New York: Metropolitan Books.
Thompson, V. A., & Newman, I. R. (2018). Logical intuitions and other conundra for dual process theories. In W. De Neys (Ed.), *Dual process theory 2.0* (pp. 121–136). New York: Routledge.
Tibbetts, E. A., Agudelo, J., Pandit, S., & Riojas, J. (2019). Transitive inference in *Polistes* paper wasps. *Biology Letters, 15*(5), 20190015. doi: 10.1098/rsbl.2019.0015
Tomasello, M. (2014). *A natural history of human thinking*. Cambridge, MA: Harvard University Press.
Trippas, D., & Handley, S. J. (2018). The parallel processing model of belief bias: Review and extensions. In W. De Neys (Ed.), *Dual process theory 2.0* (pp. 28–46). New York: Routledge.
Turiel, E. (1983). *The development of social knowledge: Morality and convention*. Cambridge, UK: Cambridge University Press.
Turiel, E. (2008). The development of children's orientations toward moral, social, and personal orders: More than a sequence in development. *Human Development, 51*, 21–39.
Wainryb, C., Shaw, L. A., Langley, M., Cottam, K., & Lewis, R. (2004). Children's thinking about diversity of belief in the early school years: Judgments of relativism, tolerance, and disagreeing persons. *Child Development, 75*, 687–703.
Wason, P. C., & Johnson-Laird, P. N. (1972). *Psychology of reasoning: Structure and content*. Cambridge, MA: Harvard University Press.
Wellman, H. M., Cross, D., & Watson, J. (2001). Meta-analysis of theory-of-mind development: The truth about false belief. *Child Development, 72*, 655–684.
West Virginia State Board of Education v. Barnette, 319 U.S. 624 (1943).
Whittington, K. E. (2018). *Speak freely: Why universities must defend free speech*. Princeton, NJ: Princeton University Press.
Wilkins, M. C. (1928). The effect of changed material on ability to do formal syllogistic reasoning. *Archives of Psychology, 16*, 1–83.
Wimmer, H., & Perner, J. (1983). Beliefs about beliefs: Representation and constraining function of wrong beliefs in young children's understanding of deception. *Cognition, 13*, 103–128.

Witherington, D. C. (2011). Taking emergence seriously: The centrality of circular causality for dynamic systems approaches to development. *Human Development, 54*, 66–92.

Woodworth, R. S., & Sells, S. B (1935). An atmosphere effect in formal syllogistic reasoning. *Journal of Experimental Psychology, 18*, 451–460.

Zentall, T. R., Peng, D., & Miles, L. (2019). Transitive inference in pigeons may result from differential tendencies to reject the test stimuli acquired during training. *Animal Cognition, 22*, 619–624.

Zillmer, N., & Kuhn, D. (2018). Do similar-ability peers regulate one another in a collaborative discourse activity? *Cognitive Development, 45*, 68–76.

AUTHOR INDEX

SUBJECT INDEX

For Product Safety Concerns and Information please contact our EU representative GPSR@taylorandfrancis.com
Taylor & Francis Verlag GmbH, Kaufingerstraße 24, 80331 München, Germany

www.ingramcontent.com/pod-product-compliance
Ingram Content Group UK Ltd.
Pitfield, Milton Keynes, MK11 3LW, UK
UKHW022120190926
475702UK00013B/1553
9780367312770